SAFARI PRESS

Make Every Shot Count!

Make Every Shot Count!

Get the Most out of Your Hunting Rifle under Field Conditions

by

J. Scott Olmsted

Safari Press Inc.

Olmsted, J. Scott

First edition

Safari Press

2014, Long Beach, California

ISBN 978-1-57157-388-9

Library of Congress Catalog Card Number: 2010939012

10 9 8 7 6 5 4 3 2

Printed in China

Dedication

To Charlie Titus, who made sure I became a hunter after my father died; to my brother, Marc, whose example inspired me to become a United States Marine, probably the best move I've ever made; to John Zent, who took a chance that a news photographer could become a gunwriter; to Bryce Towsley, who always had a moment or sixty to lend advice; and to Frank Miniter, who showed me how this whole book publishing thing works.

Table of Contents

Introduction

"The possession of a good rifle, as well as the skill to use it well, truly makes a man the monarch of all he surveys."

—Jeff Cooper

In the predawn blackness on the first morning of my first elk hunt, I stood huffing at 8,000 feet with other hunters waiting to step off with our guides. One guy glanced at my rifle.

"What'd you bring?" he asked.

I explained my setup, a Winchester Model 70 chambered in .338 Winchester Magnum topped with a Leupold Vari-X II 3–9X scope.

"I just got it this fall," I explained. "It's the biggest gun I've ever owned, or shot. But I shot it a lot the last two months; I didn't want to come out here without knowing it well."

"Wish I'd brought something lighter, and easier on my shoulder," the guy lamented. "My boss said, 'You're hunting in the West. You need a bigger gun, and a bigger scope.' I wish I'd stuck with my deer rifle; I know it better. Hell, I've only fired this thing once," he said, referring to the cannon on his shoulder. "It weighs a ton. And it kicks like a mule."

I glanced at his rig, a .30-378 Weatherby Magnum with something atop it that looked akin to the Hubble telescope. "Looks heavy," I agreed. "Did you bring some shooting sticks?" I knew there were no tree stands or shooting house windows at 8,000 feet. "They might help you steady it."

"No," he replied. "You?"

"Yep."

"Didn't think of them," the fellow sighed.

I was new to the "business" then, if you consider thirty-five years old "new" at anything. Only a year before, I'd left the newspaper life behind for a chance at a dream job as assistant editor of the NRA's *American Hunter* magazine. But I wasn't new to hunting or shooting. As the elk hunt approached, I knew I wanted a new rig, something besides my .270 Winchester bolt-action or .35 Remington lever-action.

I knew once I acquired it I'd need to practice extensively with it to be sure I could wield it properly. In shooting sessions accompanied by my brother and uncle, I made sure that happened. Although I struck out on elk on that hunt, the training time paid for itself, at least during that moment in the predawn darkness when one fellow from Georgia realized he was overgunned and inexperienced, and I realized I was not.

Over the years, as the anecdotes and the experience piled up, I realized a book on the subject of marksmanship for hunters wasn't such a bad idea. To my mind, there are a lot of folks in the field who could use some help, from beginners to experienced hunters taking on new game, or simply those who like to collect as much knowledge as possible.

Some of my peers didn't agree. "Oh, you mean like the book O'Connor wrote? Or Boddington? Or Cooper?" they asked. Another guy said, "A book? Sounds like a feature article in your magazine to me, not a whole book."

Yes, field marksmanship and choosing a rig have been covered before. And texts on riflecraft, bullet construction, and shot placement have been published, too. I've read everything on all these subjects that I could find; each of them are noted in the bibliography in the back of this book. But I have never seen one book that encompasses everything from choosing your hardware to marksmanship fundamentals to exterior ballistics to situational awareness while afield.

This book is organized into four parts. Part I guides a shooter through decisions he must make long before he heads to the range or the field: deciding what he wants in a good rifle, choosing a sighting system, and choosing a bullet. Part II takes us to the range: We test-fire our rig to ensure dependability and accuracy, learn the fundamentals of marksmanship and the field-shooting positions, learn to spend our range time wisely, and noodle through the math required to make shots at long range, in the wind, and on moving targets. In Part III we enter the field: We learn how to do the little things that can help us steady a rifle, how to handle ourselves in the bush, how to carry our rig over hill and dale while remaining ready for a shot at any moment, why we must own every shot we fire, how to recover after a bullet whistles downrange, and how to choose a big-game battery. In the Afterword, we learn why the National Rifle Association and shooting schools like Gunsite and Sportsman's All-Weather All-Terrain Marksmanship are vital to anyone who spends a life in pursuit of game. And in "A Hunter's Library" I list the books I refer to time and again whenever I encounter a question about guns and shooting I cannot answer off the top of my head.

Feel free to jump around if you like. Although each part builds upon its predecessor, there is no reason to start at the beginning if you feel you do not need a primer on some subjects. Hunters who are experienced rifle and scope buyers, and those who have spent years performing post-mortems to find and examine bullets in the game they have shot, likely will wish to jump straight to chapters on training time, long-range shooting, and situational awareness. Those teaching others to shoot might wish to begin with Part II, which examines the principles behind every good shot. I assure you there is something here for everyone—novice and experienced shooter alike.

In writing this book, I drew on experience gained throughout my life as a hunter, Marine infantry squad leader, NRA-certified firearm instructor, and graduate of shooting programs at Gunsite Academy and Sportsman's All-Weather All-Terrain Marksmanship training. To that end, this book is not about the Marine way, or the NRA way, or any other way. It's my way.

Good luck.

Part I

Before the Shot

How to choose a rifle and a sighting system, and why premium bullets command premium prices

Chapter 1

Know Your Gun

A brown bear hunt on the Alaska Peninsula is neither the time nor the place to admit you have little familiarity with your firearm. Yet that's exactly the situation I found myself in when I carried a .444 Marlin lever-action rifle to the Last Frontier a few years ago. I had no choice in the platform I used, for the plan was to shoot then-new Hornady LEVERevolution bullets designed for lever-action rifles.

It had been a long time since I'd carried a lever-action rifle regularly, so I made sure to get in some range time before the hunt. The sessions helped only a bit. In Alaska, I really missed my bolt-action—any bolt-action.

Over the course of eleven days in bear country, I was always uncomfortable with the Marlin. It never felt right cradled in my arm or carried in any other way. When I threw it to my shoulder, I had to search to get a proper cheek weld and find eye relief behind the scope. The trigger was anything but the crisp, light, three-plus-pound pull I set on my bolt-actions. Unlike my old Marlin, the new rifle wore a cross-bolt safety button. My old Marlin has only a half-cock hammer

A controlled-round-feed bolt uses a claw extractor to grip the cartridge from the moment the round springs from the magazine until the empty case is ejected.

safety (I like this better). In Alaska I used both safeties, repeating in my mind throughout the course of every day, "Thumb cross-bolt, thumb hammer," so I'd remember what to do if I needed to shoulder the gun in a hurry. Perhaps I should have used one or the other safety, but not both. But presented with new technology, I thought I should use both to be safe.

This is the first story I tell people when they seek shooting advice from me. Stick to one model, and you won't face the same worries I did in Alaska. Fortunately, I never needed to use the gun to face a charging bear—a fact that feels better now only in hindsight.

Aside from your prowess as a marksman, I believe the most important component to success in the field lies in muscle memory—the kind that comes from familiarity with your shooting platform. Any rifle you pull off the rack must feel the same in your hands as another. Each one should shoulder and point with ease, without conscious thought. The trigger squeeze should not surprise you because you've set up each rifle to fire at three pounds or so of pressure. Each rifle should load and unload similarly, so you can do it blindfolded. Ideally, the safety on each one is located in the same place and operates similarly, and each rifle is scoped similarly. To my mind, only a bolt-action repeater delivers all those characteristics.

The Bolt-Action: Queen of the Field

The bolt-action design enjoys a long and fruitful history beginning with Germany's adoption of Paul Mauser's Model 98 as its military service rifle in 1898. Although militaries around the world have long since switched to semiautomatic or fully automatic service rifles, the bolt-action still receives the bulk of research-and-development attention among sporting arms makers. It is the flagship bolt-action in a company's lineup that generally is the first to get space-age metals and weatherproof coatings. In recent years, bolt-action receivers made entirely of titanium, a super-strong alloy half the weight of steel and impervious to the elements, have appeared in more than one catalog. Add synthetic stocks, new chamberings, and modern triggers to this list. To spur sales, companies distribute

Imagine carrying each of these rifles on three consecutive days. Note that neither the ergonomics nor the controls are even close to the same with the three different types of actions. It is impossible to build and maintain muscle memory if you constantly switch between rifle platforms.

these flagships first and foremost among the shooting press. Favorable reviews speak volumes.

Three bolt-actions, the Mauser Model 98, Winchester Model 70, and Remington Model 700, form the basis of all commercially available sporting bolt-action rifles in America today. The former two use a controlled-round-feed system, and the latter uses a push-feed. This isn't to say all others are copycats; gunmakers create their own designs all the time. But there's no use reinventing the wheel, as they say. So whenever a company makes its own rifle, engineers are wise to look at existing designs first, perhaps modify them, add their own features, then tweak the final product to their liking.

Compared to other action styles, the bolt-action is a straightforward and open design. That is, when the bolt is open, all mechanisms that control the storage, feeding, chambering, extraction, and ejection of cartridges lie in plain view. Contrast this with lever-action, pump, or autoloading designs, where cartridges disappear inside the receiver and the action does all its work "behind closed doors," as it were. With a pump or lever it's possible to watch the cartridge's journey from magazine to chamber, sure, but generally one needs to cant the rifle to see the process. And with an autoloader, the process is so speedy you'd better not blink or you'll miss it.

With any of these three designs, once a hunter loads the magazine, he might not see the cartridge again until the firing sequence is completed, when the action opens and the case is ejected. Is a round chambered? If there is any doubt, it's a noisy and sometimes lengthy process to verify it. Conversely, when he closes a turnbolt, a hunter knows he's got a loaded and locked firearm in his hands. If there is any doubt, he can quickly and quietly open the action ever so slightly for a visual and tactile check of the chamber. Such simplicity of design makes the bolt-action the easiest to operate and, therefore, to my mind, the easiest to master.

The key feature all bolt-actions share is a turning bolt and the lugs at its head. Twin opposed lugs are common, though three and even as many as nine may be used. The lugs, in concert with the turning bolt and its integral handle, put great power in the hands of the operator. Most problems with feeding can be overcome with requisite force.

As simple as it is, a turnbolt is also strong. Great leverage is brought to bear by the bolt handle and internal cams, which effectively serve to make the bolt and firing unit act as lead screws during opening and closing. The receiver threads deeply onto the barrel where, together with the bolt, a solid locking unit is formed around the cartridge. The design handles high-power cartridges with aplomb, even in conditions that would foul up other designs.

A bolt-action is also capable of great accuracy, greater than any other sporting arm in use today, notwithstanding recent advances with semiautomatic AR-15s, some of which now rival bolt-actions. The key lies in the concentricity of the design. Unlike lever guns or autoloaders that may utilize square receivers, everything in the bolt-action equation—the receiver, the bolt, and the barrel—is round, which helps because, of course, the cartridge is round. In this equation,

The author shot this kudu with a Browning A-Bolt in .300 WSM in Namibia in 2005.

all components are manufactured and fitted to function around the line central to the axis of the bore. The round bolt glides through the centerline of the round receiver, picks up the round cartridge, and guides it into the centerline of the round barrel. If accuracy is lacking, it can usually be cured by lapping the bolt to ensure even contact by all lugs.

Given all that, why would a hunter choose anything but a bolt-action? The best argument I can think of comes from the firepower crowd—the characters who fire not one, but two and even three rounds in quick succession to check their zeroes in camp. Downrange, if a round or two is outside the ten-ring, they fall back on the "more is better" argument. By contrast, the well-trained rifleman fires one carefully aimed round at a time, knowing the first one is the most important regardless of which action type is employed. Firepower is never a match for well-aimed rounds on target.

Pick a Stick and Stick with It

In the end, it doesn't matter what your platform of choice is, as long as it's uniform. If you like lever-actions, so be it. If you've tapped the latest trend and carry an AR-15 into the field, that's fine, too. But stick with your platform until you master the techniques in this text, or else be prepared to rebuild your muscle memory every time you switch guns.

An experienced hunter who travels the world might own one or two deer rifles; a similar rig in a magnum chambering for elk; a lightweight mountain rifle for sheep or goats; a medium- to heavy-caliber rig for dangerous game in Africa; an all-weather rig, appropriately chambered, for caribou, moose, or bears in Alaska; a heavy-barreled, long-range rig for varmints; and a .22 rimfire for plinking and practice.

Personal taste, specific needs, or an overwhelming desire to own a gun for no other reason than your attraction to it may vary the makeup of your list, but six or

NRA Publications editorial director John Zent hunts in Alaska with a Sako Model 85 Brown Bear.

ten rifles outfitted and chambered appropriately is pretty much all anyone needs in his or her hunting career.

Regardless of which rifle you choose to carry on any given day or how it's chambered, it should operate similarly to all your other rifles. When the bull elk of your dreams is lined up and you're thinking only "breathe, squeeze, and follow-through," you need to know exactly where your thumb needs to slide to slip off the safety. When you empty the magazine on a Cape buffalo bull and the bugger comes running, you need to know without thinking whether you can chamber a round in an empty gun by simply throwing another atop the follower, or whether you need to seat it before closing the bolt.

While I use numerous action designs in my capacity as an editor for a hunting magazine, carrying various new guns into the field to test and evaluate, the rifles in my personal collection are predominately bolt-actions. What's more, the majority of them are controlled-round-feed designs with three-position safeties—Winchester Model 70s or Kimber 84Ms or 8400s. Thus, when I have a choice of what rifle to carry, I know I can pick up any one of these three models and rely on certain similar characteristics.

You should do the same. Limit the variables, build proficiency with your chosen style of rifle, and the rest becomes second nature. To help you figure out what style of rifle will work best for you, let's take a look at the three major aspects of a bolt-action rifle: lock, stock, and barrel.

The Lock

Controlled-round-feed vs. push-feed

In hunting camps everywhere, the battle rages over which bolt-action design is better: controlled-round-feed or push-feed. Both are proven designs, and both will do their job well. Despite what you might hear around the campfire, you're not at a disadvantage against dangerous game when using a push-feed rifle, although devotees of controlled-round-feed reject such a notion.

Controlled-round-feed traces its heritage to the Mauser Model 98. The hallmark of this design is a claw extractor, so-called because it reaches around the

The author used a Remington Model 700 CDL in 7mm Remington Ultra Magnum on this Wyoming mule deer.

locking lug like a crab claw. When the bolt is pushed forward, the bottom edge of its face pushes against a cartridge in the magazine. The claw engages the cartridge rim as the round rises, gripping the cartridge throughout its journey into and out of the chamber. So throughout the act of feeding, firing, extraction, and ejection of the cartridge, the claw is in control of the case rim.

The design produces few failures to extract. Ejection is achieved when the bolt is pulled to the rear, whereupon a standing blade under spring tension at the left rear of the receiver applies pressure on the left side of the case and pushes it to the right and free of the grip of the claw. Yank back the bolt with force, and the ejector contacts the case with force, sending the brass flying; pull back the bolt gently, and the ejector gently pushes the case clear. A drawback of the design is that the cartridge has to be chambered from the magazine so that the claw engages the case rim. That makes single-round loading a pain. A hunter who wants to throw one more round into an empty gun to finish off game or to defend himself must remember to push forcefully during those tense seconds in order to first seat the cartridge in the magazine. To counter this, many riflemakers bevel the front of the extractor so it snaps over a chambered round.

By contrast, the extractor and ejector on push-feed designs reside on the bolt head. The most notable examples employ a hook extractor that pushes the cartridge from the magazine. When the round pops up in line with the bore, the bolt pushes it into the chamber, and the hook snaps over the cartridge rim when the bolt is turned down and the round bottoms in the chamber. Once locked down, a spring-loaded plunger ejector applies pressure to the bottom left side of the case. When the bolt is pulled rearward and the case clears the receiver ring, the plunger tosses out the empty case. Controlled-round-feed devotees like to point out that in this system, the cartridge is not controlled until the bolt handle is turned down. Thus, hook extractors leave

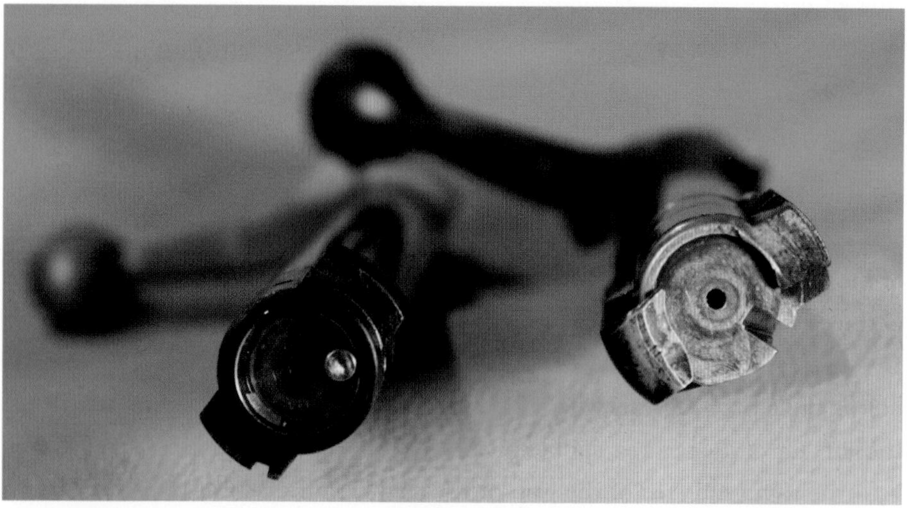

The stark difference between a push-feed system, left, and a controlled-round-feed system, right, is embodied in the bolt face. The push-feed bolt merely encloses the case head, and uses a plunger-type ejector in its face. The controlled-round-feed bolt uses a claw extractor to grip the cartridge during its journey from magazine to chamber and back out of the chamber when the empty case is ejected.

It takes a lot of experience to determine the pull weight of a trigger by feel. To be sure, use an electronic trigger pull weight gauge like this one from Lyman. Take an average of three trigger pulls to see if your trigger pull weight varies.

the cartridge floating for at least part of its journey into the chamber. It's possible for an excited hunter to double-feed his rig by short-stroking the first round and feeding another one atop it, which results in a jam. But hooks extract cases just fine as long as the rifleman locks down the bolt. Plungers are reliable and provide consistent ejection, which is why they are favored in autoloading designs.

Still, controlled-round-feed enjoys almost deitylike devotion among dangerous-game hunters, perhaps for reasons even they don't understand. Though it's worth noting that controlled-round-feed actions perform the acts of feeding and extraction better than push-feed systems, the latter, as noted, hardly suffer by comparison. The great advantage of a controlled-round-feed action lies in stealth, which is important on the trail. Quite often (unless on the trail of dangerous game), safety dictates that a hunter stalks game with

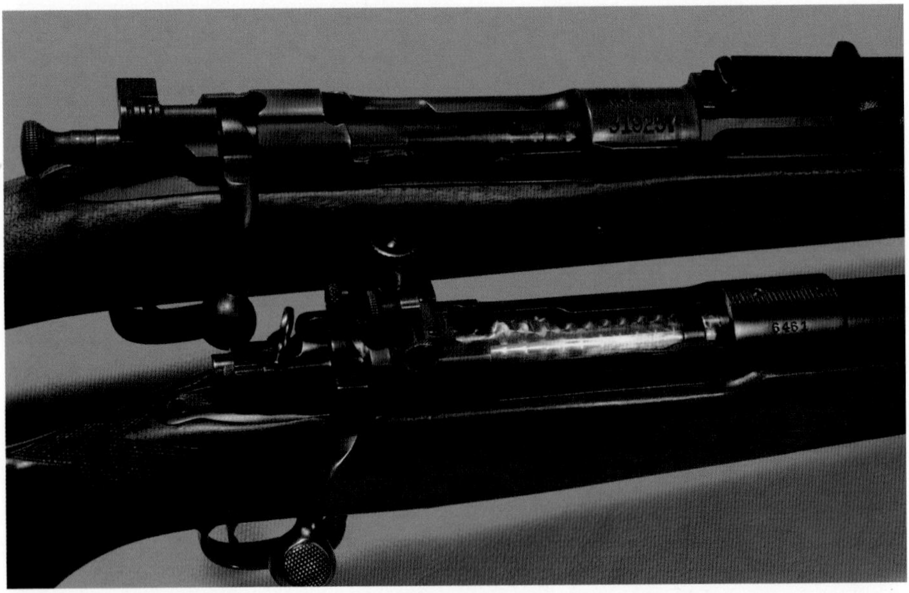

The 1903 Springfield rifle (top), was adopted by the U.S. military in the early twentieth century. It borrowed so heavily from Paul Mauser's Model 1898 that the United States government actually paid a royalty to Mauser. But its proven controlled-round-feed design was a hit. In 1936 Winchester introduced the Model 70 (bottom), another gun that adopted Mauser's design. Both guns feature claw extractors.

The claw extractor on the bolt in a controlled-round-feed action holds the cartridge securely during the entire time it is being pushed from the magazine into the chamber.

an empty chamber. With controlled-round-feed, a hunter may chamber a cartridge more slowly and quietly than with any other system, and he never loses control of the cartridge during the process.

By contrast, slowly push forward the bolt of a push-feed rifle, and notice how the cartridge rattles about when the bolt face pushes it free from the grip of the magazine; notice how the bolt never actually grips the case before it pushes it into the chamber. It's noisy. It's also why a push-feed system sometimes fails to extract a case. The point is largely academic, for push-feed designs today are quite reliable.

Long-Action vs. Short-Action

Action length can affect the weight of the rifle and the way it handles. I have a Model 28 Short built by Melvin Forbes of New Ultra Light Arms on his own Model 700-inspired action that weighs five and three-quarter pounds. It's chambered in .300 Winchester Short Magnum, a short-action caliber usually associated with lightweight mountain rifles. On the other hand, I have a rifle built on a Model 70 action by Lex Webernick of Rifles Inc. chambered in .338 Winchester Magnum, a long-action caliber, which weighs just a bit more than six pounds. Neither rifle is difficult to handle and shoulder, despite the difference in action lengths. In fact both feel like wands in my hands; I carry them easily, point them surely, and both are supremely accurate.

Such similar characteristics won't always hold true across the board, however. Short-action rifles are generally easier to carry and come more quickly to one's shoulder. Long-action rifles, especially those chambered in bigger calibers, generally weigh more and are longer and more robust. Carrying such a rig over hill and dale and shouldering it under stress while wearing heavy clothing won't come easy to someone used to carrying a short-action rifle.

Chambering

Sometimes choosing a certain model of rifle limits one to certain chamberings; many rifle models are introduced only in long- or short-action lengths before a complete lineup is developed in later years. But generally speaking, you should pick the action that suits your sensibilities and your budget, and then decide how to chamber it.

With the game you seek in mind, study trajectory tables to get a good idea of the capabilities of various cartridges, paying close attention to downrange energy to determine whether a particular caliber will deliver enough energy at the maximum range you will use the gun. Notwithstanding the obvious limitations of some cartridges, the decision can be made less difficult if one breaks down the list into short- and long-action calibers.

While short-action calibers like the .22-250, .223 Remington, and .243 Winchester bag plenty of deer-sized game across the country, in my view the serious choices in this category for any critter bigger than deer or pronghorns start with the .308 Winchester and quickly proceed to the short magnum lineup including the Winchester Short Magnums (WSM), Remington Short

Haden Olmsted killed this impala with a Kimber 84M in .243 Winchester. So chambered, the 84M is a svelte little gun with mild recoil. Quick-handling and nimble, it features a controlled-round-feed action.

Action Ultra Magnums (RSAUM; now discontinued), and the Ruger Compact Magnums (RCM). But don't mistake "short" as less powerful than "long." If a small, lightweight rifle is what you need for a mountain hunt, you'll pack plenty of punch with anything chambered in a short magnum. You'll also enjoy a shorter bolt stroke, which can mean a faster reload. But you won't enjoy more firepower. Short magnums are also fat magnums, thus the magazines of many short magnums won't hold as many rounds as those chambered for their longer, more slender brethren. All else aside, they perform well and are the chambering of choice among many mountain hunters.

Many hunters, including me, enjoy the romance of a long-action caliber. There's something intrinsic to working the extra length of a long-action bolt, a satisfaction in the mechanics of the motion that can't be put into words. Besides, calibers in this category carry quite a bit of history. The .30-06 was adopted by the U.S. Army in 1906 for use in the 1903 Springfield rifle. It is the most useful, all-round cartridge available to big-game hunters in America, and the many available bullet weights and types solidify such a claim. The .375 H&H Magnum, introduced by Holland & Holland in 1912, is considered by many to be the finest all-round hunting cartridge of all time. Its mild recoil (compared to other medium and big bores) makes it the first suggestion of African professional hunters when recommending a caliber to first-time buffalo hunters. The .300 Winchester Magnum was introduced in 1963 by Winchester for the Model 70. Complaints about its short neck and the need to seat its heavy bullets deep into the powder charge aside, the .300 Winchester Magnum is a supremely accurate cartridge (used extensively by civilians and the U.S. military alike in long-range competition and combat) and a fine long-range big-game cartridge for anything in North America. Ammunition for any of these three calibers is widely available even in some of the most remote locales. Come to think of it, a hunter who owns one of each of these has a good battery for hunting the world.

Trigger

This component, above all others, has the greatest effect on accuracy. Without a trigger that breaks cleanly the instant you will it to, accuracy will forever be a moving target.

A hunter is served best by a single-stage trigger, a trigger that moves smoothly rearward to release the sear at its set weight without any interruption. Two other kinds of triggers are sometimes found on rifles, but neither system is best for hunters. Let's look at each of them to understand what's at stake before we explore the qualities common to a good single-stage trigger.

Two-stage triggers used to be commonplace on military rifles. Apply just a bit of pressure to one and it moves rearward about half an inch before stopping; apply more pressure and it moves again before the sear is released and the rifle fires. The long movement of the first stage and the hard "bump" of the second stage gives a soldier a safe mechanism while under stress and yet a good idea when his rifle will fire when facing the enemy. But it's not ideal for sporting purposes because when the first stage of the trigger is taken up, sear engagement is reduced so greatly the rifle is capable of firing with little further manipulation.

Set triggers—also called "hair" triggers because it is said a gun so outfitted can be fired by the touch of a hair—present a different problem for hunters because they must actually be set before a gun will fire. Double set triggers, one lying before the other, are most popular on European guns. Pull one trigger to create an audible and tactile "click" and set the mechanism. Pull the other to withdraw the spring-powered lever now cocked by a precarious sear arrangement and fire the gun. At one time the "setting" trigger usually lay at the rear, the "hair" trigger in front. The modern arrangement places the set trigger in front, where it is cocked by pushing it forward. Either way, the motion takes time and concentration. Will you remember to do so when it's time to shoot? Every time? What's more, most set triggers are designed for extremely light pull weights that range between mere fractions of an ounce and perhaps two pounds—a bit light, to my mind, for a hunting arm.

Three parts are common to any trigger group: the hammer, sear, and trigger. To fire the rifle, one pulls the lever that is the trigger to release the sear (the component that retains the hammer in the cocked position), which activates the spring-powered hammer that strikes the firing pin. In bolt-action rifles, the hammer is replaced by a cocking piece, and there is no half-cock like that found on a lever-action rifle. When the bolt is pushed forward and locked in battery, the cocking piece comes hard against the sear. The contact surfaces of the two must be large and strong to stand up against wear, and to prevent the cocking piece from slipping by the sear and firing the gun when the bolt is closed.

To pick out a good trigger you should understand what occurs when you pull it. Break, pull weight, creep, over-travel: Most hunters know what these things mean but they're pressed to explain how each influences performance.

When a trigger "breaks," it releases the sear, firing the gun. Some triggers are said to break cleanly or crisply; others are described as sluggish.

"Pull weight" refers to the pressure required to break the trigger, release the sear, and cause the rifle to fire. It's expressed in pounds and ounces. Most shooters judge a trigger's pull weight by simply squeezing it and making a guess; use a trigger pull weight scale for accuracy. A trigger is nothing more than a lever, so weight of pull needed to break it is less at the lower tip, where leverage is greater, than at the upper portion of the blade. Weight of pull is measured at the midpoint, which will be the rearmost point of the curve.

The best pull weight for a hunting rifle is three to four pounds. That's a lot lighter than it sounds, particularly since most hunters have never really felt such a good trigger. The average pull weight of factory rifles not long ago was more than five pounds. And it was getting heavier, thanks to a litigious society. If you're used to a heavy feel, three pounds of pull weight seems like a hair trigger. It's not. Shooters not accustomed to an extra-light pull weight tend to fire before they are ready. Three to four pounds is the lightest most of us can pull while exercising some control over the exact timing of the shot. Set up your trigger accordingly, practice with it, and soon you'll be able to manipulate it quite well, even with cold fingers or while wearing gloves.

If you're conscious of the pressure you're applying to break the shot, the trigger pull is too heavy. This is not only annoying but it robs your concentration, which takes your attention off your front sight post or scope reticle. Also, the muscular effort required to pull a heavy trigger introduces jerks. Then there is abrupt relaxation of strong tension just after the trigger breaks, which interferes with a smooth follow-through. No one shoots a heavy trigger particularly well.

A three-pound trigger alerts your subconscious that the trigger is being manipulated—there's just enough resistance but not too much. If the pull is too light, the gun fires before you're ready.

Linked to weight of pull is consistency of pull. Many triggers do not break at an identical pressure from shot to shot. Bad triggers vary their break by

Timney of Arizona makes aftermarket replacement triggers for many rifles.

as much as two or three pounds. The worst thing about this is it keeps the shooter guessing as to when the rifle will fire.

"Creep," or drag, describes the motion of the trigger before the break. It is not desirable because it's annoying; the shooter never knows exactly when the shot will break. Excessive creep tends to create a gritty feeling when pulling the trigger caused by friction on poorly finished parts. Ideally, there should be no creep, and a trigger should break cleanly under sufficient pressure as the shooter deems appropriate by adjusting pull weight.

Military bolt guns of yesteryear, such as the Mauser and Springfield rifles, featured a lot of creep. That was desirable on military rifles then, as they were predominately used by men under stress with little or no experience with guns. But a hunter must have instantaneous connection with the trigger when the gun is brought to the shoulder; the minute the eye lines up with the reticle, the rifle should fire. Too much creep in any trigger tends to confuse one's muscular control and thus reaction after the rifle fires.

"Over-travel" is the movement of the trigger after the sear breaks. One would think this isn't a problem, as at such a time the bullet is already on its way to the target. But the problem with over-travel is it disturbs the gun during dwell time, that instant of time when the bullet is still in the barrel, when the momentum of your rearward-moving and now accelerating trigger finger is abruptly halted when the trigger comes to a stop at the end of its travel. If over-travel is great the rifle is buffeted, altering sight picture. Over-travel is most damaging when combined with a heavy pull weight because the trigger finger moves proportionally faster and harder.

The best triggers are consistent and reliable, with little motion and vibration so your trigger press is almost imperceptible. A hard trigger pull—that is, one with a heavy pull weight—causes too much exertion during trigger press, and even fatigue in some cases. Worse, the muscular contraction necessary to manipulate the trigger tends to throw off the sight picture.

Today almost all triggers on factory-produced hunting rifles function at minimal pull weight with little or no creep or over-travel. New rifles produced by Remington, Winchester, Browning, Kimber, Thompson/Center, Savage, and others break cleanly at three to five pounds, and several are user-adjustable.

If your trigger is not user-adjustable, or if it displays more creep or over-travel than you'd like, it's best to hire a gunsmith to adjust it to your liking. Beware, however, that too much tinkering can lead to an unsafe condition.

Sometimes a factory trigger worked over by a gunsmith isn't the best option. An aftermarket trigger can cost no more than the labor of a gunsmith, and in many cases may be safer. If you have a factory trigger with creep, a lot of over-travel, or more pull weight than you'd like, a drop-in aftermarket trigger, such as those made by Timney, might be the answer. Most installation jobs take less than an hour. With few exceptions none take gunsmith work, but some require inletting of the stock around the new trigger. A typical installation involves removing the factory trigger by driving out two pins and installing the new trigger with the same two pins—that's about it.

The Stock

Material

Riflestocks may be made of wood or some synthetic material—plastic, fiberglass, Kevlar, graphite, carbon fiber, or some combination thereof. A finely grained wood stock is a beauty to behold; a synthetic stock is cold and unpleasing to many eyes. Aesthetics aside, terrain and weather dictate the stock material you should choose.

Originally, of course, wood was the only material used to make stocks. Gunsmiths in colonial times favored curly maple on flintlocks for its beauty, and

Both these guns have stainless steel metalwork, but other features differ greatly. The Remington Model 700, back, uses a synthetic stock and wears a nylon sling—a good combination for the rigors of wet weather in places like Alaska. The Kimber 84M, front, wears a walnut stock, good in arid climates but likely to swell if exposed to a week of rain.

it is still in use, but the most popular wood today is walnut. In the deer woods, in many parts of elk country, and in Africa, walnut stocks predominate.

There's simply no denying the beauty of finely grained walnut. Coupled with nice bluing on the metalwork, a walnut-stocked rifle attracts admirers. You'll pay for that admiration, though. Walnut is becoming scarce; many of the stock blanks used in the United States today come from overseas. While any number of factories and custom gunsmiths use walnut these days, remember that the nice stuff with fine grain draws a concomitant price. If you plan to use the rifle mainly in dry conditions, a walnut stock will serve nicely. Over time, it may acquire scratches and dents, or "beauty marks," as owners like to call them. You will never regret taking a finely grained piece of walnut to most elk camps or to Africa.

If you want to take the rifle to Alaska, however, it's wise to consider a synthetic stock. Wood warps in wet weather, and wet weather is a fact of life on the Last Frontier. Synthetic material, however, is impervious to the elements. It also resists scratches and dents. It's also generally lighter, which is why custom gunsmiths like Lex Webernick of Rifles Inc. use it almost exclusively. If your aim is a lightweight rig to carry up and down the mountains of elk or sheep country, a synthetic stock material should be your sole consideration.

Design

The style of stock is mostly a matter of personal taste, although there are caveats to consider. One is whether your rifle wears a one- or two-piece stock. Generally, bolt-action stocks are one-piece; there simply isn't any reason to split up the material, as the stock may flow from buttplate to fore-end tip without interruption and function perfectly. One-piece wood stocks are susceptible to warping in wet weather, however, which can affect the accuracy of a bolt-action rifle because as the stock twists it applies pressure to action parts and even the barrel bedding. Two-piece stocks are generally found on semiautomatics, pumps, and lever-actions because the action type dictates interruption of the lines between buttplate and fore-end; we can't work a lever, or pump a fore-end, on a one-piece stock. While these stocks are also susceptible to warping if they're made of wood, the problem is mitigated by the two-piece design.

Another choice in stock design is whether to weld your cheek to a straight-comb or a Monte Carlo-style stock. When I was a boy, I loved to play with G. I. Joes. In those days, the 1970s, army Joe was being phased out in favor of adventure Joe. My main Joe was a tiger hunter, and he carried a bolt-action rifle with a Monte Carlo stock. Thus I grew up thinking of a Monte Carlo as the only stock design to be considered. It's not. In fact, while the Monte Carlo is still popular in Europe, the straight-comb style is more popular in America. The difference is more than aesthetic; there are practical considerations.

A Monte Carlo stock has a high comb to position a shooter's eye in line with a riflescope mounted atop the action. The high comb also helps a rifleman obtain a solid "cheek weld," a critical component of marksmanship. The hump in the comb is easy on the eyes; it's as if all riflestocks should be shaped this way. Generally it works well, too, especially if a large-objective scope is used. Sometimes, though, the comb is too high for low-mounted, low-powered scopes, the kind you'll want to use on lightweight mountain rifles. What's more, some say that the high comb sends much of the recoil into your face, instead of straight back into your shoulder where it belongs, although many hunters disagree with this. The Monte Carlo stock is a distinguishing feature of Weatherby rifles, and most Weatherbys I've shot have not done this; then again, they were moderately chambered. But there was that .378 Weatherby Magnum I borrowed for a brown bear hunt that was brutal, to say the least.

A straight comb is an almost exclusively American aesthetic, at least on sporting guns. A stock of this style is rather ordinary looking, but it functions perfectly as long as the proper scope is used with low- or medium-height rings. What I like most about this design is its simplicity; a straight comb against my cheek feels similar to the military rifles I've carried. Most importantly, it sends recoil straight back into my shoulder, where my body—not my face—is more apt to handle the force without strain.

There are certain design considerations involving the fore-end. Do you want two forward sling swivel studs in order to mount a bipod? If they're present on a factory rifle, they generally indicate a heavy-barreled rig. If your rifle is a lightweight model, you'll have to install a second one on your own. Big-bore magnums used for dangerous game generally place the front stud on a barrel band, which prevents your hand from being pinched during recoil.

Most bolt-action rifles employ a drop floor plate with a box magazine. Study the magazine release to be sure it's of proper design, and to make sure the parts are sturdy. Some rifles leave the factory with too-weak or too-strong spring pressure here, or with release buttons inappropriately sized. Either problem can lead to dumped magazines when least expected, or to a rifle that is a bear to unload.

You can save some money, and shave weight, by eschewing a drop floor plate. If you do, though, you'll have to unload the rifle one round at a time by chambering and ejecting each cartridge. That can be problematic in the dark. Removable magazines are popular among hunters who climb in and out of vehicles all day. Carrying two isn't a bad idea for a quick reload in the field.

Fit

Length of pull is the last variable to consider with stock design. Here, again, we'll deal mainly with bolt-action rifles, for lever-actions are all pretty much the same and single-shot, pump, and semiauto designs are made within more or less the same parameters as turnbolts.

Notwithstanding "youth" or "bantam" rifles, a quick look through any manufacturer's catalog will reveal that most bolt-action rifles are cut for two lengths of pull: 13½ and 13¾ inches long. If you're a big fellow, 13½ inches may be too short. If you're a man of standard height, as I am, 13½ inches may feel just right. Some shooters, especially youngsters and women, may need a shorter length of pull, in which case they will in all likelihood need to consult a stockmaker to cut the stock of the rifle to match their dimensions (although there are a few models available with shorter lengths of pull).

Consider clothing you may wear on a hunt because it alters your length of pull. A 13¾-inch length of pull may feel fine on the range when you are wearing a lightweight shirt. When you are wearing bulky clothing, however, it may be tough to shoulder the longer length of pull; thus, consider a 13½-inch length if the situation warrants it. I own guns stocked with both lengths of pull and shoot both well. While my physical frame suggests a 13½-inch length of pull is more

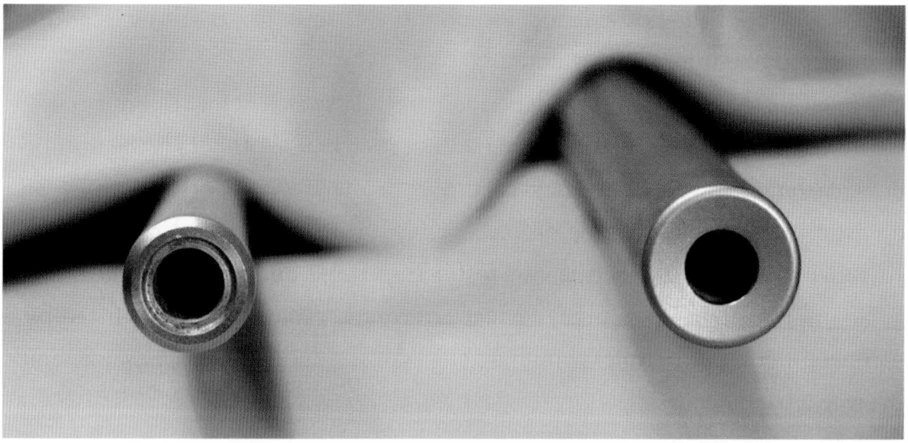

The standard weight and contour barrel on the left is nice to carry all day or all week, but its light weight can make it whippy when it's time to hold steady on a target. The heavy barrel on the right is more rigid, which should produce better overall accuracy. The trade-off is a lot more weight than that of a standard contour. The standard barrel also has a recessed crown, a feature increasingly popular with hunters who are worried about damaging the very last part of the rifle to touch the bullet before it travels downrange.

comfortable for me the majority of the time, I would never venture afield with a .375 H&H Magnum thus stocked. To do so would be to invite "scope eye."

The rifle's fore-end should be ample enough to aid your weak hand as you grip the rifle, but not so thick that it adds weight or bulk. On hunting rifles, this generally translates to a slender profile. So-called "beavertail" fore-ends have wide, flat surfaces designed to nestle in a benchrest or on a sandbag, and are not suitable on most big-game rigs.

The Barrel

The barrel is the heart of the rifle and a major determining factor in accuracy. Without a good one, a rifle is worthless.

Not long ago, anyone who wanted an accurate rifle replaced its factory barrel. Today, computer-numerically-controlled (CNC) machinery and better materials have made many of the rifles produced by high-volume gunmakers today as good as anything made in a custom shop, all other factors being equal. In fact, it's likely an average out-of-the-box rifle today shoots as well or better than any fine-tuned custom gun of our forefathers' era.

Even so, there are a lot of independent barrel producers for the aftermarket. Custom gunmakers will tell you that a desire to change calibers is the number-one reason. Improved accuracy is also a prime desire. Both accuracy and ballistic performance can be enhanced with a new or higher-quality barrel. In general, re-barreling a rifle can result in a three-quarter to one minute of angle improvement in accuracy. Most aftermarket barrels must be fitted by a competent gunsmith; unless you have the training and the tools, never attempt to swap a barrel yourself.

Taper and Length

You can make your rifle longer, shorter, thinner, fatter, or prettier with your choice of barrel. With various contours from soda-straw thin to beefy, match-grade thick, and overall lengths ranging from eighteen to twenty-six inches, the barrel of your rifle has a profound effect on aesthetics. How it performs in the field, however, is your paramount concern. A long barrel may be necessary to eke out velocity from magnum cartridges, but it will be prone to getting caught in thick brush. Conversely, a very short barrel may make for a whippy rifle that does not settle well on target.

A lot of people think fluting looks cool, but it was developed to serve a purpose. It not only lightens the weight of a barrel, but it increases its surface area to speed cooling. At the business end, a recessed crown protects the muzzle from damage—important since this is the last surface the bullet will have contact with before it travels downrange.

Most rifles come in one of three common barrel lengths. Rifles in standard calibers generally wear twenty-two- or twenty-four-inch barrels; rifles chambered in magnum calibers generally have twenty-six-inch barrels. The extra two inches of barrel on the latter provides more burn time for the extra powder used in magnum chamberings. That's all well and good on the plains of Africa, but it can be a hindrance in heavy brush. Go shorter if you like, even in a magnum, if you will use the rifle exclusively in places like Alaska where fighting the alders is a daily chore.

Rifling

High-volume gunmakers usually use one of three methods to form the rifling inside the bore: cut rifling, hammer forging, or buttoning. Cut rifling is the oldest method. With it, cutters physically remove metal from the bore to form grooves. There are two methods. Single-point uses a single cutter that removes just a small amount of metal (about one-ten-thousandth of an inch) with each pass. It cuts one groove at a time; multiple passes precisely indexed to each groove are required to complete the barrel, which makes this method time-consuming. The second method pulls a gang broach with a series of cutters, each slightly larger than the previous one, through the barrel. The gang cuts all the grooves in a single pass. With either method, cut barrels must be lapped by hand to produce a proper finish. These barrels are expensive, but their rifling is uniform throughout the length of the bore. Many custom gunmakers and competition shooters prefer cut rifling.

With hammer forging, a barrel blank slides over a mandrel that is a mirror image of the expected finished bore. Then the barrel is radially hammered under pressure and compressed around the mandrel in the barrel to form the rifling. The blank may be cold before forming (cold hammer forging) or hot (hot hammer forging). Either style leaves an excellent bore finish and a barrel of great strength. Hammer-forging equipment is expensive; this method is usually used by companies that manufacture a high volume of rifle barrels.

Button rifling uses a bullet-shaped, carbide "button" with the rifling form and twist rate built into the body of the button. The tool is pushed or pulled through the barrel blank to physically displace, or "iron out," the grooves in the bore. The button may rotate freely with the grooves on the body, controlling the twist rate, or it may be held rigidly and positively rotated to keep variations in twist rate to a minimum. Button rifling is fast and results in a smooth, hard bore. Machinery for the process is inexpensive, making it the preferred method for most barrel makers today.

Chapter 2

Iron Sights: There When You Need Them

If you're using iron sights, it's probably because you need them, not because you want them. Sure, you can go afield with irons and do just fine on a big-game hunt. But why bother, when a riflescope can reduce the margin of error? Lest you discount the difference between "need" and "want," take into account two immutable facts.

First, as we age our vision deteriorates and it becomes difficult to focus on the front sight. This fact of life prompts many hunters to give up on irons at some point in their lives. Secondly, while a "throwback" hunt with irons can be great fun from time to time, regardless of the quality of your vision you will be effective with them only when the shots are close. How close? That depends on a lot of things. In the eastern United States shots can be close, sure, but thick woodlots there produce a lot of vegetation that not only obscures your vision but makes it difficult to obtain a sight picture. In the American West or in Africa, open terrain may prevent stalking close; often you'll be lucky to get within two hundred yards. In either case, I'll use a scope every time.

So where does "need" come in? Answer: In the pursuit of dangerous game. If you hunt critters that bite back, you'd better understand how to use irons and know what separates the good ones from the crud. When stalking bears, buffaloes, elephants, and such, it's critical to get close for the first shot or else risk an error. Sometimes it's necessary to follow wounded dangerous game into the thick stuff, leading to heart-pounding moments when a split-second reaction might be the difference between life and death. If you find yourself in such a situation, you'll likely need a wide field of view, and that may require you to remove your optic and rely on open sights. Whether it's the first shot or a follow-up, by default that animal will be practically in your lap when you give it the news.

Principles at Work with Iron Sights

All open sights function under the same premise: Your eye positions the front sight in one of several positions relative to the rear sight then, while maintaining this arrangement (sight alignment), you place the front sight on the aiming point (sight picture). If you're using an open V, U, or square-notch setup, you can get on target and place an accurate shot quickest by burying the front post in the bottom of the rear notch. Alternatively, more precise aiming is possible by centering the front sight in the rear notch and lining it up flush with the top leaves of the rear notch. Since the front post is so prevalent, however, this method tends to cover up the aiming point, leading in fact to coarser aiming. Thus preciseness may not be what is called for during fast-moving situations when open sights are used. Depending on sight construction you may not have time for finesse—a desire for preciseness may lead in fact to slower and more inaccurate aiming. Lastly, if you're using a rear aperture sight, you center the front post in the circle. Any way you cut it, the process is complex compared to using a riflescope.

The problem is we are capable of focusing only on one object at a time. Thus, the eyes of shooters unaccustomed to using iron sights will tend to wander between target, front sight, and rear sight. Stock fit, too, is a concern. Bring a gun to your cheek slightly differently from shot to shot and the sights may not line up the same way from one moment to the next, producing errors in aiming that are difficult to address.

Shooters accustomed to using iron sights are capable of extraordinary accuracy. Others will curse them. To make sure you're not a member of the latter group it helps to understand a few principles of aiming that apply to any sight system.

Sight alignment is the relationship between the front sight post and the rear sight. It's critical to achieve when aiming with open sights because errors in the process grow in proportion to the distance fired; a one-inch mistake at one hundred yards expands exponentially at four hundred yards, which can be the difference between a dead or wounded animal, in some cases.

Sight picture, by contrast, is the placement of the tip of the front sight post in relation to the target. It can be described as a 6 o'clock hold, a 12 o'clock hold, center mass, or whatever. The point is sight picture must be attained after sight alignment is achieved, and it must be maintained while simultaneously maintaining sight alignment.

Focus must remain on the front sight after you achieve sight alignment and sight picture. Remember the human eye can focus on only one thing at a time, which explains why we hear shooting coaches preach "front sight, front sight" repeatedly to their pupils. Whether it's a pistol or a rifle, the concept is the same: Focus on the front sight post when you begin your trigger squeeze.

The sight radius is the distance between front and rear sights. For precise aiming, the longer it is the better because there will be less margin for error in sight alignment. Think about it: The distance between the front sight post and a rear peep on a rifle with a twenty-six-inch barrel may be twenty-nine inches, and on a pistol with a four-inch barrel sights are likely only five or six inches apart, which explains why it's more difficult to accurately shoot a pistol than a rifle. But a long sight radius does not induce speed. Remember, we need to achieve sight alignment and sight picture, and then focus on the front sight. Also remember that we cannot focus on more than one thing at a time. With a rear peep, you'll spend precious seconds achieving sight alignment, which might cost you a shot. A quarter-rib rear sight mounted perhaps five inches forward of the receiver is much quicker, particularly for older eyes. The reduced sight radius will magnify errors in aiming, sure, but what is lost in preciseness is made up in speed. Speed, if you're using open sights, is most important, as the animal is likely close and the situation fluid.

Eye relief is the distance between your aiming eye and the rear sight. Creep up the stock too much and you'll be hard-pressed to achieve sight alignment; you'll have too much room for error when aligning front and rear sights.

All this should point out two things. One, it's critical to maintain the same eye relief from shot to shot in each shooting position. Two, open sights are not necessarily quicker to employ than a riflescope. They are quicker in the hands of those familiar with their use—folks like professional hunters of dangerous game who must back up their clients in thick bush, for instance. But "client" hunters of dangerous game unfamiliar with open sights should invariably stick to a scope.

Moreover, since open sights are not capable of magnifying the image of the target, zeroing your rifle precisely will be more difficult. That also makes them ill-suited for long-range shooting. The worst sights ever created are perhaps the full buckhorn style on American lever-actions; their wings cover the target during aiming. The very best might be a leaf sight with a top-edge V or, my favorite, a wide-aperture peep.

You should know that not all "open" sights are the same. Most are usually made of some sort of metallic material, but the term "open" is not a catchall to describe all iron sights. An "open" sight, to my way of thinking, is a rear sight with a notch through which the front sight is aligned for aiming. There are several kinds of rear notches with a V, U, or square-shaped cut on their upper edges—none of which is an aperture, which is another kind of "iron" sight. The term "irons" generally describes any sight, front or rear, not containing optical elements. Irons may be fixed or adjustable, but they are not all open. Also, they are not universally available as standard equipment these days on most big-game rifles. When present, iron sights are rarely anything more than simple "open" sights, which can leave much to be desired, as we shall see.

So what makes a good set of iron sights? First of all, they should actually be iron, or steel or aluminum, as it were. Beyond that, there are a number of different types.

Fiber-Optic Sights

Fiber-optic sights are all the rage these days. Why not, since they glow like dimes on cow pies? The glow alone makes it easier to achieve sight alignment and focus on the front post. This makes fiber optics popular additions to many guns. Keep in mind, however, that with fiber-optic sights there is not really a front post—it's a fiber-optic pipe laid horizontally to produce a red or green dot. As such, there is nothing to be done should the front sight need to be trimmed (a rare occurrence). Also, fiber optics are often encased in plastic—not a very robust material. I can't tell you how many times I've cracked the fiber-optic front pipes on my muzzleloaders (enough times that I now mount XS Ghost Ring irons when I hunt where scopes on smokepoles are not legal). Don't be fooled into thinking you're getting a valuable feature on any centerfire rifle fitted with fiber-optic sights unless they are encased in steel or aluminum. And if you want to mount aftermarket sights on your rig, don't be swayed by the glowing embers in the blister packs at the gun shop unless they're surrounded by steel.

Another reason I generally don't like fiber-optic sights is because they invariably use a rear V and front ramp setup, which is not conducive to accuracy. That's not to say such a system can't be accurate; it can be, but you have to know what you've got in hand. The last reason I don't favor fiber-optic sights is I have yet to find such a system that allows me to mount the rear sight on the rear bridge of a bolt-action, thus increasing the length of the sight radius.

TRUGLO's Rifle Sight Set features a red front and green rear for eye-catching contrast. Machined aluminum ensures durability, and they are adjustable for elevation and windage. However, I can find them only for late-model Remington rifles.

The Williams Gun Sight Company makes a couple models suitable for our purposes. Its Fire Sight system uses a red front sight with an adjustable peep or U-notch rear. The latter, featuring a nice three-dot pattern for quick sight alignment wherein two green dots on the rear line up with a red front pipe, is available for Remington bolt-action rifles as well as Browning, Winchester, and Marlin lever-actions. The company's WGOS Replacement Slide/Blade combo fits all standard-size Williams adjustable, rear-guide, open-sight bases if you insist on replacing your rear irons with fiber optics. With this system, an aluminum blade contains a U-shaped green rod; use it with an existing front blade or replace that, too. Better still is the company's Fire Sight Ghost Ring system that fits all standard-size Williams adjustable rear-guide open-sight bases. It's aluminum, adjustable, and features a large-aperture aluminum ring with two green dots on either side for quick sight alignment. There's a Fire Sight hood, too, to protect the front pipe.

New England Custom Gunworks offers a fiber-optic front sight for Ruger No. 1 and M77 rifles; it is encased in steel with fully machined bodies that feature either white or red pipes.

Buckhorn Sights

The standard American buckhorn setup—a rear V-notch atop a ramp with a built-in elevator and a front ramp (with either a brass bead or fiber-optic pipe)—is usually found on lever-action, rimfire, or muzzleloader rifles these days. Any of the three guns will be used at perhaps one hundred yards or slightly more, which makes the room for error inherent in a buckhorn setup acceptable. The rear sight is invariably mounted forward of the receiver, which shortens the sight radius, producing a lot of "air" around the front post when achieving sight alignment, the same drawback I find with most fiber-optic sights.

A typical buckhorn rear sight on a lever-action rifle: Note the wide margin of error. There's plenty of room here to achieve sight alignment, but there's also plenty of room to mess up the sight picture. A buckhorn sight is quick-handling, but it's not very precise.

The way the front-sight post is mounted on this lever-action gun shows poor quality. If that barrel band were wrapped around the barrel of a bolt-action rifle, one would expect the front sight to be a part of it. Don't count on this setup to last very long, especially on a rugged hunt. The spot weld that holds the sight post is very likely to fail.

Marble's offers a variety of replacement barrel-mounted rear sights if you want more precision than your factory buckhorn setup delivers. The Bullseye model is designed to center your eye within two steel rings; the moment the rear sight is misaligned, the theory goes, the front sight drifts out of the center ring. I have not used such a system, and I have my doubts about looking through two concentric rings. Seems like a lot to overcome. Perhaps a better solution is the company's Folding Sporting Rear Sight. It's steel, too, and it folds to prevent damage when not in use. Best yet, it uses a standard buckhorn notch more precisely cut than you'll find on most lever-actions as they come from the factory. The long shank replaces the rear buckhorn on lever-actions. It's screw- and drift-adjustable for elevation and windage thanks to a center plate and lock screw, so there's no elevation ramp needed. The folding leaf has a white-diamond insert to improve sight alignment.

Express Sights

The other kind of V-notch rear sight setup lies in the blades of express sights found on dangerous-game guns, and these can be quite accurate. Don't confuse a buckhorn V with an express V. The former is simply stamped metal, and it's not very robust. Because it's mass-produced, the setup produces a lot of "air" around the front bead when you achieve sight alignment. The latter, on the other hand, is machined steel, and it's usually made by somebody who knows what he or she is doing.

Express sights feature between one and three V-notches. Usually only the first one is fixed; the others fold down when not in use. Often only the first one is regulated, or cut precisely, a bit at a time, to place rounds on target at a given range. The other one or two blades are generally left for the buyer to cut for use at whatever ranges he or she sees fit. When cut precisely, these blades produce amazing accuracy. The V-notches are very fine, not nearly as wide as those in a buckhorn, and the front post nestles nicely into position when achieving sight alignment.

Sight alignment can be a problem, as express setups usually feature a rear sight mounted somewhat forward of the chamber, thus limiting the length of the sight radius. But that's done with target acquisition in mind. At close range, where these sights will be used, these sights need to come to your eye quickly; there's little time to find the sweet spot of a peep when a Cape buffalo is bearing down on you.

The front post is usually made of brass. It can tarnish over time, which makes it hard to find it and concentrate on it. You can solve this by keeping it polished, or you can opt for the bright white or fiber-optic post many makers use instead of brass. Stay away from the fancy "solutions" some gunmakers employ these days, the ones that veer from the standard setup and instead use rather ridiculous "square peeps" with white outlines designed to supposedly lead your eye to proper sight alignment. Express V-blades have been used for more than a century, and there's nothing wrong with them a little practice and familiarity can't solve.

Express sights should be standard equipment on a dangerous-game gun. Whether it's a magazine rifle or a double, a gun like this is built for Africa, and it won't come cheap. You should expect its factory sights to be of high quality, and you should expect accurate regulation. I watched a peer settle into a benchrest setup behind a Heym PH double rifle and hit his point of aim at 200-plus yards. Now, nestling behind a .450/400 (3") double gun on a bench isn't my idea of enjoyable shooting, but it's nice to know such a gun is capable of this kind of accuracy. That being said, hunters of dangerous game should expect to engage their quarry at a hundred yards or less. That's where express sights shine—providing your eyes are up to the task.

New England Custom Gunworks makes a nice line of steel aftermarket express sights—in fact they are factory-installed on many dangerous-game guns. (Why reinvent the wheel?) They sell aftermarket bases with one leaf or two, and banded ramps, too, to protect the front sight.

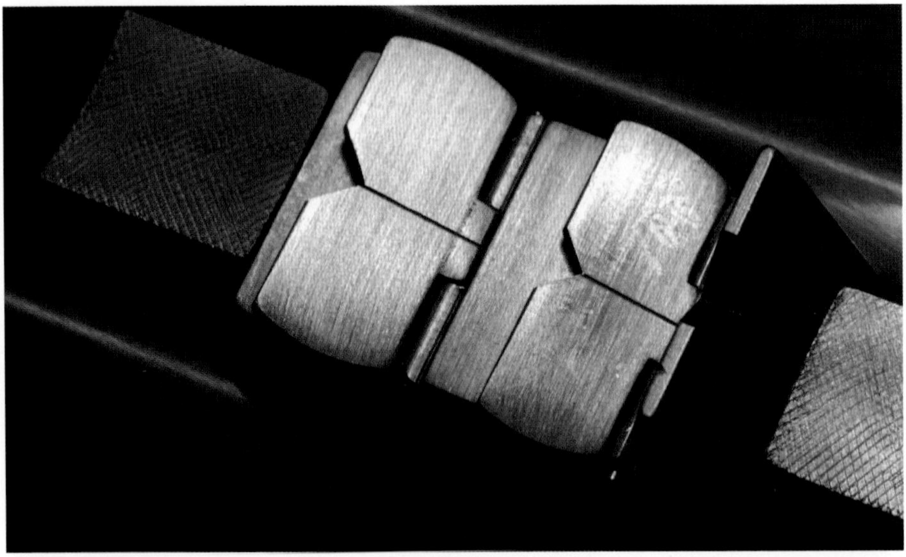

A three-leaf express rear sight on a double rifle: Note the standing leaf and two folding leaves. Normally, a gunmaker regulates the standing leaf to whatever range the user wants—usually fifty or a hundred yards. The user then cuts or files the two folding leaves to be accurate at other desired ranges. Because the Vs in the leaves are cut sharply, this sighting system can be very precise.

Peep Sights

My favorite iron sight setup features a rear peep, or "ghost ring"—so-called because your eye does not focus on it, so it forms a ghostlike ring of gray in the peripheral vision of your sight picture. At first blush, it might seem logical to assume a peep is not any more accurate than a plain old V and ramped front blade. It seems intuitive, after all, that once you settle in behind that rear ring you'll see too much "air" around the front post. But a ghost ring works because our natural tendency as human beings is to center any object within a circle. (Ask the six-hundred-yard shooters at the NRA National Matches what they use for the High Power Rifle event.) Not only is a peep sight the most precise iron sight, it's also the most consistent and the easiest to use.

Nowadays, the term "ghost ring" encompasses basically any large-aperture sight used for quick shooting in low light. Jeff Cooper, former Marine, founder of Gunsite Academy, author of the book *The Art of the Rifle*, and the guru of defensive pistol technique, swore by its use. Of course hunting is a far cry from combat of any kind, but the fact is game seldom stands still, and we usually encounter our quarry at dawn and dusk—two times of day when a ghost ring shines.

Peeps are generally tang-mounted, on the steel above the pistol grip behind the receiver, or receiver-mounted, atop the action of the gun. A tang-mounted sight was once more popular among hunters than a bolt-mounted setup, and it was once standard equipment on most lever-action, autoloading, and slide-action rifles. It was also found on some bolt guns—in fact, the 98 Mauser was offered with a tang-mounted peep sight that folded down when the bolt was pulled rearward then popped up when the bolt was pushed forward. Tang-mounted sights offer a longer sight radius and thus more precision than a receiver-mounted setup, but they can be dangerous when the shooting angle is severe because the shortened eye relief can put that piece of metal in your eye. For hunters with bolt-action guns, a receiver-mounted peep makes the most sense because they are easy to install, they weigh next to nothing, and the good ones are fully adjustable for windage and elevation.

Every hunter past the age of forty, though, needs to remember that peering through a peep increases the focus depth of field. Think about how a camera lens works. When we decrease the size of the aperture the depth of field increases, but the amount of light that passes through to the film plane

The Lyman peep sight was standard on bolt-action guns of yesteryear. This is a fine setup for durability and preciseness, but note the small aperture. It's difficult to achieve sight alignment and maintain sight picture quickly.

is decreased. Thus, a longer shutter speed is required to make an image. The same thing applies to using a peep sight: The image through the peep will appear dim; it will take longer for aged eyes to achieve sight alignment and then focus on the front sight. Conversely (particularly if you're farsighted), if you have trouble focusing on the front sight when peering over plain old "open" sights you will see it sharply when viewing it through a peep, but a small-diameter peep will be most effective. If you're farsighted, try using the smallest peep that still allows enough light to pass through to your eye in order to bring the front sight into focus.

If you need to mount aftermarket irons on a bolt-action or muzzleloader, check out the XS Ghost Ring Hunter series from XS Sights. The setup is simple, adjustable, robust, and made of steel. You won't knock it out of zero on a hunt.

The larger ring is ideal for hunting because it lets in more light than the smaller version and therefore is a good choice when encountering game at dawn and dusk. With practice, I've put shots into a six-inch or smaller circle at one hundred yards with a muzzleloader. Not very accurate, you say? Well, a peep sight is no match for a riflescope. Five- or six-inch groups at one hundred yards should be about what any of us can expect without the help of an optic.

The company includes detailed instructions with every pair of sights it sells, but there's not much to mounting this system. The holes on the rear aperture should line up with the holes drilled and tapped in your rifle's receiver (and they will if you explain your needs to company reps when ordering). You can use a rail instead, if you prefer, but either way be sure to mount the rear sight as far back as possible. This is critical, for a longer sight radius ensures better accuracy. The aperture threads up/down and left/right for fine adjustments in elevation and windage. The front sight comes in two parts. If your rifle barrel is drilled and tapped for a front sight, you need only screw the ramp/dovetail into the same holes. (If the rifle, as is usual these days, did not come with factory sights, you'll need to engage the services of a gunsmith to drill and tap the barrel.) Once the dovetail is attached, tap the post into it. A sight pusher, available from Brownells, might come in handy here. Regardless, most shooters should appreciate the tight fit, which ensures the post won't disappear in the field. If you're not a do-it-yourself type, a call to XS customer service can answer any questions that arise.

Other companies make peep sights—New England Custom Gunworks, Marble's, and Lyman prominent among them. Lyman has three styles of aluminum rear apertures that fit hundreds of rifles—even one for tang installation on muzzleloaders. Audible clicks tell you the quarter-minute adjustments to elevation and windage are indeed taking hold. An elevation stop screw permits instantaneous return to zero. A quick-release mechanism allows the slide to be removed at the press of a button. There's a reason Lyman sights were factory equipment once upon a time—they are well made. The Lyman peep on my 1937 Winchester Model 70 still functions flawlessly.

Chapter 3

Riflescopes: Focus on What Counts

It was Dad's gun. Mom bought it for him for Christmas in 1971 with half the money Dad won at blackjack when the two of them vacationed in the Bahamas. It was a Marlin Model 336C in .35 Remington, a good, old-fashioned East Coast brush gun. Moreover, it was a lever-action, a gun that I, a fan of Chuck Connors and the TV show *The Rifleman*, simply loved.

After Dad died, the Marlin was my main connection to the man I watched build our family's first deer stand. At that time telescopes had yet to become mainstays atop hunting rifles, mainly because hunters still didn't trust them to remain accurate and fog-free. Thus at the time Dad died in 1974, he'd yet to mount one atop the Marlin.

I eagerly began my hunting career with that gun, but without a scope I was outclassed. This was especially true in Pennsylvania, where I accepted invitations to accompany my childhood friend, Andy, and his father, Charlie, in the late 1970s. There, deer could appear at long range, so for the first season or two Charlie loaned me his Winchester Model 70 chambered in .30-06, which, naturally, wore a scope. I used the loaner gratefully, but I felt less than whole around the old-timers in Pennsylvania; I was itching to use my own rifle.

One fall Andy said, "You need a scope. Maybe my dad has one you can borrow."

Charlie did. It was a 4X Redfield Widefield, which featured an oblong ocular lens shaped like a TV screen to widen a hunter's field of view. The scope was the perfect addition to a gun that fired a fat, .35-caliber slug—the package was the ultimate East Coast brush buster.

I hunted with my own gun that season, finally feeling complete among the old-timers in camp. But I didn't get a deer, and I wondered how I'd do the

You should match your scope to your rifle in terms of size, weight, and capability. This Remington Model 700 Mountain Rifle in .30-06 is served well with a Leupold Vari-X III 2.5–10X40 riflescope with a Boone and Crockett reticle. It's an ideal setup for a mountain hunt.

following year with a rifle that once again would be devoid of an optic. Then, on Christmas Day, Charlie called me.

"You know that scope I loaned you? Keep it. Merry Christmas."

The Redfield "made" the gun. It was an awesome Christmas gift for a boy whose mother couldn't afford to outfit him with everything he thought he needed. I bagged my first deer with the Marlin/Redfield rig, and many more deer over the years.

Finally, in the mid-1990s, I retired the lever-action with its limited range and the scope with its limited magnification in favor of a bolt-action Winchester Model 70 chambered in .270 Winchester, fitted with a 3–9X Leupold Vari-X II.

Now, I thought, I'm ready for long range.

Was I truly ready? Well, I thought I knew why I wanted a variable-power riflescope. No doubt most of us think we do, but without a rudimentary understanding of what's at work within a scope that provides magnification and a single sighting plane, we're shortchanging the process.

It's akin to my days as a budding photojournalist, when college professors made me shoot all photos in manual mode before switching to the "idiot-proof" automatic modes available on my camera.

"You need to understand what's at work," they said.

To do that, I learned to first visualize the picture, then capture the image I wanted by manually manipulating the controls on the camera. Only after I understood what calculations in exposure, aperture, and focal length produced the precise images I envisioned could I confidently switch to an "auto" mode and take the pictures I wanted in fast-moving situations. Once it all clicked, I could concentrate on framing images rather than the nuances of exposure.

That "speed of thought," if you will, is critical in photojournalism, where photographers don't so much make images as take them. When shooting sports or spot news, the scene unfolds quickly. It's important to watch, to learn, and record the event rather than think of oneself as an artist who has the benefit of time to think through everything. The difference between using iron sights and using scopes is similar, I believe. A hunter may use a scope effectively for an entire hunting career, but without a rudimentary understanding of what's at work within the sight, how can he or she appreciate the benefits it provides?

The main tube of my Redfield Widefield is steel, a desirable feature in the 1960s and '70s when many hunters didn't trust the strength of aluminum scopes. It has "coated" lenses and a "cross hair" reticle, also two qualities considered state-of-the-art at one time. It has never failed to hold zero, but as we shall see, that's likely a testament to Spartan use rather than superior construction (although the Redfield brand did enjoy a sparkling reputation). The view through it is rather milky today, despite that "coated" glass. And its cross hair is difficult to pick up in low light now that I'm accustomed to using a plex reticle. How times change. What once was considered cutting edge now seems antiquated.

Scopes first appeared on rifles in the United States in the 1840s, and snipers used them in the Civil War. Military use of optics was unquestioned a hundred years later, at the outbreak of World War II, but it took a while longer before hunters trusted them. Just about everyone was used to seeing and concentrating on a front sight post, so simple "post" aiming points made the transition to optics seamless. The desire for a more precise aiming point was answered by a cross hair, which sufficed to keep one's field of view uncluttered.

There were other misgivings to overcome, however. Many considered the erector systems of early scopes to be too delicate—thus the instruments could never be trusted to hold zero. Even if they could, a scope was bound to fog, causing one to miss a golden opportunity. Today, in an age of waterproof construction, high light transmission, and repeatable adjustments, when one may custom-order any reticle, it's hard to fathom such resistance.

It's easy to define the qualities of a good riflescope: optical brightness, robust construction, and sufficient eye relief teamed with a reticle you can use effectively. Seems like simple advice. Too bad so many hunters don't follow it. Instead of the big picture, they focus on features that matter little.

When shopping for a scope, remember you are choosing a sighting device, nothing more. It is not an instrument to enable you to see the rings of Saturn, though the magnification of some scopes today will give you a pretty good view of the heavens. It is not the best device you can use to determine range, although many scopes do just that. It is not a cure-all for bad shooting, despite the fact that many hunters expect whatever they view through a scope to die if they will it to happen by pulling the trigger. Brightness, construction, eye relief, and a reticle you use effectively, in that order, are the keys to marksmanship when using a riflescope.

Note I said nothing about parallax adjustment. Parallax is the apparent movement of the target when you view it from an angle through the scope at either very close or very long range at high magnification. It's a function of distance—the targets lie at different points between the objective and the erector of the scope—and it can't be corrected with lenses. The reason? The reticle does not move along the scope's main-tube axis to compensate for this disparity, so it meets a focused image only when the target is a certain distance from the rifle. Big scopes with big objective lenses and high magnification feature parallax adjustment so you can program the scope for zero parallax at the range you want to shoot.

A big-game rifle, however, has little business wearing a scope with a magnification greater than 10X, the point beyond which you'll need to worry about parallax shift. If your eye is centered in the axis of the scope, you don't need to worry about parallax regardless of range.

Instead of gadgets, worry about qualities that count. What you need to know is most scopes made for big-game hunting are set to be parallax-free at roughly a hundred yards. Likewise, you don't need to worry about relative brightness, twilight factor, or other arcane terms. Focus on the following features.

Brightness

A bull elk looks good through almost any scope at high noon when it has answered your guide's cow call after an hour of entreaties. Place an inexpensive

These two newer riflescopes represent the trend toward bigger objectives and more bells and whistles. The Zeiss Victory Varipoint 2.5–10X50, top, provides excellent light gathering with its 50mm objective, and it features the company's Lotutec, a water-shedding exterior lens coating. The Weaver Grand Slam 3–10X50mm, bottom, features a mil-dot reticle and finger-adjustable turrets. Both scopes are rather large, but because of their length there is plenty of margin for mounting them on either short- or long-action rifles.

scope next to a premium-priced Leupold, Nikon, Zeiss, or Swarovski at dawn or dusk—the times when you're much more apt to see that bull—and you'll see a major difference.

An experience I had at Wingmeade Plantation in Arkansas some years ago illustrates my point. The plantation managers wanted to thin the whitetail herd, and hunters were asked to shoot as many does as we wanted. We could also shoot any buck of a certain size, but, above all, the biologists wanted us to take does. I was happy to oblige them.

After a couple days of hunting, everyone had killed a sufficient number of does, and by dusk on the third night I hoped a good buck might materialize. I peered into the waning light with a Swarovski EL binocular—an optic widely recognized as one of the best in the world. There, in a staging area where I expected to see activity as day turned to night, was a magnificent 10-pointer. The buck never stepped into position and I left my stand without getting a shot at it, but the point is, with a cheap optic I would have seen only shadows. With the Swarovski, I saw details in the shadows. Most hunters think two factors—30mm main tubes and big objective lenses—are responsible for brightness in a scope. The truth is, lens quality and magnification affect brightness more.

The majority of optics makers do not make their own lenses. They order glass from one of only a handful of lens producers in the world. Save for special considerations outlined by the ordering company, glass is glass. What optics makers do to the lenses during their own production processes makes a heap of difference. Further, what they've learned to do with them over the years makes old scopes pale by comparison to what's on the market today—the reason my old Redfield will never be as bright as anything produced today.

Uncoated glass admits only about 50 percent of the light that strikes it; the rest is reflected off the surface of the glass, away from our eyes. A coating effectively creates two layers—the coating and the glass surface itself. Stray light that bounces off the glass beneath a coating is reflected by the coating back through the lens to our eyes. The coatings on "coated" glass are no thicker than half a wavelength of light, because a full wavelength of depth would be similar to no coating at all—it would reflect light. Single-coated lenses transmit 85 to 90 percent of light.

But light is made of many wavelengths, which, as photographers know, is why we see color. And each color occupies its own frequency, just as different sounds occupy different frequencies. So multicoated lenses gather more light waves than single-coated lenses, and transmit 99 percent of the light that strikes them.

A mere two layers qualify an optic to be labeled "multicoated," but that may mean the maker has covered only one or two lens surfaces in its proprietary coatings. The top makers use three or more coatings to produce their best lenses, and they coat all air-to-glass surfaces, which produces "fully multicoated" optics, the best you can buy. It's an important distinction, for it means you can count on reduced flare. Point a single-coated optic toward the sun and notice how the image washes out. Good multicoated lenses practically eliminate flare.

The more lenses in a scope, the less light will be transmitted. Remember, each multicoated lens transmits 99 percent of the light it gathers. Four multicoated lenses in a fixed-power scope transmit only 96 percent of the gathered light to your eye. To perform their feats, variable-powered scopes have more lenses, which can consequently make them less bright at a given magnification than a fixed-power of the same magnification.

Light passing through any telescope isn't funneled down by the scope tube but by the lenses it houses. Hold the scope at arm's length and view the circle of light in the center of the ocular lens. This is the exit pupil, and it's the source of the image we see. The diameter of the exit pupil is critical to the brightness of the scope.

The easiest way to measure exit pupil is to divide the diameter of the objective lens by the magnification of the scope. An 8X40 scope has an exit pupil of 5mm. Exit pupil diameter, however, changes with magnification.

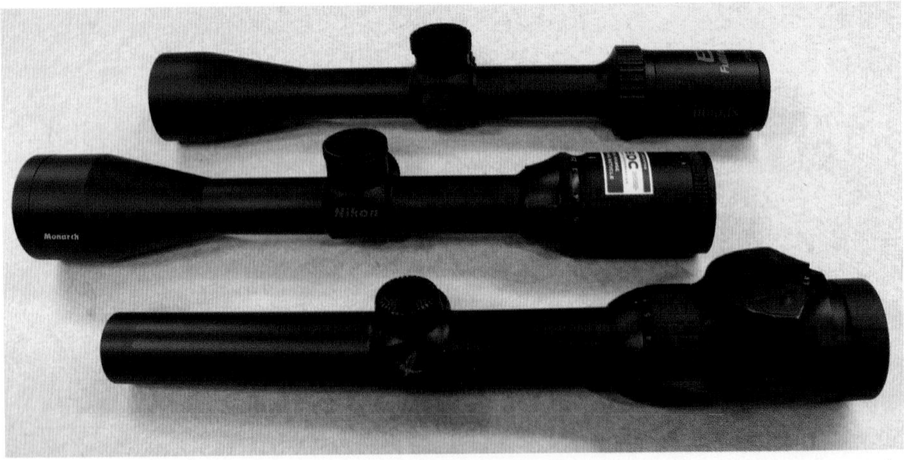

These three scopes run the gamut of length, overall size, and features. The Burris Fullfield E1 3–9X40, top, features the company's E1 Ballistic reticle. The Nikon Monarch 2.5–10X42, middle, features the company's BDC reticle and is a good all-round scope both in size/weight and in magnification range. The Swarovski Z6i 1–6X24, bottom, represents the latest development from the revered Austrian optics maker. Z6 scopes feature 6X magnification range for maximum bang-for-the-buck in versatility. The illuminated reticle on this model, however, necessitates the bulky housing for the electronics atop the ocular lens.

So a 3–9X40 variable will produce an exit pupil of 13.3mm at 3X and an exit pupil of 4.4mm at 9X.

Our own pupils expand and contract, respectively, in dim and bright light to regulate the amount of light that strikes the rods and cones of our eyeballs. When we're young and healthy, they shrink to about 2.5mm in bright sunlight and expand to perhaps 7mm in dim light. By the time we reach our mid-forties, most of us can expect dilation of no more than 6mm, and a loss of perhaps a millimeter per decade after that. No matter how big the objective lens is, your eye can use only so much light, about 7mm, as we've seen. So a big objective benefits you only when shooting at high magnification in low light. The reason bell-shaped objectives are used, even on fixed 4X scopes, is because they provide latitude for head placement.

Beyond 5X, tube diameter has little effect on brightness. Do the math again. At 10X, a scope with a 50mm objective lens produces an exit pupil of 5mm; at 10X a scope with a 40mm objective produces an exit pupil of 4mm. You won't see the difference in the field. So don't weigh yourself down with a 5–15X50 variable scope on your big-game rifle. European optics makers produce 30mm scopes not because the larger diameter produces more light, but because they use the metric system. (Where 30mm tubes shine is in the range of adjustments enabled by their larger diameter, a point we'll discuss later.)

The diameter of a scope's exit pupil, and thus its brightness factor, is dependent on three things: magnification, objective lens diameter, and the interior dynamics of the scope itself.

Lean hard toward small objectives. More magnification shrinks exit pupil; 8X produces half the diameter of 4X. And remember it's the objective lens, not the main tube, that gathers light. A 40mm objective lens on a 4X scope produces an exit pupil twice the diameter of a 20mm objective lens, regardless whether the lens is mounted on a 30mm or one-inch tube. You don't need anything larger than 40mm, and if you find a scope with magnifications to your liking with a 36mm or even 32mm objective, all the better.

The guts of all scopes are not created equal. In much the same way as camera lenses use apertures to "stop" down the light they collect and thus "sharpen" the transmitted image, some scopes use field stops, interior light-blockers, to reduce diffracted light—the fuzzy wavelengths that reduce image quality. This comes at a price: It reduces exit pupil size, which reduces the size of the circle of light your eye sees. It reduces the brightness factor of the scope.

You can tell whether a scope uses a field stop by literally measuring the exit pupil with a ruler. Shine a flashlight through the scope from front to rear, place a piece of paper behind the ocular lens at a point where the image is sharpest, and measure the resulting circle of light. At 8X a scope with a 40mm objective should produce an exit pupil of 5mm, right? If the exit pupil measures, say, 4mm, you've effectively discovered a scope that, despite exterior dimensions, functionally has a 32mm, not a 40mm, objective lens. That's not too bright, despite what the manufacturer may print in advertising. The best scopes don't have field stops.

The interiors of all decent scopes should be painted, or baffled, to reduce reflection. You can see this yourself by shining a flashlight into the objective lens of a scope. Is the inside solid black? It does little good to use multi-coated lenses to gather all that light if a bright main-tube interior bounces it every direction except toward your eye.

Construction

My Redfield Widefield has a steel tube. When it was made steel was considered the way to go, despite the plethora of aluminum scopes then on the market. But while steel is inherently stronger than aluminum and is still used for some scopes, notably tactical models, the material has its inherent problems.

Steel is heavier than aluminum. Tote an extra couple ounces up the mountains of sheep country if you like, but also understand that steel, since it doesn't give, will transmit the shocks of inevitable bumps and bruises to the guts of the scope. I doubt the innards of any quality scope would shake loose,

This is a nice gun/scope setup. The Kimber 84M in .243 Winchester is a small rifle that demands a small scope. The Leupold M8 fixed 4X scope atop the rig is a nice accompaniment both in terms of size/weight and magnification.

but I'd rather not find out. Aluminum, on the other hand, merely dents when it's bumped, rather than transmit any shock to the guts or lenses. Steel is unnecessary; you don't need a scope to be as strong as your rifle barrel. Also, steel tubes as light as aluminum are stretched, thinning their walls enough to negate any strength advantage.

Be sure it's waterproof. You can't count on sunny weather during any big-game hunt, so don't count on coddling a scope that isn't rated for the elements. In 1947, Leupold & Stevens was the first manufacturer to use nitrogen purging to prevent fogging. The gas prevents any condensation from temperature swings within the scope. Since then, leakage has been further reduced as better seals and one-piece tubes have come on line. You can test manufacturer claims by dunking the scope in warm water, which will expand the nitrogen inside the scope and push bubbles through any leaks. Next, you can check it against fogging by placing it in a freezer.

If you do these tests, be aware of two things. First, some waterproof claims are valid only when the turret caps remain in place. Check manufacturer literature, or better yet quiz company reps at trade shows to learn which models feature O-rings in their adjustment turrets. Second, it's impossible to eliminate absolutely all moisture within a scope when it's assembled, even with the best nitrogen-purging system. Expect any scope to fog if first dunked in warm water, then placed in a freezer.

One-piece main tubes are sturdier and better sealed than two-piece tubes. But two-piece tubes have served well for decades, and they're still popular mainly because they reduce cost. Other things might be more important for your application. How much room does the tube allow for mounting atop a receiver? Is the turret located conveniently? The tube sections of many scopes locate turrets in bad spots, or have such long ocular housings it's impossible to find a suitable ring location. Many 30mm tubes use the same erector lenses as one-inch units. However, a 30mm tube allows more room for erector movement, thus providing more elevation or windage adjustment than a one-inch tube.

Adjustments must be repeatable. If you turn a quarter-minute turret four clicks, you should get one inch of adjustment at one hundred yards. Shoot the square to test this. Fire a three-shot group at one hundred yards; move eight clicks left and fire three shots; then eight up and fire; then eight right and fire; then eight down and fire. The fifth group should print on the first.

Tactical turrets—those that allow you to make adjustments without unscrewing caps—are popular nowadays. I like the M1 turrets calibrated in quarter-minute clicks on a Leupold Mark 4 scope I've been using lately. If you grow accustomed to dialing in elevation and windage rather than simply holding over, such a system can pay dividends. It's not for everyone. For one, the turrets add weight. Most hunters are better served with simple, covered turrets that require the user to unscrew the covers before making adjustments.

The less weight the better. A smaller objective often will serve your style of hunting. Scopes in the 3.5–10X range are as popular today as 3–9X scopes used to be. But they weigh perhaps an ounce more than the old standbys. A 2–7X does anything the aforementioned variables do, but at about an ounce less.

Glass elements already add all the weight you want in a scope; the rest of the components should be as light as possible. Not long ago, titanium scopes looked like they'd be the next big thing. A quick look through manufacturer Web sites recently revealed only Nikon still offered such a unit. There's a reason 99 percent of all scopes made for the sporting market are made of aluminum: The material does everything we need it to do in a lightweight package.

Too much weight does a lot of things. It adds to the overall weight of your rifle; it raises the center of gravity because a big scope will likely have a big objective lens, which requires a high mount; and it adds to the inertia of the scope during recoil. Too much weight can cause a scope to slip in its rings during recoil. Depending on tube dimensions, a steel scope may add 30 percent over the weight of an aluminum scope. An increase in objective lens diameter from 40mm to 50mm adds another couple of ounces. Batteries add weight, too.

Scopes will fail. If you hunt long enough you'll find one that does. I've seen three scopes kick the bucket. One was brand-new, and its reticle broke after its owner took three shots. The others were not old, but they had been used by hunters who did a lot of shooting. Both failed to respond to turret twists (likely indicating broken adjustment springs).

A third type of failure, reticle shift, is also common, especially on hard-kicking rifles. Reticle shift is exactly what's occurred with a five-year-old scope mounted on a .300 Winchester Magnum I've carried from the Rockies to Africa, which is quite a bit of use for such a young scope. The symptom is usually increasingly larger groups, or failure to hold all three shots of a group within established averages. It may take merely a few shots, it may take hundreds or even thousands of rounds, but no scope can withstand the effects of recoil atop a high-power rifle forever.

Finger-adjustable turrets are becoming increasingly popular, and with good reason. They allow shooters to dial in windage and elevation adjustments without first having to unscrew turret caps. This one from Leupold is designed specifically for a 55-grain .223 Remington load.

Tough as they may be, riflescopes are complex instruments, and multiple complex steps are involved in their manufacture. Despite the best quality-control measures, any company can and will build a bad one occasionally. The majority of scopes sold will never see heavy-duty, repeated use. Optics makers know this. They know the average buyer is a deer hunter who shoots a box or two of ammo per year through his trusty '06. Less expensive scopes, therefore, simply don't need to be particularly tough because most hunters will never shoot them enough to break them.

If you buy a new gun for Africa, buy a new scope for it. Don't transfer the ten-year-old scope from your deer rifle to it, for two reasons. That scope is old, and the magnum may deal it the inevitable recoil-driven death blow. Or, switching it to the big kicker may reveal an inherent defect the little kicker never had enough stones to muster.

Remember, the bigger the cartridge, the smaller the scope. Any animal you hunt with a .460 Weatherby Magnum is big enough to see well through a small, low-powered scope. You don't need 15X to see a Cape buffalo. Plus, the heavier the scope, the more likely it will succumb to recoil.

These days, lightweight rifles are all the rage. Not long ago the average .30-06 weighed perhaps nine pounds. Nowadays, it's not uncommon to see .30-caliber magnums that weigh less than seven pounds. I know, because I've got three of them. Couple this with the public's current desire for bigger scopes (and the industry's desire to sell anything hunters want). Then imagine the forces of recoil at work on a heavy scope atop a lightweight gun.

Eye Relief

Eye relief is the distance between your eye and the scope when you obtain a full field of view—it's the complete circle of light you see when you nestle into the sweet spot on the stock. It's as important to note on mild-recoiling rifles as it is on hard-kicking ones because it affects the field of view you'll have while looking through the scope.

There are two measurements of eye relief—optical and practical. It's the latter that keeps recoil from giving you "scope eye," and it can sometimes differ from the advertised number by half an inch. Check eye relief by reading company literature, but beware of caveats. If you suspect that the generous four inches of eye relief touted in a catalog is something less than three, measure it yourself. As you did to measure exit pupil diameter, shine a flashlight through the scope from front to rear; place a piece of paper behind the ocular lens at a point where the image is sharpest; and measure the exact distance with a ruler.

If it's a variable scope, rotate the power ring and you'll notice that eye relief varies with magnification. It can lengthen at low magnification and shorten at high magnification. It's why you may sometimes have difficulty finding the sweet spot when you crank up the magnification of a variable-power scope. This isn't a big problem on deer rifles, but a mere three inches of eye relief at 6X on a .458 Winchester Magnum could deliver a bloody brow—another key reason to stick to low-powered scopes on big kickers.

Science dictates that the shorter the eye relief, the wider the field of view. Long eye relief can be designed into any scope, but it comes at the expense of field of view. A large ocular lens can provide both, but such a scope must be mounted high on bolt-actions to make room for bolt throw. My Redfield Widefield did this too, of course, with a horizontal lens that resembled a TV screen, but it was long ago discontinued.

Nowadays scopes are mounted low on receivers, thanks to high combs on riflestocks. This negates the need to have both long eye relief and field of view. Field of view is less critical in such a setup because the ocular lens lies right before your eye, not off to the side. So pick one. My vote is for long eye relief, because a few extra feet of field at two hundred yards matters little.

Reticles

Once upon a time you could have any reticle you wanted, as long as it was a cross hair. Well, that's not entirely true—there were also posts and dots. But cross hairs were the predominant reticles on the market when hunters began using scopes in earnest seventy years ago.

Leupold & Stevens changed all that in 1962, when it released what is now the most widely used reticle on the market: the Duplex. It's a cross wire with thick outer sections that thin as they cross in the center of the field of view. The thick lines grab your attention and carry it inward, where the thin lines stand ready to help you aim carefully. In poor light, you can find a point of aim quickly thanks to the thick lines. And if you know the subtension of the center wire at a given magnification and yardage, you can use the Duplex as a rangefinder. No wonder it's so copied nowadays. You'll be hard-pressed to find any maker of riflescopes that doesn't offer some sort of plex reticle in its catalog.

The Leupold Duplex is a mechanical reticle—wire suspended on a mount within the erector tube. Leupold begins with micro-thin platinum wire, then flattens and thins it even more to make the outer lines appear thicker than the middle. Some companies make their plex reticles by crossing flattened wires in the middle to make the center cross wire super-thin. Others twist ribbon wire at the middle of the lens. All three of these wire reticles are soldered in place.

Another process uses chemicals to etch away all excess material on metal foil to reveal the reticle pattern. The remaining foil is quite thin and must be cemented to the mount. Proper tension is crucial; too little, and the foil will shake under recoil, too much, and it won't withstand extreme temperatures. Point a scope with an etched reticle at the sun too long, and you'll melt the reticle. Reticles may also be etched on glass. A lot of shooters like them because there is no wire to break under recoil. However, remember our discussion of brightness—the more lenses a scope has, the less light will be transmitted to your eye. A glass-etched reticle adds another lens.

In light of plex reticles, cross hairs don't make much sense—their thin wires make it hard to find the center of the reticle in low light, or make it out against a cluttered or colored background. Posts don't make much sense either; heavy ones obscure the target if you must hold over. And in dim light there is only one thick wire rising from the 6 o'clock position to guide your eye to the center of the field. Posts were widely used seventy years ago because shooters at the time were used to focusing on a front sight blade. A post reticle seemed to make the transition to optics easier.

Simple dots were also popular when scopes became commonplace on hunting rifles. Today they are mainly used on tactical rifles at short range. Hunters should use a dot larger than they think they need, but consider two things: your specific application and your scope's magnification. A four-minute dot might look right in a 2.5X scope on a lever-action used for hunting whitetails in the woods, but appear too big in a 6X scope used on a .30-caliber bolt-action for pronghorns on the plains. Regardless, remember they provide nothing to guide your eye to the center of the field of view in dim light or thick brush.

A rangefinding reticle can be quite useful in the right hands. With one you can determine holdover at great distance—greater than you'll ever need to shoot at any game. The simplest use stadia wires (cross bars), but indicator marks might be specially sized and spaced round dots or football-shaped dots. Any of them bracket a known dimension at a given range—eighteen inches, the chest depth of a deer, is an industry standard. If you know the wires should span a buck's chest at two hundred yards and you're looking at a deer that fills only half that space, you can figure the animal is standing at four hundred, not two hundred yards.

Many of the newest rangefinding reticles are a hybrid of tactical and hunting features. My Leupold Mark 4 2.5–8X36 MR/T with M1 turrets fits this mold. It's a blend of many of the best features I've outlined throughout this chapter: a 30mm tube for 90 minutes of adjustment range; the smallest objective lens I can find in such a package; finger-adjustable turrets; and a special reticle that took some time to master. Leupold's Tactical Milling Reticle (TMR) employs various sized and spaced hash marks on each stadia to aid rangefinding and accuracy. With it I can determine range to the target using the mil system then pick a corresponding aiming point matched to my cartridge (in this case, a .308 Winchester).

Still, the mil-dot is the primary design. Contrary to popular belief, "mil" stands for milliradian, not military, despite the fact the U.S. Marine Corps devised the mil-dot in the 1970s for sniper use. Milliradian is the mathematical measurement at the root of the system. That should tell you something about the level of sophistication involved in its use. (We'll discuss the mil-dot system in greater detail when we explore exterior ballistics.)

Some rangefinding reticles use the more familiar minute of angle (MOA) as the basis for their measurement systems. You must understand the difference because a milliradian is not the same as a minute of angle. (We'll discuss why I prefer thinking only in terms of MOA later when we discuss exterior ballistics in chapter 9.) Although it is the premier optical rangefinding method, few hunters will make the effort to master the mil-dot system because it is complicated and too dependent on a user's math skills.

Regardless whether it's a mil-dot or MOA system, user interpretation is involved; you must decide how high or wide the animal is relative to the spacing of the dots. Since game will rarely fit exactly to the marks, you must estimate its size on an imaginary scale. Then you must make a calculation to determine distance, which can be time-consuming. Add to that a quick check on a cheat sheet or another calculation to determine holdover. Not only that, rangefinding reticles are calibrated at only one magnification. Forget this fact when using a variable, and you'll hit nothing.

Many plex reticles help hunters estimate range with posts spaced to coincide with the chest depth of common game (eighteen inches, as stated, is an industry standard). Key distances for referencing are between the ends of the two opposing posts (thirty-six inches) and from the center of the reticle to the end of the post (eighteen inches). Bracketing the animal by varying the magnification then referring to a distance scale on the magnification ring will indicate distance to target. Leupold and Burris include range-estimation scales on the magnification rings of many of their scopes.

Using any reticle for range estimation is like learning a second language: It must be practiced regularly to be maintained. If you use a laser rangefinder in the field (you should), a bullet-drop-compensating (BDC) reticle is a step up from a basic plex system. With range determined, a BDC provides all the information you need for determining holdover without the extra calculations required in mil-ranging.

BDC reticles have been around for some time, but the designs coming online these days are better than ever. They work for a broad range of cartridges because many factory loadings share similar trajectory arcs. Thus shooters intuitively see what's at work with the holdover bars placed on the vertical wire. But complexity still varies widely. As with the mil-dot system, the most accurate BDC reticle on the market does little good if it provides more information than you can process at the moment of truth. Conversely, a simple, intuitive reticle may not be as precise as a complex one.

In terms of complexity, the Zeiss Rapid-Z and Swarovski BR reticles rank high. The dots between lines on the Rapid-Z 800 lie at fifty-yard increments out to six hundred yards, then in twenty-five-yard increments from six hundred to eight hundred yards. Swarovski's BR reticle consists of five main "bars" and five smaller "dots" between each bar, for a total of ten aiming points. Both models require online augmentation to printed instructions. On the Swarovski Web site you find data for your load, then write down yardages that correspond to each graduation. Zeiss requires you to enter data and get the correct magnification setting for your load and then adjust the scope accordingly.

Such steps are not unreasonable considering the level of sophistication at work here, but they are not required for other systems. Once they understand what they're dealing with, many shooters prefer these systems. Others (myself included) think they are overly complex, with too many bars and numbers filling the field of view.

By contrast, the Burris Ballistic Plex and Leupold Boone and Crockett systems are simpler to use. They use modified plex reticles with holdover marks between two hundred and five hundred yards. You zero the scopes at two hundred yards (three hundred if using a magnum) and adjust the power ring to the standard mark. Neither is as precise as those above, but they are more intuitive and don't require a hacker's skill online. You must use either one at its correct magnification setting for the holdover lines to work. Leupold's system also provides a ten mile-per-hour hold point for wind at both ends of its three hundred and four-hundred-yard lines.

Lying somewhere between the four previous models is Bushnell's DOA (Dead on Accurate). It's a plex reticle that provides not only holdover marks but a bit of range estimation and marks for windage, too. Four holdover lines for yardages between two hundred and five hundred yards lie beneath its central aiming point, and a six-hundred-yard hold can be had at the bottom of the vertical wire. Its Rack Bracket system helps you gauge the size of a deer's antlers—if the ears fit between the vertical lines of a given holdover wire, you know the approximate distance to the deer. The holdover wires are not load-specific, and you must use DOA at the highest magnification. Bushnell offers an optional glass-etched reticle if you prefer one.

If all this has your head spinning but you still insist on buying a BDC reticle, take a look at Nikon's BDC. It uses a series of two MOA circles beneath the center aiming point. At first blush, intuition would suggest one simply uses the circles like aperture sights, centering the target within them. That's partly true, because it does work. But the circles can be too coarse at long range. The system shines when you realize that each circle provides not one but three aiming points at its top, center, and bottom. That, too, can equal a lot of information—more than the average hunter needs. But for shots out to three hundred yards (about the practical limit for most hunters), it's fast and easy.

Perhaps the telltale sign of the complexity surrounding the use of any BDC reticle lies in the instructions accompanying Nikon's scope: They suggest shooters learn for themselves how each aiming point works with a given cartridge at a given range. That's good advice regardless of which system you choose, for no amount of hypothetical number-crunching or instruction can replace real-world experience.

The ultimate rangefinding, bullet-drop-compensating system is a laser scope. These electronic instruments (they're not simple sights) calculate the precise horizontal distance to the target whether they are pointed uphill or down. Aim at the animal, push a button, and in a split second the scope factors the distance, the angle of the shot, and the ballistics of your cartridge, and presents an illuminated dot to tell you precisely where to hold. Three models predominate: the Burris Eliminator, Bushnell Yardage Pro, and Nikon Laser IRT. Here's a secret: They're all made in the same factory.

Once you get the hang of things, any of them are extremely simple to use, but there are caveats. They aren't as bright as standard riflescopes due to many glass elements. They are extremely heavy: about a pound and half (remember what I said about heavy scopes). Before sighting-in, a specific load must be picked and its ballistic data entered into the scope. I suspect we'll all use laser aiming systems someday—when they are foolproof, brighter, lighter, and smaller. Until then, most of us will do things the "old-fashioned" way with a standard riflescope and reticle.

Lighted reticles are catching on fast. They show up well in dim light and help you obtain a sight picture quickly in thick brush. Too many of them, however, are too coarse and too bright; their glow dominates your field of view. Choose one with adjustable brightness; you need less illumination in dim light, more at high noon.

Of course, batteries complicate things and add weight. The battery bubble does nothing for looks, and the adjustment knob for brightness adds another turret and more weight. I wouldn't worry much about battery life, though. These days they all seem to last as long as you need them to, and even if they don't you still have a plex reticle in place. I suspect more sophisticated lighted reticles with finer aiming points will come on the market in the years ahead. Leupold's VX-R, with the firm's Fire Dot reticle, is a good example. It's sleek enough to suit most hunters' tastes, it comes in a wide range of variable magnifications, and it has an interesting feature to preserve battery life: After five minutes of inactivity it switches to standby mode. Simply shake the rifle and the unit powers up.

No matter what type of reticle you choose, be sure you understand where it is located. There are two locations where designers can place it within a variable-power scope tube—in either the first focal plane (in front of the erector) or the second (rear) focal plane. The reticle in most European scopes is placed in the first focal plane, so it changes size as magnification is increased. The reticle in most American scopes is placed in the second focal plane, so it remains centered and its size stays constant relative to magnification.

A first-focal-plane system subtends the same measure on the target no matter what the magnification, so you can use it as a rangefinder. It also eliminates point-of-impact shift when magnification changes in variable scopes. But it must be finer than a second-plane reticle; otherwise, it would appear too bulky at even the lowest magnification. To compensate for this, many makers use glass reticles, adding another light-robbing element to the scope.

See Clearly

A scope provides a bright, clear, flat sight picture to enable fast, precise aiming. It does you no good if it is not compatible with your rifle and suited to your style of hunting. If you follow the advice outlined here, you'll probably pay more for a scope than you had in mind. Think of it as money well spent.

To get the brightest scope, you must pay for it. But don't be fooled by the high price of European units, which may have more to do with the monetary exchange rate and European labor costs than quality components. The fact a particular model may cost twice as much as a similar unit made in America or Asia doesn't mean it's twice as bright. Still, a higher price tag should indicate some level of quality.

When it comes to magnification, remember you can do plenty with less. You can't go wrong with fixed-power scopes in the 4X, 6X, and 8X range. Variables of 2–7X, 3–9X, and 3.5–10X are all good, too. These variables employ a three-to-one zoom range; that is, the erector system provides magnification no greater than three times the lowest setting. Lately, five-to-one and even six-to-one zoom ratios have come on the market from Swarovski and Leupold. These make sense, as they offer a greater range of magnification in a package otherwise the same size as traditional scopes.

True, lower magnification may not provide all the precision you think you want, but it will give you enough to keep rounds on target at whatever range you choose to ethically engage game. With my 2.5–8X Leupold Mark 4 mounted atop my Kimber 84M .308 Winchester, I hit gongs at seven hundred yards. Assuming normal eyesight, a 4X scope will give you a clear shot at an elk at four hundred yards. Most of us can't shoot well enough to put eight of ten shots in a pie plate at that distance, so why buy anything besides a standard variable? You'll also save money by sticking to the popular units, as they're the most competitively priced.

Check used markets if you like; if it looks good chances are the scope is fine. But beware the cumulative effects of recoil. If you can quiz the original owner, do so—maybe the scope saw only limited use on a gun he never shot much. Stay away from third-hand scopes and anything a decade old. Chances are they've seen a lot of use, and the recoil bug may bite you.

Don't confuse sophistication with quality. Rangefinding reticles are a good idea only if their use is second nature. Too many dots, bars, circles, or numbers fill one's field of view with a lot of information. A cluttered view begets a cluttered mind in the moment of truth. Try as you might, it's hard to beat a simple plex.

As it was with your choice of rifle, the aspects of a scope bear directly on your marksmanship. A rifle that feels lively, one that's quick to shoulder and quick to line up with your eye, is usually topped by a scope with the qualities outlined here. It hurt to spend the money you did on your rifle, did it not? Spend enough on your scope to make it hurt just a bit more.

How to Mount a Riflescope

The main advantage of a riflescope lies not in its magnification, but in its ability to provide us with a clear image of the target on a single plane. That capability is negated if you are using a poorly mounted optic. I've never paid someone to mount my riflescopes. I learned to do it as a boy. To this day, I'm always amused to see someone pay for the service. The process is not difficult. Pay attention to the following tips and you'll never again pay a gunsmith to do it for you.

Choosing Rings and Bases

The wide variety of styles and brands of scope mounting systems available makes choosing rings and bases almost as confusing as choosing a rifle or scope. For starters, understand there are two kinds of mounting systems: fixed and detachable. However, that only begins to decipher the options. There are also one- and two-piece bases that use single or dual dovetails; horizontally and vertically split rings; single- and dual-dovetail mounts; and quick-detach setups if you think you might need to access the open sights on your rifle in a hurry.

Fixed systems are just that—fixed to your rifle. Once installed, they cannot be removed without tools. Detachable systems usually include removable rings, but sometimes the bases can be removed without tools, too. A fixed system is generally more aesthetically pleasing, and it weighs less than a detachable setup. Extensions for fixed-mount systems are available for scopes that don't provide enough mounting space between the bells and the center hub to sufficiently mount them on long-action guns. A detachable system, however, allows you to quickly remove a scope from a gun in the field if the optic fails, or if you need to follow-up dangerous game in vegetation that negates the advantages of an optic. Also, if you plan to use one scope on two different rifles, use a detachable system.

Rings may split horizontally or vertically. You may choose one or the other based on ease of installation, strength, or aesthetics; either one works fine. Only the bottom half of each horizontally split ring engages the base. Each half of vertically split rings engages the base, producing a strong mount, but one that's difficult to install properly. Both systems use between two and six screws. More screws may provide insurance against stripping or other failure, but they require more work during installation/removal. Some use Allen heads, others slotted heads, and others Torx heads, which resist "boogering" better than their counterparts and usually come with their own installation tool. Rings come in 1-inch, 30mm, and 34mm diameters to accommodate scope main tube sizes, and in different heights.

Bases are either one- or two-piece. On one-piece units, rings clamp onto an angular Weaver or Picatinny base (or rail). These are stronger because they help the scope resist the forces of torque during recoil, but depending on design they may interfere with access to the chamber. Some two-piece systems use a dual dovetail design, but two-piece Weaver or Picatinny bases also are available. Sako and Ruger use their own proprietary, integral bases.

Rings and bases are produced differently, depending on the material used. Steel, aluminum, and high-grade alloy systems are machined. Sintered steel (compressed iron and graphite) is cast, then machined. Some bases feature integrally attached bottom ring halves.

Universal fixed-mount systems (generally sold under the Redfield and Leupold brands) use either a dual dovetail setup or a dovetail front ring and opposing screws in the rear to provide windage adjustments. The latter setup allows you to use coarse adjustments to line up the reticle with the scope's centerline, so as not to use up the finite adjustments built into the scope during sight-in. The dovetail is a wedge, really, machined into the bottom half of each ring. It rides in the front base; insert it, then turn it 90 degrees to lock it into position. This setup is not as strong as dual dovetails. Universal rings from Burris, Leupold, Redfield, Weaver, and others are so similar as to be interchangeable.

Tools Needed

To mount any scope you need a few tools: a good gunsmithing screwdriver set (Brownells sells a popular one) with hollow-ground bits to prevent damage to mount and ring screws; a gun cradle to hold the gun firmly; dowel rods to torque the rings into place (never use the riflescope to straighten rings, as this may bend the main tube); rosin; electrician's tape; and a scope level (optional).

Eye Relief

Eye relief typically reduces when you adjust a scope from low to high power. Be aware that optics makers may only list eye relief at the low end of magnification. Check when mounting to make sure there's enough distance between your eye and the scope at high magnification, but also that there's an acceptable distance at low power. Some variable riflescopes provide constant eye relief throughout their range of magnification, a desirable feature.

Eye relief is critical when you don't have much back-and-forth room for adjustment when mounting a scope. Big-game scopes should have plenty of eye relief because sometimes you must aim quickly from unorthodox positions, such as steeply uphill, which place your eye closer or farther than usual from the ocular lens. Big kickers, in particular, should get lots of eye relief.

Don't settle for eye relief of less than three inches. Can't find the sweet spot? Your eye is too close or too far away from the ocular lens either because of a poor cheek weld or poor scope mounting.

Always mount a scope as low as possible. Most modern stock designs use a comb designed for scope use, which puts your eye in the scope axis as long as the scope is mounted low. Big objective lenses force the scope to be mounted higher, which can come at the expense of a good cheek weld. What's more, the rifle's center of gravity will be higher, and handling may suffer. If you plan to hunt from horseback, you may find such a mount won't fit in a saddle scabbard, either.

Tips for a Level Scope

A misaligned scope can prove costly. Take care to level the reticle and keep it level when you clamp down on the ring screws. It helps to tighten ring screws in a roundabout fashion, moving from one to the other, right to left, front ring to back ring, as you clamp the scope in place. Work slowly. Periodically shoulder the gun or, if it's clamped in a vise and you're sure it's level, peer through the scope to ensure the reticle remains level as you tighten the screws. This usually prevents uneven torque from rotating the scope as you put the final clamps on the rings.

The Level Level Level—yep, that's its name—from Wheeler Engineering levels the scope relative to the receiver, rather than the top of the scope base. It's available from Battenfeld Technologies, and it's simple to use. Level your scope as best you can as you mount it in the rings, and avoid cranking down on the screws. Bridge the bolt raceway with the rifle level. When that's established, use the scope level to double-check reticle alignment, then tighten screws on the rings.

Focus

Be sure to focus the eyepiece (ocular lens), and thus the reticle. You must do this with every new scope. Depending on the manufacturer, the ocular lens will have either very fine or coarse threads. Coarser threads are quicker and easier to turn into focus. American scopes use eyepieces finely threaded to the main tube, kept in check by a lock ring. Turn the eyepiece in or out (sometimes a great number of times) until the reticle is focused, then cinch down the lock ring. European scopes use a different system. Their eyepieces remain stationary, and the ocular lens cams in and out; there is no lock ring. The threads are coarser than American systems, and one turn may provide all the adjustment you need for focus.

Point the scope at a uniform surface just a few yards away, the better to see the reticle clearly. Don't focus the reticle in bright light, as your pupil will be contracted to limit the amount of light it gathers. Then, when you peer through the scope at dusk, when your pupil has expanded to see greater depth of field, the reticle is likely to appear fuzzy. Instead, focus in low light, when your pupil has dilated to perhaps the shallowest depth of field of your vision, and the reticle will stay sharp throughout your range of use.

Riflescope Mounting in Ten Easy Steps

1. **Bases and rings:** Many mount systems exist, but two predominate: Weaver-style and Redfield-style. Bases for both systems are available as one- and

two-piece units. Cross-slotted Weaver mounts make it easier to remove and reattach a scope. Dovetail-style Redfield mounts offer what many believe to be a stronger forward ring connection; and their rear setup offers built-in windage adjustment. Rings for both systems come in progressive heights from low to high to accommodate objective bells, bolt lift, and comb height. Choose the height that provides clearance for your scope and bolt, while simultaneously positioning your aiming eye in line with the ocular lens. Be sure to buy the right ring size; some scopes require 30mm rather than one-inch rings. Scope adjustment fore and aft in the mount to provide proper eye relief, and thus ring placement problems, can be solved by extension rings.

2. **Proper tools:** Damaged screw heads can result from slippage of ill-fitting drivers, making it difficult to remove the scope in the future. Invest in a quality kit with a hollow-ground bit like those available from Brownells and Lyman.

3. **Start clean:** Traces of oil left over from machining and cutting receivers and mounts/rings can prevent proper purchase of screws. Degrease mounts, rings, screws, and screw holes on the action with an evaporating agent like that available from Birchwood Casey.

4. <u>Securing bases:</u> Turn each screw into the hole individually. Check for looseness, making sure it clamps to the base securely. At least four or five threads must engage the receiver taps to ensure strength; replace screws that are too long or short. A drop of thread-lock ensures durability. Don't overtighten the screws, else risk stripping their threads or breaking off their heads.

5. <u>Mounting rings:</u> With Redfield rings, turn rear base screws evenly to begin with the scope centered; pivot the front ring into position with a dowel (never use the scope to do this, else risk bending the main tube). Protruding cross-bolts may interfere with tightening of Weaver rings; Brownells V-bit driver solves the problem.

6. <u>Check ring fit:</u> Check rings for burrs left from machining and file lightly if needed. For a tight, even fit, and to prevent scratching the main tube, line inside ring surfaces with electrician's tape or dust them with rosin. Trim tape with a razor blade.

5
BUSHNELL
BROWNELLS, Inc.
MONTEZUMA, IOWA

6

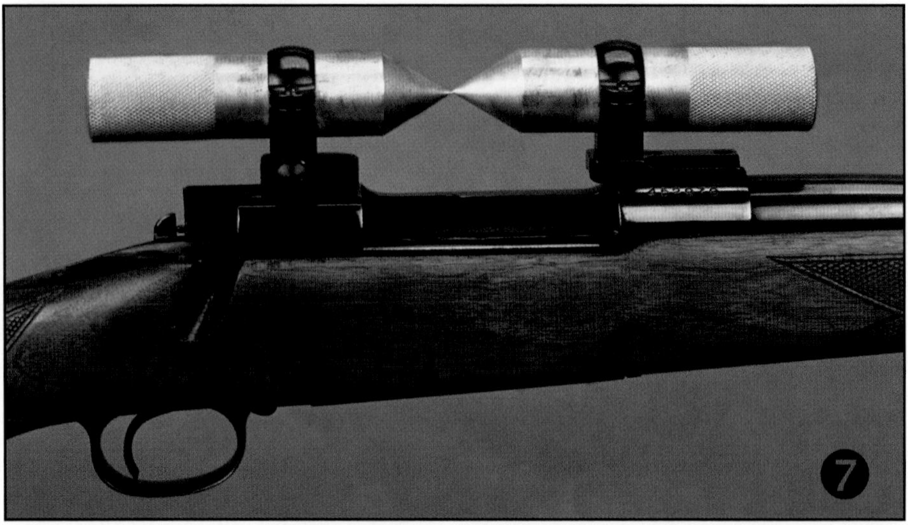
7

8

7. <u>CHECK ALIGNMENT:</u> Rings must be precisely aligned for the scope to fit without binding. Visually check to ensure ring edges are parallel with the main tube, or use a pointed alignment gauge from Brownells for absolute precision.

8. <u>POSITION THE SCOPE:</u> Snug up the scope under the top ring halves, but leave enough slack to allow you to move it fore and aft to adjust for eye relief or rotate it to level the reticle. To check your adjustment, close your eyes, shoulder the rifle, then open your eyes; eye relief should be correct and the reticle level. The Level Level Level, available from Battenfeld Technologies, ensures perfection on this part of the job.

9. <u>LOCK IT DOWN:</u> Remove remaining slack from all screws. Gaps between ring halves should even on all sides. To prevent stripped or broken screws, do not overtighten. To prevent disorientation of the reticle, tighten the screws in a cross pattern, side-to-side and front-to-back.

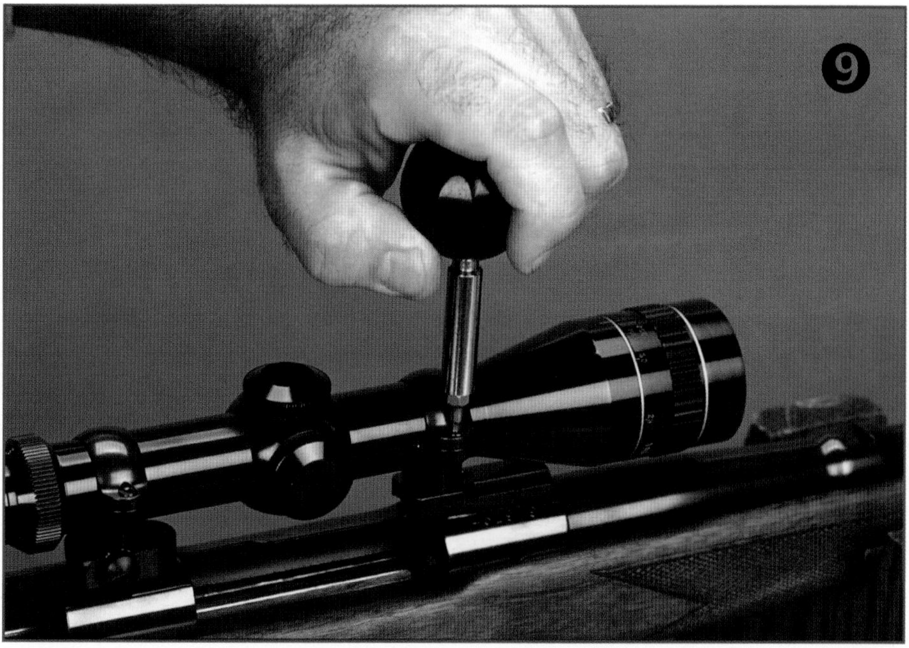

10. **<u>Bore sighting:</u>** Remove the bolt of a bolt-action rifle, peer through the barrel, and center it on a small object across the room. Alternately look through the barrel and scope, then, taking care not to nudge the rifle, adjust the reticle over the aiming mark. For more precision, or for rifles without removable bolts, an optical collimator (available from Brownells) will provide a good initial zero. Always check and fine-tune your zero at the range before hunting.

Field Note: Keep It Clean

- Carry an optics cleaning kit, and use it often. In my duffel I always carry lens-cleaning fluid and tissues in the same kit as my eyeglasses. If the scope takes a plunge, or if the weather is particularly bad, a good cleaning in camp usually keeps the picture bright.
- In the field during the day I carry two items in my pocket: a Lens Pen and a microfiber cleaning cloth. The Lens Pen has two ends, a soft brush that clears large debris and bits of dust that might scratch the exterior of the lens if it slides about underneath a cloth; and a squeegee-type wad designed to be used with a bit of pressure to clean and polish the lens of dried water marks. I keep both items inside my coat or pack, where they remain ready to clean and dry the most sophisticated instrument on my rifle.

Chapter 4

The Bullet: Where the Metal Meets the Meat

The first time I traveled to Africa I carried two guns, a .270 Winchester and a .338 Winchester Magnum. The plan was to use the .270 and 130-grain Sierra GameKings on smaller game like springbok, blesbok, and the like, and the .338 with 225-grain Nosler Partitions on larger game like nyala, kudu, and zebra. Upon arrival, however, the .338 shot poorly during a zero check. A loose scope was made worse when I sheared off the head of a screw trying to cinch down the optic in the rings.

"Forget it, Scott," said my professional hunter. "You've been shooting your .270 beautifully. Leave the .338 and let's go hunting."

Thereafter I proceeded to shoot everything in my bag—even the 400-pound kudu and 500-pound zebra—with a type of bullet that has performed marvelously for decades, but by today's standards doesn't run in the same league as newer designs like the Partition.

That's not to say the Partition is a new design—it's been around since 1948. As such, it was the gold standard in hunting bullets for decades. In fact, it wasn't until the 1980s that a new class of bullet—super-premium bullets, if you will—began to be produced by several manufacturers. Even today, the Partition remains one of the best choices in this category.

The science of ballistics is divided into three parts—interior, exterior, and terminal. As hunters, we're not too concerned with interior ballistics, the study of the processes within a gun as it is fired. We do care about exterior ballistics, the study of the motion of bullets in flight—an entire chapter is devoted to this subject later. We also care about terminal ballistics: how bullets strike, penetrate, and kill, which we'll discuss here.

Terminal performance is one of the most important factors in any killing shot. When all things work according to plan, a bullet expands (or not, as we shall see) on impact with the animal, creates a wide wound channel, and retains enough weight to penetrate to vital areas on the toughest game. Ideally, it does all this across the full spectrum of impact velocities, from fifty yards to several hundred yards. Of course, all this is moot if we don't do our job and place the bullet properly. So manufacturers work to control the only variables they can—exterior ballistics and terminal performance.

The GameKing and the Partition are traditional "cup-and-core" bullets; the cup is the copper jacket, the core is the lead surrounded by the jacket. In fact, the Partition is a double cup-and-core design; John Nosler created the first one by accidentally drawing two bullets together. It may have been an accident, but he knew a good thing when he saw it. For years, cup-and-core bullets were the standard, but today there are several designs that, to my mind, perform remarkably better.

Barnes Triple-Shock X-Bullet. (Photo courtesy of Bryce M. Towsley)

Many peers remind me that the GameKing performs very well on deer-sized game. In fact, my experience with African plains game years ago proves it does even better than that with proper placement. Still, why leave anything to chance when there are so many super-premium bullets available? The bullet we fire is the last chance we get to affect the outcome of the hunt. A super-premium bullet isn't cheap, but its cost is a drop in the bucket compared to the cost of a hunt in both time and money.

The Partition is but one of four types of super-premium hunting bullets available today. It's a mechanical locker, accomplishing its task with a design that smashes together on impact, mechanically locking the core and jacket together to prevent separation. (The Swift A-Frame also does this.)

Bonded bullets, the most prevalent design among premium hunting projectiles today, use heat or chemical processes to fuse the core and jacket together to prevent separation. These include the Swift Scirocco, Federal/Speer Trophy Bonded Bear Claw and Trophy Bonded Tip, Hornady Interbond, Remington Core-Lokt Ultra Bonded, Nosler Accubond, Federal Fusion, and the now discontinued Barnes MRX.

A third design, exemplified by the now-defunct Winchester Fail Safe and newer Winchester XP3, uses a combination of the two processes to bond the core and jacket and lock the two together upon impact.

Monolithic bullets use uniformity of materials (solid copper or copper mixed with gilding metal) to present one solid mass that, upon impact, smashes through to the vitals. These include expanding bullets like the Barnes Triple-Shock X and Hornady GMX, and "solids" like the Barnes Banded Solid and Nosler Solid. The result is nearly 100 percent weight retention. All premium bullets, however, deliver high weight retention in addition to outstanding terminal performance.

The majority of bullets mentioned above are expanding designs—they open up upon impact with game to deliver their terminal performance. As hunters, we are concerned primarily with these designs. If we pursue large, dangerous game like elephants and buffalo, however, we need to understand the terminal performance of "solid" bullets, which do not open but instead

Barnes Banded Solid. (Photo courtesy of Bryce M. Towsley)

stay uniform to penetrate and kill. In fact, many of these bullets remain so pristine they can be used again after they have been recovered from game.

When choosing a bullet, pay attention to its ballistic coefficient (BC), which is expressed mathematically to indicate a projectile's ability to overcome air resistance, or, conversely, its tendency to decelerate in flight. The BC represents drag, so for any given bullet at a known muzzle velocity, its expression represents the bullet's trajectory. Generally speaking, the higher the BC the higher the bullet's retained velocity, the greater its striking energy, the flatter its trajectory, and the less the wind deflection it will suffer. Nevertheless, BC is but one measure. In the final analysis, you want a bullet sufficient to perform on the game you hunt and one that your rifle shoots well. If you must sacrifice a few decimal points of BC to find that load, so be it.

No matter what kind of bullet you use, all this performance has a price; good ammo isn't cheap. That's mainly a function of worldwide commodity markets, the markets frequented by American ammunition makers, who must compete with, among other things, a Chinese economy that continues to grow. To save a few bucks, by all means shoot cheaper ammo through your gun during practice sessions on the range. Just about anything that groups well in your rifle will suffice, but don't resort to rock-bottom-cheap, corrosive stuff from some parts of the world; it can wreak havoc on your rifle.

How Expanding Bullets Work

The basic premise of expanding bullets is that they work when their front ends are weakened, allowing them to expand. Sometimes the weakening is facilitated with a hole in the front end, as on a hollowpoint; sometimes the lead core is merely left exposed. Either design can be further weakened by longitudinal cuts. The recovered bullet displays a mushroomed front end because it collapses outward when it hits game.

Even though humankind has used firearms to kill game for hundreds of years, there are many misconceptions about how bullets fired from guns actually work. The first misconception involves bullet speed. Many hunters believe magnum

Barnes MRX. (Photo courtesy of Bryce M. Towsley)

Hornady Interbond. (Photo courtesy of Bryce M. Towsley)

Hornady GMX. (Photo courtesy of Bryce M. Towsley)

chamberings or even the .270 Winchester develop too much velocity to allow a bullet to open upon impact. The truth is almost all bullets expand completely by the time they penetrate their own length—the biggest hole they ever make is immediately after they enter the game, not several inches into it.

Sure, some bullets expand less than others do, fostering a misconception that they open more slowly. The difference lies in fragmentation of the bullet upon expansion. Varmint bullets that deliver their terminal performance through disintegration upon expansion are a good example. They make a big hole upon impact and seldom exit. On the other end of the spectrum are heavy-duty big-game bullets that retain most of their weight. They make a smaller hole upon impact and then plow through the animal, making a long "wound channel" and, generally speaking, exit the other side.

The slow-expansion theory has no basis in fact. The truth is the exit wound produced by a heavy-duty bullet is not much bigger than the entrance wound. Expanding bullets often punch through hide on the off side, and many hunters point to this as proof the bullet did not expand, even though a post-mortem will clearly reveal a wound channel.

The Hornady Dangerous Game Solid, left and center, and Dangerous Game Expanding, right. The Dangerous Game Expanding has an exposed lead nose.

I proved this to myself on the African safari mentioned above, when the fast-shooting, .270-caliber, 130-grain GameKing I shot at a twenty-pound steenbok neither exited nor disintegrated. I shot that animal stem to stern. The bullet entered its chest; I found it under the hide on the off rear quarter, fully expanded. Although I shot this twenty-pound animal with a high-power centerfire rifle in a large caliber, the animal did not come apart, as one might expect. The reason was that the bullet did not disintegrate. It did expand fully.

Most expanding hunting bullets these days have hollow points to initiate expansion. In theory, a hollowpoint opens when the cavity in the bullet encounters fluid or flesh. In reality, there aren't many such bullets that won't open up in any medium.

Another misconception is that shock is the major factor in expanding bullet performance: "Arrows induce death by loss of blood," old-timers will say. "Bullets induce death by shock."

Trophy Bonded Tip, left, and original Trophy Bonded Bear Claw, right. (Photo courtesy of Bryce M. Towsley)

Trophy Bonded SledgeHammer Solid.

Hardly. The "shock" alluded to here means the collision of the bullet with game; many hunters mistakenly believe a bullet hits with so much energy ("a ton of it") that it must "shock" an animal into the contortions seen when it rears up and dies. They cite numerous examples, such as a deer that rises up violently upon being struck by a bullet. They quote theories of kinetic energy (the "ton" of energy delivered). In this case, these theories hold no water.

Think about it. A 2,000-pound car traveling sixty miles per hour (a mere 88 feet per second) produces roughly 240,000 foot-pounds of kinetic energy. That's about 100 times greater than the energy a 180-grain bullet fired from a .30-06 rifle delivers at 100 yards. If a rifle actually delivered that much energy, it would knock us down when we fired it. Remember Isaac Newton's rule: Every action has an equal and opposite reaction.

Bullets sometimes knock an animal down because the game is hit in the spine or its nervous system otherwise goes haywire. It isn't knocked down with energy—it falls down violently due to interior damage.

Still another misconception holds that a bullet that stays inside an animal rather than exiting is more "deadly" than one that does not. The truth is, bullets that do not exit still expand greatly. They stay inside an animal precisely because of that expansion; when they encounter resistance, their velocity is slowed. Consequently, the now-wider bullet creates a wider wound channel—that, not energy or "shock," is what kills the animal.

Related to this misconception is the theory that energy otherwise capable of being delivered to or inside the animal is somehow "lost" when the bullet exits. To refute this, let's say a bullet that exits game is still traveling about 1,000 feet

Nosler Partition. (Photo courtesy of Bryce M. Towsley)

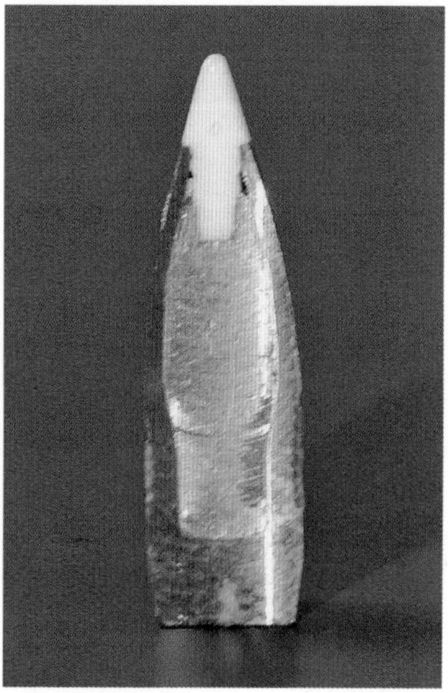

Nosler Accubond.

per second. Often the velocity will be much less, but the point is a 180-grain .30-06 bullet (now weighing perhaps only 120 grains) would be carrying about 266 foot-pounds of kinetic energy. When we fired the bullet, it carried 2,500 foot-pounds of kinetic energy. Subtracting 266 from 2,500 leaves 2,234 foot-pounds of energy, which is more than enough to be lethal. Living flesh is elastic. That explains why bullets are often found just under the hide on the off side of an animal (like my steenbok). Smashed into a classic mushroom shape, many expanding bullets cannot cut their way through the elastic hide at such reduced velocity. They might push their way out the off side. But more often they merely push until the elastic hide produces sufficient resistance.

Nosler E-Tip. (Photo courtesy of Bryce M. Towsley)

Although the classic mushroom shape of an expanded bullet is what many of us are accustomed to seeing, other designs are becoming prevalent nowadays. The Sierra GameKing and even the Nosler Partition turn into mushrooms, the same as many good hunting bullets on the market. But others, notably the Barnes X, Nosler E-Tip, and Hornady GMX, expand to create four sharp petals, which cut through hide instead of pushing on it. They also tend to retain more weight than their mushroomed peers.

Frontal area is also key to understanding terminal bullet performance. It—not retained weight—is the primary factor in penetration. The steenbok I shot is a good example of this. The little animal was shot with a high-power, large-caliber rifle, which would suggest the bullet should have steamed right through it. Because the bullet opened up about two times its original diameter and retained about two-thirds of its original weight, it lost a lot of velocity, enough so that it did not have enough steam left to punch through the elastic hide on the far end of the steenbok.

Barnes Triple-Shock X, Tipped Triple-Shock, and Banded Solid

Randy Brooks of Barnes Bullets developed the X-Bullet in 1985 not long after he bought the company. The name came to him easily when he noted the X-shape of the petals upon expansion. Today the Barnes X is the most imitated big-game bullet on the market. The X family has expanded, and every family member is worth knowing.

The patriarch is the X, a monolithic design made of solid copper. If ever a bullet came close to 100 percent weight retention, this is it because unless it hits something solid at high speed, it keeps everything. The X also penetrates deeply, partly due to that high weight retention but also because of the X-shape of the expanded petals, which cut flesh as the bullet travels through the wound cavity. The gaps created between those expanded petals act as relief valves, allowing tissue to flow by the bullet. So unlike conventional cup-and-core bullets with lead hearts and mushroom shapes that must push their way through an animal, an X-Bullet resists drag and cuts through tissue. The result is a wound channel smaller than hunters who use lead-core bullets are used to seeing, but with better penetration and an overall deeper wound cavity.

The X is offered in three designs. The first is the Triple-Shock X (TSX), an all-copper design with a small, but quite deep, hollow point. On impact the nose expands to the depth of the hollow point then stops when it meets solid copper. This is essentially a modern X bullet with three concentric rings cut in the shank (hence the Triple-Shock name) to bleed off metal as the bullet engraves the rifling, which reduces fouling and improves accuracy. In addition, the characteristics of the X have been improved so the window of impact velocity that can create expansion has been widened. A .30-caliber, 180-grain TSX has a BC of .453.

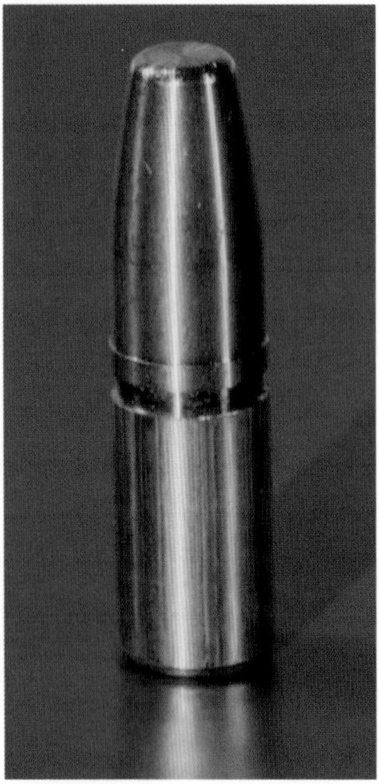

Nosler Solid.

Remington Core-Lokt Ultra. (Photo courtesy of Bryce M. Towsley)

The Tipped Triple-Shock X (TTSX) adds a plastic tip to provide a slightly better BC and more rapid expansion. At first, it looked like Barnes launched this bullet as a light-for-caliber offering, as the initial products included a 130-grain bullet for the .30 caliber. This projectile and others like it proved that the new design gave excellent penetration to bullets previously considered too light for bigger game. Today the TTSX is loaded in all manner of weights for all manner of calibers. A .30-caliber, 180-grain TTSX has a BC of .484.

The Maximum Range X (MRX) took the whole X-thing a step further. It featured a tungsten core fused together by a machine not unlike that used to compress aspirin into tablets. The core was surrounded by a copper jacket with a hollow nose topped by a polymer tip. Tungsten is heavy, so such a core reduced the length of the bullet in any given weight. Since all-copper bullets are long, this created a huge advantage in some chamberings since the shorter bullets made of tungsten and copper did not have to be seated as deeply as all-copper bullets. This allowed a case to be loaded to spec and achieve its velocity potential. The BC of a .30-caliber, 180-grain MRX was .473. The MRX, in my opinion, was the best hunting bullet ever designed. Alas, it was discontinued; it was so expensive it simply didn't grab the market share the company had hoped for.

The Barnes Banded Solid is a monolithic bullet made of a homogenous copper/zinc alloy available with a flat or round nose. Rings cut in its shank, similar

Swift Scirocco II, left, and Swift A-Frame, right. (Photo courtesy of Bryce M. Towsley)

to the TSX, allow displaced metal to escape into the rifling. Barnes designed this bullet to deliver no impact shift when used in conjunction with a TSX in the same caliber and weight. Many hunters have used it on the toughest game; they generally retrieve bullets that can be used again. The Banded Solid is a long bullet that must be seated deeply in the case. This is a problem with some cartridges like the .458 Winchester Magnum that already present too little case capacity. The BC of a .375 300-grain roundnose is .230; the BC of a flatnose .375 300-grain is .307.

Federal Trophy Bonded Bear Claw, Trophy Bonded Tip, and Trophy Bonded Sledgehammer

Federal Premium Ammunition, based in Anoka, Minnesota, was the first company to put the best bullets available in its factory loads. When the ammo maker began the practice, it used any bullet, regardless of what company made it. Today Federal doesn't have to rely on other bullet makers—it has its own thriving division of bullet geeks.

Jack Carter's Trophy Bonded Bear Claw, developed in 1985 and produced and loaded exclusively by Federal since 1992, was the first bullet to take on the Nosler Partition in the super-premium class. With a bonded lead core nose and a shank of solid copper, the Trophy Bonded Bear Claw was unique for its time. The bonded core expanded until it hit the solid rear end. Since the core was bonded to the copper jacket, the bullet demonstrated excellent weight retention.

In 2007, Federal redesigned the bullet. The Trophy Bonded Tip uses a lead-core nose bonded to the jacket for nearly 100 percent weight retention. The rear is a 95 percent copper, 5 percent zinc, gilding metal shank. The result: The transition from lead nose cavity to nearly solid copper rear presents a barrier to further expansion—it's impossible for the front end to expand past that point.

A series of rings cut around the shank reduce friction in the bore and provide an escape for displaced metal as the bullet engraves the rifling, reducing fouling and improving accuracy. Federal engineers "pre-programmed" the nose for expansion to ensure the jacket splits exactly as designed. A polymer tip initiates expansion, and boosts accuracy and trajectory. The BC of a .30-caliber, 180-grain Trophy Bonded Tip is .500.

Loaded in dangerous-game cartridges, the Trophy Bonded Bear Claw now incorporates all the improvements of the Trophy Bonded Tip, with the exception of the polymer tip and boattail base. Big cartridges used for big critters need all the magazine capacity they can get; a polymer tip (and to a

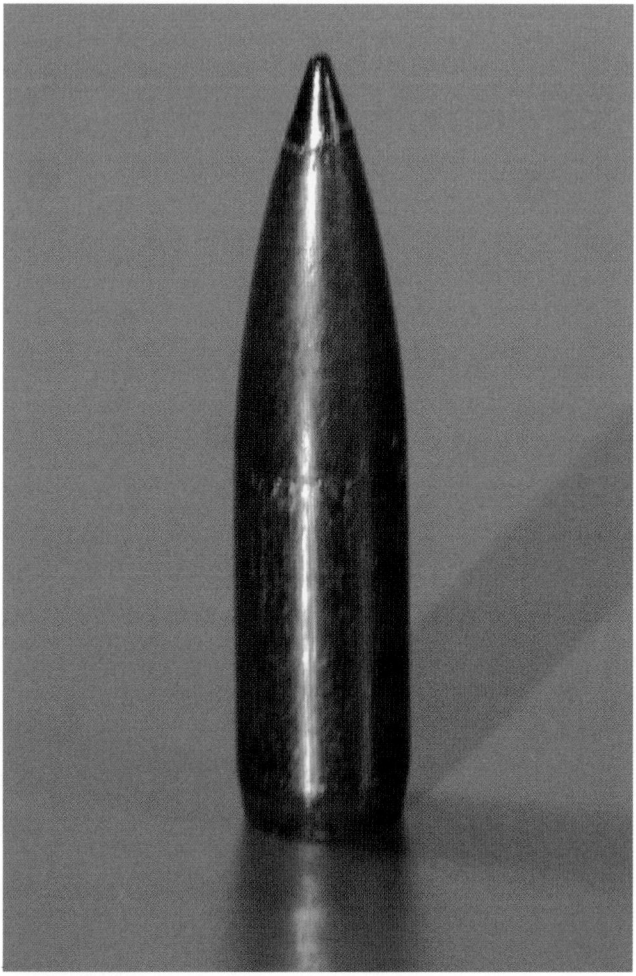

Winchester XP3.

lesser extent a boattail base) creates a longer bullet, robbing magazine capacity or case powder capacity because the bullet must be seated more deeply. Both roundnose and flatnose designs are produced. A .375-caliber 300-grain Bear Claw roundnose has a BC of .230; a flatnose has a BC of .307.

The Trophy Bonded Sledgehammer is a solid bullet that fuses a thick bronze jacket to a bonded lead core. It's a flatnose design for big, big game that produces a deep, straight wound channel. Since lead has a high specific gravity, the result is a slightly shorter bullet compared to other solids. That's good news, since the bullet does not take up as much case powder capacity, comparably speaking.

Hornady Interbond, GMX, DGX, and DGS

As one of the largest bulletmakers in America, Hornady is represented in the super-premium bullet class by the Interbond and GMX. The former is a bonded design, the latter a monolithic one.

You'll recognize the Interbond stacked up against other bonded bullets when you see the bullet's red polymer tip—red being the trademark color of Hornady. The Interbond features a boattail design and a lead core bonded to the jacket for high weight retention. The jacket is thin at the nose of the bullet to produce expansion. Partway down the bullet's sleek profile is an "expansion control ring" of thick jacket material followed by a thicker jacket wall to stop expansion. The bullet was designed to open up more quickly than other bonded bullets. It's particularly well suited for long-range work on big game. A .30-caliber, 180-grain Interbond has a BC of .480.

Hornady's latest creation is a monolithic design called the GMX, which stands for Gilding Metal eXpanding. It's got a boattail base and a polymer tip. Two rings cut in the forward portion of the shank allow displaced metal to escape into the rifling, reducing fouling in the bore and improving accuracy. It's designed to expand into a mushroom shape similar to conventional lead cup-and-core bullets, which increases the frontal area of the GMX compared to other monolithic solids. A .30-caliber, 180-grain GMX has a BC of .447.

The DGX (Dangerous Game eXpanding) and DGS (Dangerous Game Solid) are produced for big, big game. In both, a copper-clad steel jacket surrounding a high-antimony lead alloy core produces deep, controlled expansion (or none, as in the case of the DGS) and deep penetration. A smooth, flat nose produces straight wound channels. The DGX has an exposed lead nose. The BC of a .375-caliber 300-grain in both units is .275.

Moose are tough critters; even the little ones rarely acknowledge any shot. That makes it critical to use a good-performing bullet like the Swift A-Frame. This moose was taken with a Thompson/Center Dimension rifle at just twelve yards with a .300 Winchester Magnum.

Nosler Partition, Accubond, E-Tip, and Solid

The Partition was the first super-premium bullet, and it's still one of the best. It is a mechanical locker that features two cores, one in front and the other in back, separated by a "partition" of jacket metal. The bullet can expand only forward of the partition, thus it will often lose its front core—after creating massive damage. Even if or when that happens, the nose jacket folds back against the shank, and the rear core continues to drive through vitals. Sometimes that creates a rather small exit hole. Some think that indicates poor expansion. It does not. A .30-caliber, 180-grain Partition has a ballistic coefficient of .361, which isn't the highest. But it is usually quite accurate.

The Accubond uses a bonded core and polymer tip. Its terminal performance is similar to, albeit slightly less than, its brother the Partition. A .30-caliber, 180-grain Accubond has a BC of .507, indicating good long-range flight characteristics.

In 2007 Nosler released the E-Tip, a monolithic design. This is a boattail-base bullet made of gilding metal with a hollow point and a polymer tip. Recovered bullets generally demonstrate greater expansion than other monolithic designs. The nose deforms into a conventionally shaped mushroom, but the hollow point creates two times expanded diameter. This can result in decreased penetration, but larger-diameter wound channels. The BC of a .30-caliber 180-grain is .523. Nosler sells the bullets only; Winchester loads and sells them in factory offerings.

Nosler's monolithic solid offering is the Solid, a homogenous, lead-free alloy bullet with a flat nose. It is designed to deliver nearly the same point of impact as similar calibers in similar weights as the Partition. A .375-caliber 300-grain has a BC of .300.

Remington Core-Lokt Ultra

The plain old cup-and-core design of the Core-Lokt has served hunters well for decades. In fact it may be the most popular bullet sold in

America. When bonded-core bullets took off a few years ago, Remington went back to the drawing board. It bonded the core of the Core-Lokt to its jacket. The jacket is tapered and made of gilding metal. That helps expansion, and the bonded lead core retains its weight. A .30-caliber, 180-grain bullet has a BC of .402.

Swift A-Frame and Scirocco II

Like the Partition, the A-Frame is a mechanically locking design. It has two lead cores separated by a thick wall of copper. Its jacket walls are tapered up front to aid expansion. Its front core is bonded to the jacket to prevent separation. The rear jacket is folded over the heel of the bullet to lock the lead core in place, producing quick expansion that stops precisely. So the bullet expands well, but continues to penetrate deeply with a large frontal area to create a wide wound cavity. Weight retention is nearly 100 percent. A .30-caliber, 180-grain has a BC of .400.

The Scirocco II is a bonded-core bullet developed in the late 1990s with the addition of a polymer tip to aid trajectory and expansion. Its tapered copper jacket is bonded to a lead core. The thin front end of the jacket works with what Swift calls the "wedging" action of the polymer tip to initiate expansion. As it expands, the jacket peels back to the middle of the bullet; then expansion is controlled by the increasingly thick jacket. It's a long bullet with a boattail base that produces excellent flight characteristics. A .30-caliber, 180-grain has a BC of .520.

Winchester XP3

Many hunters remember and revere the Fail Safe. Many handgun shooters remember and revere the Black Talon. The thing is, they are one and the same. When Black Talon handgun bullets were released in the early 1990s along with the Black Talon rifle lineup, the media lambasted them because they were said to be so sleek they could penetrate body armor. So

Winchester dropped the Black Talon—and re-released it as the Fail Safe. Evidently the anti-gun media didn't realize it.

Many hunters regard the Fail Safe as the best bullet ever created. It was the last bullet designed by Winchester engineers after the company partnered with Nosler to form Combined Technologies. Its construction was complex—more than thirty steps were required—and expensive. Its hallmark was a steel cap wrapped around the front end of a lead core. The rear core was sealed at the base by a brass cap. A solid copper front end had a hollow point with an interior scored to help expansion. It punched through just about anything, which endeared it to many hunters. Many others disliked it for the same reason. They complained it didn't open up and didn't make a big enough exit hole.

What its detractors didn't understand was the front of the Fail Safe cut its way out of the animal, unlike other bullets that would tear their way through hide to make big exit wounds. While the bullet expanded on the front end, it did not expand at all in the rear. This design enabled it to penetrate more deeply than a mushroomed bullet.

In 2005, Winchester replaced the Fail Safe with the XP3. Its design represents a mix-and-match approach. It has a polymer tip like the Swift Scirocco and Nosler Accubond, and it's a bonded design. At first it looks like a Fail Safe without the steel insert. That's because it uses a copper-alloy jacket with a homogenous hollowpoint nose like the Barnes X-Bullet. Combined with a bonded lead core in the rear, the XP3 produces what some call a "double expansion" upon impact. The nose expands in a classic four-petal manner, but then the back end collapses forward, as it does with the Partition, and also "expands." The bonded lead core keeps the weight-to-length ratio reasonable (shorter bullets take up less powder space in the case and present less bearing surface in the bore). The overall result: higher velocity and lower pressure in any given bullet weight. The shorter overall length also allows the addition of a plastic tip, which improves flight characteristics. The BC of a .30-caliber 180-grain XP3 is .527.

Part II

On the Range

Only perfect practice makes perfect. Here's how to make the most of training time before heading afield, and how to make sense of exterior ballistics

Chapter 5

Test-Fire

On an airliner headed to Africa it's easy to spot the hunters—we're all dressed alike. I was waiting to use the head on one such trip when the hunters in line started talking about our plans.

A squat, round-faced guy in back asked me, "What are you shooting?"

"A .375 H&H," I replied.

"Me, too," he said. "But I also brought a .458 Winchester."

"Ah, hunting a couple head of dangerous game," I ventured.

"Nope," he replied, "just one buffalo. I like both guns, so I thought I'd bring them both. I just bought the .458, and I couldn't stand to leave it home."

Then my companion, who experienced difficulty with a new .375 she was carrying, asked him, "Did you break in the new gun? Which one do you think you'll use?"

"Yeah, I shot it," the guy said. "About five times. I don't know which one I'll use yet."

I thought he meant about five different range sessions, which, I hoped, meant he fired at least fifty rounds. But amazingly, he had fired a mere five rounds through a new .458 Winchester Magnum before packing it up and heading to Africa for dangerous game.

Poor bedding between action and stock can lead to poor accuracy. Many bedding problems need the attention of a gunsmith, but you can eliminate some variables with a simple test. Separate the action from the stock, then check the stock for cracks near the action-screw holes. If that checks out, replace the action in the stock. Stand the rifle on its butt and hold it at the junction of action and stock, then tighten the front screw, followed by the rear screw. Alternately loosen and tighten each one. You should be able to feel unwanted movement you can't see. Finally, tighten each screw to a uniform torque, front one first. The proper amount of torque depends upon design, manufacturer recommendations, and, frankly, on individual practice. (Photo courtesy of Bryce M. Towsley)

LEUPOLD

This is a good time to determine your "ammo management" system—in other words, to decide how you will carry rounds "on station," in the field. This leather cartridge wallet on the stock keeps extra rounds handy for quick reloads, but it can also be cumbersome, add weight to the rear end of the rifle, and subject cartridges to the environment.

Clearly, the guy was not a fan of shooting big-bore rifles. Back in our seats, we hoped for his sake the guy would use what we had to assume was his tried-and-true .375. We nicknamed him Mr. Five Shot, and throughout the trip we wondered what became of him.

Don't be Mr. Five Shot.

Shooting any game proficiently requires absolute faith in one's hardware. Shooting dangerous game adds a level of commitment found only by those few who venture into the temple of the big-bore rifle. No matter your level of commitment, you can't gain faith in your rifle, scope, and ammo with a mere five shots.

Long before you head afield, you should spend ample time at the range wringing out your hardware, with an eye on dependability and accuracy. Those two factors are listed in their appropriate order, for they are separate considerations. First and most importantly, dependability is measured as repeatable function without fail. Hunters cannot rely on performance observed only once or twice; we need to know our hardware will perform the same way every time. Accuracy is secondary, not because it is unimportant but because without dependability the most accurate rifle is good for perhaps only one shot. It's never wise to enter the field with such a small margin of error.

Moreover, if dependability is present, tight groups typically follow. Using modern, sophisticated manufacturing techniques, gunmakers today churn out rifles capable of better accuracy than the majority of consumers who buy and shoot them. That's not to say most of us can't shoot, but I know what I've seen in the field, and I'm reminded of the letters and verbal queries I've received over the years. If they are any indication, I'd say many hunters can improve their shooting skills. If that sounds like you, don't fret, for there is help to be found in the following pages.

That said, it's possible those misses may not ride solely on your shoulders. Despite modern CNC machinery, gunmakers can and do produce some lemons. Machines grow old, tolerances fall, and quality suffers; not often, mind you, but often enough to warrant this chapter on evaluating your rifle.

This pad was installed in the channel of the stock's fore-end to improve accuracy. (Photo courtesy of Bryce M. Towsley)

Break in new equipment during numerous range sessions—six at minimum; a dozen or so is even better. Over the course of these range sessions, fire at least fifty rounds downrange; firing more than a hundred is even better. Besides breeding familiarity, these sessions will establish consistency of operation. If your system is going to break down, you want it to happen now, when you have the tools and other resources at your disposal to fix it—not in the field, a thousand miles from civilization.

Firing so many rounds during so many range sessions is easier with light-recoiling calibers. A .30-caliber rifle can be fired numerous times with only a T-shirt between your shoulder and the butt pad. Big bores are another matter; with them you might be limited to only a half-dozen rounds during each session. Use a slip-on recoil pad with either gun to lengthen your session and to lead to more productive time on the range. There's no need to "suck it up" here. You're building skills and testing your equipment, not engaging in a tough-guy contest.

Most guides and professional hunters will tell you the number-one problem they see with clients is folks who show up with rifles they can't shoot, or worse, rifles they're afraid to shoot. Your job is to not be one of them. Start all this prep work months (not weeks and certainly not days) before your hunt. It may take time for problems to manifest themselves, but the following guidelines will ferret out most culprits in time to make a fix.

Safe Gun Handling

As we move to the range, it's important to remember safe gun-handling practices. The three primary rules are:

Always keep the gun pointed in a safe direction.

The gun must always be pointed so that even if it accidentally discharges it will not cause injury. The key to this rule is muzzle awareness, which applies not only on the range but also in the field.

Always keep your finger off the trigger until ready to shoot.

Guns are so ergonomic it's easy for humans to naturally place their finger in the trigger well. Instead, rest your finger alongside the trigger well until you are on the target with the safety off.

Always keep the gun unloaded until ready to use.

Usage is defined personally by the shooter. If you're hunting, you're using the gun; it does no good to walk around the woods with an empty gun. Conversely, when you place the gun in its case for the ride home, it is not being used for its intended purpose; unload it (remove all rounds from the chamber and magazine) before travel. As a general rule, a gun stored for any purpose other than personal protection should never be kept loaded.

Remember to treat every gun as if it were loaded!

- Some other guidelines to remember include:
  - Know your target and what lies beyond it.
  - Know how to use your gun properly and safely.
  - Be sure the gun is safe to operate.
  - Use only the correct ammunition for the gun.
  - Wear eye and ear protection as appropriate.
  - Never use alcohol or drugs before or while shooting.
  - Store guns so they are inaccessible to unauthorized persons.

Stress Check

Inspect the action for hairline cracks thoroughly before, during, and after shooting. We've all heard stories about cracks developing on old rifles, but new ones are capable of displaying them, too. Gunmakers essentially solved this problem long ago by incorporating gas vent holes in their designs. So unless you're shooting "hot" handloads and producing pressures that exceed the manufacturer's recommendation, you shouldn't see this kind of problem develop.

More common is a cracked stock generated by the forces of recoil. If an action isn't bedded properly, it can rock backward in the stock, breaking free of the bedding surface used to wed the action to the stock. This can occur if a recoil lug shears. If you spot the broken lug before the stock cracks, you're in good shape—it's not too difficult to replace the lug. It's likely you won't notice it, though, and a broken stock will result before long. It will usually crack around the belly of the stock, just rear of the recoil lug on magnum actions, or around the tang. Either way, the action will rock backward under the full force of recoil, and the motion produces more torque than the stock is designed to take. If this happens, it's best to take the rifle to a qualified gunsmith and have the gun bedded in a new stock.

If you use a recoil-absorbing rifle cradle like a Caldwell Lead Sled to zero your rifle, do not exceed the manufacturer's weight recommendations in the tray. That is, if the manufacturer recommends twenty pounds of weight in

Thousands of miles from home in Africa is no time to learn your rifle is not up to the task. Be sure to wring it out before you leave home to learn of any shortfalls. This is how your rifle will ride during most African safaris—in a rack in the rear of a Land Cruiser.

the tray, load twenty pounds, not fifty. Too much weight eliminates any chance of recoil and produces tremendous stress, something the gun is not designed to take. The result can be a broken stock, sometimes in places you would never imagine.

Stress cracks are severe problems, but they are rare. Modern manufacturing techniques should ensure you never see them.

Function Check

If you encounter any mechanical problems, they're likely to be found in the firing sequence. Any firearm must properly feed a cartridge into the chamber, fire it without delay when the trigger is pressed, extract and eject the empty case, and repeat the process without fail. When a rifle fails to function properly, take a moment to remember these steps to find the problem quickly.

Failure to Feed

Check the magazine lips, follower, and spring. Sometimes the lips are crushed enough from use or abuse that they won't hold onto a cartridge. If it's a removable magazine, you can usually fix this by bending them back to their proper position. On smallbore rifles, the magazine lips are sometimes made of metal so soft they fail to hold cartridges. I've loaded rimfires and then watched in consternation as half my cartridges spit out rapidly as I tried to chamber a round. Unload the magazine and bend the lips back into place.

Sometimes if you load the magazine in an internal drop-box design absentmindedly, you can torque the follower, and none of your cartridges will ride correctly inside the box. Likewise with springs; they can break, but usually they've simply been compressed poorly due to improper loading. Pay close attention to either of the latter two problems; they could indicate a rifle with a design flaw. A gun that forces you to pay close attention to the loading process might be problematic in the field. The problem might be fixed by simply loading one less round than is called for in the design. You want to learn that trick on the range, not in the field.

Failure to Fire

Check for debris in the chamber that prevents the firing pin from striking the cartridge primer. If you keep your rifle clean, you should find none.

Check your ammo. Sometimes primers are seated too deeply to be struck adequately by a firing pin. If you handload your own ammo, or have a friend do it, pay attention to best practices. It's highly unlikely to encounter this problem with factory-loaded ammo—but it's not out of the realm of possibility.

The firing pin may not be traveling far enough or strongly enough to impact the primer adequately. This a problem for a gunsmith to solve. I've encountered two guns with what I believe were weak firing pin springs that failed to fire cartridges. Inspection showed the primers to be dented too lightly to induce firing. Neither gun did this all the time; I don't use either one anymore.

It's also worth mentioning some no-brainers in this department. One, be sure you disengaged the safety. Two, be sure you chambered a round. It's easy to fail to do so when operating slowly and deliberately on a range—sometimes you work the action so smoothly you don't notice the bolt closing on an empty chamber. Also, if you short-stroke a bolt-action, the extractor may fail to grip a cartridge case head. (This is a problem usually encountered in the field by excited hunters during the moment of truth.) Worse, though, the extractor could be damaged, which is a problem for a gunsmith to solve.

Whatever the cause, when a rifle goes click, you've got a misfire on your hands. The best practice is to wait sixty seconds, keeping the rifle pointed downrange, then inspect the chamber, the cartridge, and the gun. If everything looks fine, try to fire the cartridge again. If it fails again, try another cartridge to begin to narrow the list of problems.

Failure to Extract/Eject

Is the empty case still in the chamber? Extreme heat has been known to produce excessive pressure in a cartridge; upon firing, the case bulges abnormally and becomes stuck. "Hot" handloads that push the recommended limits for a particular caliber can create the same problem. Worse still, hot weather and "hot" loads can be a bad combination.

Check the extractor, located on the side or face of the bolt. The large surface area of an extractor in a controlled-round-feed system is usually enough to remove any cartridge case stuck in the chamber—a primary feature of the system. Extractors on push-feed designs are small by comparison, which leads many hunters to worry about their efficiency. Then again, push-feed designs probably outnumber controlled-round-feed designs, if that's any indication of their reliability.

Check the ejector, located inside the bolt raceway or on the bolt. I once saw a standing-blade ejector in a controlled-round-feed system get buggered up by a single strand of nylon from a cleaning brush used to clean the gun. A pair of tweezers eliminated the problem, something I would not have had time to remedy had it occurred during a follow-up shot on a buffalo.

Extractors and ejectors should be made of steel so they should never, ever break. If they do, a gunsmith will have to replace them.

Accuracy Woes

As you are going through the function check, pay attention to three aspects of accuracy: group size, group consistency, and point-of-impact stability. If these are not satisfactory, the problem could be in one of several areas of the rifle itself.

Lock

A bedding surface that bends or twists the receiver can limit accuracy. Believe it or not, tightening a couple of screws can generate enough force to bend something as seemingly rigid as a heavy-walled tube of steel. With the front action screw removed and the rear screw loosened a full turn, grasp the stock and the receiver at the receiver ring, and with your other hand, tighten the rear action screw. If you feel the front end of the receiver rising out of the stock as the rear screw tightens, you've got a problem. Same thing goes for the other end; if you feel the rear of the receiver rising as you tighten the front screw, you've got a problem. Neither end of the receiver should show a tendency to rise up as an action screw is tightened at the opposite end.

Recoil lugs sometimes bear unevenly against a stock's abutment surface, affecting accuracy. Under recoil, lateral forces are exerted on the action if these two surfaces are not absolutely flush with one another. On older guns, you can determine whether this is a problem by eyeballing the recoil shoulder. If only one side of the lug is making contact, that side will appear shiny. On new guns, the best way to check for this is to apply lipstick to the rear surface of the recoil lug, reassemble the gun, and shoot it. You can remedy either problem with rasps, scrapers, and chisels—a tedious process of trial and error that requires no small degree of woodworking skill. A better solution is a new glass-bedding job.

Stock

Poor accuracy, erratic grouping, or a wandering zero can often be traced to the stock bedding. Check the action screws: Do they freely fall through the stock to engage the threads in the receiver, or must they be forcefully pushed or even threaded through before they engage? If either condition exists, the overly tight screw might prevent the recoil lug from contacting the stock's abutment surface. Accuracy will not be forthcoming. You may end up splitting the stock. The remedy involves enlarging the action-screw holes with the next size larger drill, or elongating the hole with a round file. Be sure the newly tapped holes are large enough to allow the screws to pass through freely.

Aftermarket stocks often use magazine boxes pinched between the bottom metal and receiver, which can also reduce accuracy. Regardless of whether your rifle has a drop floor plate and separate magazine box or a Mauser-type unit where the two are integral, the stock should be deep enough so it doesn't sandwich the magazine box, but rather allows it to "float." When the box is pinched, it prevents the receiver and the bottom metal from fully seating and induces torque on both units. You should be able to push against the inside walls of the magazine box and move it up and down a bit. If it doesn't move, remedy the situation by placing spacer washers beneath the bottom metal, or by filing the magazine box to reduce its height.

Barrel

The way a barrel is bedded can affect accuracy. Three schools of thought predominate here: One is to fully float the barrel to prevent all contact with the stock; another is to bed only the thick chamber area that lies in front of the receiver and float the slender portion of the barrel from the point where the straight taper begins to the muzzle; and another is to leave a spot about a sixteenth of an inch high in the barrel channel at the fore-end tip so that when the forward action screw is tightened, the stock actually bows inward, exerting a dampening effect on the barrel at that point.

Most factory-produced rifles in standard sporting configurations are bedded using a pressure band at the fore-end tip. Heavy-barreled rifles use a fully floating barrel. Both systems make sense. Thinner barrels generally shoot tighter groups when dampening pressure exists. With one-piece wood stocks like those found on bolt-action rifles, however, the amount of pressure exerted over time, and in different climates, is dependent upon the stability of that particular stock. Wood warps. Laminate stocks exhibit very little warping; on synthetic stocks, the problem is virtually nonexistent.

Regardless of stock type, a gun may or may not shoot good groups. The more pressure exerted, and the thinner the barrel, the more likely you are to experience difficulty. Point of impact may shift by a couple of inches.

To remedy this you can glass-bed the barrel (a project best left to another text, or a gunsmith). Or you can change the amount of pressure exerted on the barrel at the fore-end, or eliminate it by free-floating the barrel. Light- and medium-contour barrels generally respond to either approach, but whether they do so by displaying better and/or more consistent accuracy is debatable.

The problem is, by changing pressure we change the barrel harmonics, the degree to which the barrel vibrates as the bullet travels the length of the bore. Generally, only about ten pounds of pressure is needed on a slim barrel. Measure it with a lightweight scale by hooking the scale around the barrel at the fore-end to see how many pounds register before the two separate. You may see anything between no pressure and as much as thirty pounds. You can decrease the pressure by loosening the front action screw, but you can't always increase it by tightening the same screw. If that's the case, cut a shim from a three-quarter-inch-square piece of business card material, slip it between the barrel and fore-end tip, and reassemble the gun. You may need more than one shim to generate ten pounds of pressure. The pressure can be run up to fifteen pounds on medium-contour barrels. You can free-float the barrel by sanding away the pressure band in the fore-end tip using a wood dowel or a metal tube wrapped in sandpaper.

Sighting Systems

Are the open sights secure? As we've discussed, many open sights today aren't worth mounting on a rifle. Those that are can still be tightened too much. Sheared screws that go unnoticed can lead to lost sights. Likewise, make sure the screws on scope rings are tight, but not too tight. Check scope mount and ring screws periodically.

Observe how the scope reticle holds up on your first several range sessions. As we've noted, any scope can and will fail eventually. Of the three scopes I've seen fail, one did so within the first couple of rounds fired. The couple hundred rounds you fire before heading afield should ensure you've made a good purchase.

Check the scope's erector system and turret adjustments by shooting the square. Fire three rounds at a hundred yards; dial up eight clicks (for quarter-minute scopes); fire three more rounds; dial right eight clicks; fire three more rounds; dial down eight clicks; fire three more rounds; dial left eight clicks; fire a final group of three rounds. The final group should print atop the first, demonstrating whether the erector tube moves within the scope tube properly and whether the turret adjustments "take" as advertised.

Sling-Swivel Studs

Be sure they are secure, because they have a nasty habit of coming loose. I'm continually amazed how many rifles come out of a box with poor epoxy jobs on their sling swivels. No gun has ever fallen from my shoulder when slung, but only because I pay close attention to the studs. If they are loose, you can fix them yourself with epoxy. If you ever want to remove them, screw them into the epoxy while wet, then remove them before the glue dries (per the manufacturer's recommended drying time). You'll create threads. If you never plan to switch them out, leave the studs in place until the epoxy dries.

Ammunition

Although you may be enamored of accuracy and velocity, understand that you may not get both in a given load every time in every gun. By all means, pick a load that shoots well in your gun, but don't sacrifice terminal performance on the animal for a bit of accuracy.

Most game won't know the difference between a hit a smidge left or right, or notice a hundred fewer feet of velocity. The load that shoots best in your rifle may not be the most accurate or the fastest one you can select, but it should provide the best combination of both and tilt toward terminal performance overall.

On the big kickers, though, it's not a bad idea to check velocities. Advertised numbers don't always measure up to real-world performance. Hit dangerous game with several hundred feet less velocity than you bargained for, and it might interfere with bullet performance and lead to decreased penetration. Disparities of several hundred feet per second should be noted, because overcoming resistance against a big-bore bullet is tough.

After you've picked a load, and before leaving home for the hunt, run each and every round through your rifle, chambering each to be sure it travels smoothly. Some rifles feed well with one or two rounds in the magazine but foul up when it's chockfull; others demonstrate the opposite. Also notice whether the overall case length is within specs. Bullets seated too far out produce overly long cases that may not fit in the magazine, or may prevent the bolt from closing. Worse, they may leave the bullet stuck in the lands of the bore and an action full of powder when you extract the case and nothing else. Short cases may prevent the firing pin from reaching the primer. Minor dents in cases and buggered-up bullet tips won't affect much.

Accessories

An extra scope, and an extra set of mounts and bases, isn't a bad idea to test out now. You never know when you'll need a backup optic. Does it mount and handle the same as your primary scope? How old is it?

Lens covers are optional. I generally don't like them. Scopes are waterproof, right? I generally check so many things during the hunt I never have to worry about debris on a lens when I prepare to shoot. Snow is another matter; it piles up quickly.

Slings are mostly a personal choice (you'll find more discussion of them later). You should think about your choice thoroughly. A proper sling is not merely a means of carrying your rifle, but, used properly, can be a shooting aid. I don't like the stretchy type—they don't work well for wrapping around an arm in a hasty sling. Leather is better, if wet weather isn't a concern. Where it is, nylon or canvas may have to suffice. Make sure your sling doesn't squeak.

Some hunters consider a cleaning kit an optional, luxury item; I don't. At minimum, always pack a rod, oil, and a rag to punch out the bore should it become obstructed and to keep your rig at least somewhat clean. Better still, particularly in wet climates, take along a brush and some patches to keep the bore clean and rust-free.

Decide on an ammo-supply system, whether it's a belt pouch, a pouch on the riflestock, or merely sleeves in your jacket. Whatever you decide, be sure it holds cases firmly but surrenders them when you want them. Practice with your chosen system so the fingers of your strong hand find fresh rounds and load them without your eyes looking for them. If your belt pouch is the wallet type, be sure you can open it quickly and keep it open when action is imminent. Never leave camp without plenty of ammo. I carry at least three magazine loads; if my rifle holds four rounds, I carry twelve. If I'm hunting dangerous game and packing softpoints and solids, I carry three loads' worth of each. I carry the extra in wallets that ride in my pockets—softs on one side of my body and solids on the other. Don't walk around with a pocketful of loose cartridges.

I always load three rounds in my magazine regardless of what rifle I use. This way, I develop muscle memory; I always know how many rounds I have "on station," whether I'm unloading the magazine when shooting or doing so in the dark at the end of the day. The only exception is when I'm hunting dangerous game, in which case I keep the magazine full.

When you arrive in camp, a zero check is paramount. Never assume your rifle is safe from rough handling in transit. Use the time to perform another function check. Your guide will watch you. He wants to see how you handle yourself and your rifle. Do you demonstrate proper safety precautions through familiarity with your firearm? Do you display confidence in your rifle? You should have gained that by now. Your guide will also watch to see what kind of marksmanship you display. We'll cover this in Part II.

Field Note: How to Clean a Gun

Gun-cleaning methods are kind of like armpits—everybody's got at least two. Here's how I do it.

- Unload the gun and remove all ammo from the room.
- Remove the bolt.
- Fit a cleaning rod with a caliber-specific patch jag and a patch dampened in carbon-removing gun bore cleaner (such as Hoppe's No. 9) and run it down the bore to loosen carbon deposits; work from breech to muzzle to push debris out of the muzzle and not into the action. Run a dry patch through the bore. Continue this wet/dry combination until a dry patch comes out clean.
- Every twenty to forty shots, you should remove copper buildup from the barrel with copper-removing solvent. I like CR-10 or Sweet's; both are ammonia-based. Run a solvent-dampened patch down the bore, and let it sit according to the directions on the bottle. Then fit the rod with a caliber-specific bore brush, and coat it with solvent. Run it up, then back; this is one pass. Perform one pass for every round fired. Next run a solvent-dampened patch down the bore; repeat until the patch comes out clean. With ammonia-based solvents, the patch will turn blue. It will never come out completely white, as the patch jag is made of brass, which contains copper. Some light blue streaks are acceptable.
- You may need to repeat the dampened patch/bore brushing until all copper is removed. When you're satisfied, run a couple patches dampened in regular gun-bore cleaner down the bore to remove all traces of the copper solvent (any left in the bore will dry and attract moisture, etching the bore). Then run one dry patch through the bore.
- If you will use the gun again soon, leave the bore dry. If the gun is to be stored, run one patch lightly coated in gun oil down the bore to prevent rust (be sure to wipe it clean before firing).
- Use any cleaner designed for guns to remove residue from the action, magazine, and bolt. Wooden cotton-tipped applicators like those found in a doctor's office are handy for this, as are pipe cleaners and toothbrushes. Lightly oil the bolt (or apply a couple of drops behind each lug), but avoid getting any on the bolt face.
- Wipe down all exterior metalwork with a rag coated with gun oil.
- Apply nothing but a few drops of lighter fluid to the trigger group. It will flush away debris then evaporate. Using oil or solvent risks gumming up the small parts in the trigger group, which may lead to a frozen trigger when the shooting starts.

Chapter 6

The Fundamentals of Marksmanship

"There are only two fundamentals of marksmanship," says Jim Land. "Sight alignment and trigger control. The rest are just techniques to assist you in applying the two fundamentals.

Everything else—grip, stance, breath control, all of it—is to assist you in applying those two fundamentals."

He should know. Major Jim Land served twenty-four years in the U.S. Marine Corps. An avid competitive shooter, he has won distinguished badges in both rifle and pistol, and has set seven national records in competition. He served as captain of the USMC Pistol Team, officer-in-charge of the First Marine Division of scout-snipers in Vietnam (where he was the commanding officer of Sgt. Carlos Hathcock, the most famous Marine sniper of all time), and USMC marksmanship coordinator. As someone who grew up on a farm in Nebraska, he is also passionate about hunting. For twenty-six years now he has served the National Rifle Association. He is currently the secretary of the NRA.

Jim Land is right, of course—sight alignment and trigger control are the two most important factors of marksmanship. There are many other things we must learn, however, if we expect to ably wield the hardware we assemble into our hunting kit. Too many hunters expect miracles when they venture afield with a shiny new *uber*-magnum topped with an expensive scope. To be effective, a hunter and his rifle must be accurate. That comes not from spending money at the gun shop, but from spending time on the range.

"Scientists call it proprioception," says Il Ling New, a Californian who grew up guiding hunters (her father was an outfitter). She's a firearm instructor at Gunsite. Located in Paulden, Arizona, it is the oldest firearm training academy in the United States. She was the rangemaster in a class I took there.

"Most of us call it muscle memory," she says. "Take the time on the range to practice the crucial variables, and you will naturally do them during the moment of truth."

Applied correctly, the principles of marksmanship form the basis of everything else we will do. They consist of three simple concepts: aiming, breathing, and trigger control. Seems easy, huh? The devil is in the details.

Aiming

These days, with the widespread use of highly reliable optics, it's not uncommon to encounter hunters who have never learned the fundamentals of aiming through open sights. Who can blame them, since most sporting rifles

Cheek weld is critical; it must be the same every time you shoulder the rifle so eye relief is the same every time. Bring the gun to your shoulder; don't lower your head to bring your eyes to the scope. Squeeze the trigger steadily, straight to the rear, with the middle of the first pad of your finger. It helps to isolate your trigger finger even more by moving your thumb from behind the tang to the right side of the pistol grip.

nowadays don't even come with open sights? That's a shame, really, because while one can be quite effective with a scope, using one without a thorough understanding of what's at play shortcuts the entire process of aiming. Remember, a riflescope doesn't really magnify the field of view—instead it compresses a three-dimensional sight plane into one dimension.

Let's discuss the fundamentals of aiming, using open sights. (The process is the same when using a scope, except, as noted above, the sight plane is compressed.)

Dominant Eye

Before starting to shoot, you must determine which eye you should use for aiming. That's your dominant eye. That doesn't mean it's your right eye if you're right-handed. Some people are cross-dominant.

Determining which eye is dominant is simple. Extend both arms in front of your body and cup them together to form a small opening between them. Keep both eyes open and look through the opening in your hands at a distant object. While continuing to look at the object, pull both hands toward you until they touch your face. The opening between your hands should be positioned in front of your dominant eye.

Sight Alignment

The relationship between the front sight post and the rear sight, whether it's an aperture or a simple V, and the eye one uses to aim, is known as sight alignment. This relationship is the most critical component in the aiming process. To achieve it, center the tip of the front sight post horizontally and vertically in the center of the rear sight aperture. Imagine a horizontal line drawn across the center of the rear aperture, and imagine a vertical line that bisects the front post. Lined up correctly, the front sight post will "touch" the horizontal line, and an equal amount of daylight will appear on either side of the imaginary vertical line. This relationship must remain constant from shot to shot. Errors in sight alignment produce misplaced shots. The errors grow in proportion to the distance fired.

You can develop the right kind of trigger-finger muscle memory anywhere. Grip a ballpoint pen and practice with it until you know precisely when the pen point will "click" out. Then learn to stop your squeeze just before that happens. You need that kind of control over your trigger so you can stop your squeeze should game move before you shoot.

Sight Picture

Sight picture refers to the placement of the tip of the front sight post in relation to the target; sight picture must be attained while maintaining sight alignment. Various sight pictures are described as a 6 o'clock hold, a 12 o'clock hold, or center mass; these terms refer to the placement of the front sight post on the target, whether it's at the bottom of the target, the top, or dead center, respectively. Correct sight alignment coupled with an incorrect sight picture will misplace shots every time. In most cases, a center-mass hold will achieve point of aim/point of impact. An errant sight picture remains constant regardless of range.

Eye Relief

The distance between your aiming eye and the rear sight, or the ocular lens of a riflescope, is the correct eye relief for the sighting system in use. Creep too close to the aperture, and it will be difficult to achieve sight alignment. Stray too far back, and the aperture shrinks and emits too little light to see sufficiently, making it difficult to acquire a sight picture. With open sights, the proper eye relief is between two and six inches. With a riflescope, it's normally at least three inches. The correct distance can vary based on the size of the shooter. It can also vary from one shooting position to another, which means it's critical to maintain the same eye relief for all shots fired from a particular position.

Front Sight

The human eye can focus only on one object at a time. Therefore, after obtaining sight alignment and sight picture, it's critical that you focus on the front sight post, or the reticle inside the riflescope. When you squeeze the trigger and the round leaves the barrel, all of your attention must be on that post or reticle. Your peripheral vision will include the rear aperture or even your immediate surroundings, to be sure, but your vision of everything besides the front sight post or reticle should be fuzzy; you should be aware of them but otherwise ignore them. Try not to stare too long at the front sight. Doing so induces eye fatigue and creates distortions, which will make it difficult to determine whether your sight picture is still correct when the round fires.

Natural Point of Aim

This is the point at which the sights align when you relax as much as possible without losing control of the rifle. Holding and firing a rifle without artificial support incorporates a number of human variables. Ensuring you adopt a shooting position that accounts for a natural point of aim before firing minimizes muscle tension.

As you adopt a shooting position, be sure your rifle points naturally downrange toward the target. You should not have to strain to get the sights on target. Often your body may be twisted one way or the other, depending on position, but you should never be uncomfortable. Check natural point of aim by shouldering and sighting in the rifle once in position. Close your eyes for a few seconds then open them. If the sights still rest on the target, you've found your natural point of aim.

The author's longest shot ever with open sights occurred at 266 yards. That kind of precision can't happen without learning the fundamentals of marksmanship, practicing them often, and applying them during the moment of truth. The rifle is a Winchester Model 70 in .30-06 made in 1937.

Do you have time in the field to establish a natural point of aim? Of course you do. Again, it should be a step that occurs organically as part of adopting a shooting position.

"Whenever we use muscles, they fatigue, they will actually start to move, and in extreme conditions they will shake," says Il Ling New. "It's important to use as little muscle tension as possible. We need to relax as much as possible to reduce or eliminate muscle fatigue.

"More importantly," she says, "human beings relax momentarily as we press the trigger. When we do so, we fall back into our natural point of aim. So if we're not there to begin with, how can we expect our bullet to hit its mark?"

When dangerous game stares at you at a paltry sixty yards, you need to remember the fundamentals more than ever. The author dropped this bull head-on with one shot to the brain because he practiced for weeks before heading to Zimbabwe. The rifle is a Kimber Caprivi in .375 H&H Magnum and the load was a 300-grain Barnes TSX.

Breath Control

When you breathe, your body moves; there's no way around it. This movement transfers to the rifle, which makes it impossible to maintain a sight picture. That's why breath control is critical; the idea is to fire the rifle at the instant when you move least.

A normal human respiratory cycle lasts four to five seconds, as inhaling and exhaling each take about two seconds. Between each cycle there is a natural pause of two to three seconds—that's the time we want to leverage. During this pause, the muscles we use to breathe are relaxed, and it's easier to find and hold our natural point of aim.

When you settle into a shooting position, breathe normally. Acquire your sight picture and sight alignment then take three healthy (but not too deep) breaths. Exhale about half of the last one, which allows you to stop at the natural respiratory pause. You now have two to three seconds, and perhaps as long as ten seconds, before you run out of air. Begin your trigger squeeze. The round should be fired before you run out of breath. If you wait too long, the front sight post will become blurry as your brain becomes starved for oxygen. In that case, stop and begin the process of breath control again.

Trigger Control

You should squeeze (some say "press") the trigger by slowly applying rearward pressure until the rifle fires. Done correctly, sight alignment/sight picture will not be disturbed. A skillful squeeze takes time to develop. Think of it as a mental as well as a physical process. Engage and press the trigger with the center of the first pad of your trigger finger. Apply a gradual amount of pressure.

"When the trigger breaks, it should come as a surprise," says New. "That will allow you to avoid mashing the trigger. This means the fit of the rifle is critical. You must have correct length of pull. Too little and you'll crush the trigger. Too much and your finger will engage only at the tip, and slip off during recoil."

At Gunsite, my shots consistently grouped a bit right. Mike Moore, an instructor there, noticed the problem and suggested I move the thumb of my shooting hand to the right side of the pistol grip to better isolate my trigger finger for a better squeeze. That also eliminates cant in the rifle and positions my thumb to reach the safety, whether it's on the tang or the right side of the receiver.

You should know just how much pressure you can apply to your trigger before your rifle discharges, allowing you to stop the squeeze if needed when game moves and you need to halt action.

Practice isolating your trigger finger and applying direct pressure rearward by cupping a ballpoint pen in your hand and gently pressing the clicker until the pen point appears. Do this slowly and repeatedly, until you can stop just before the pen goes "click." Can you feel all the muscles and ligaments at work in

A steady trigger squeeze is critical even in fleeting moments. Nilgai in Texas are not only notoriously tough but notoriously nervous. As this animal rose from its afternoon nap, the author lined up a perfect shoulder shot off a fence post and squeezed off a 180-yard shot in the blink of an eye. The rifle is a Forbes Model 24 in .300 WSM; the load was a 180-grain Barnes MRX.

your hand? Now imagine what's at work when your hand grips a gun. This is the kind of muscle memory you need on the trigger. Practice on the real thing. Trigger squeeze practice is one thing you can do almost anywhere.

"Competitive shooters probably dry practice three times as much as they live fire, if they're doing it right," says Jim Land.

Follow-Through

In most sports, follow-through is defined as finishing the physical motion you begin, as in throwing a baseball or swinging a golf club. In shooting, it is the continued application of fundamentals after each shot is fired. In a way, it's more accurately described as doing nothing. That is, you do not shift position, move your head, or let the muzzle drop until well after the shot has traveled downrange. Make no mistake, follow-through is a vital part of the shot. It consists of two elements.

First, it's visual: "Train yourself to reacquire the same sight picture you had before the shot broke," says Il Ling New. "You want to end up with the same sight picture after the shot breaks."

When the round fires, continue to focus on the reticle and hold your position. This is a fine line. No one can resist the forces of recoil completely.

The second element is the end of your trigger press: "Hold the trigger back for a split second. Make yourself follow through on the trigger so that your finger and thus your hand does not fly off the trigger or the gun," says New.

Remember, the trigger is your last connection to the bullet, so don't short-change this thought process.

Game won't stand around all day. You need to rehearse the fundamentals of marksmanship until you can establish your shooting position, get your sight picture, focus, breathe, and squeeze the trigger without thinking about the steps involved. If the process doesn't come without thinking, you'll likely rush the shot and thus fail to follow through.

You need to work diligently and quickly. When I miss game, I usually isolate the problem as a failure to follow through, mainly caused by rushing. To avoid this, during the hunt I remind myself, "Breathe, squeeze, follow through." With practice, you'll be able to focus on the reticle even as the gun roars, which will help you call your shot.

Shouldering the Rifle

Most hunters have shot for so long it comes naturally, but that can't be said for all of us. Some never learned the correct method in a formal environment and have developed some mixture of good and bad habits. Some shoulder a rifle the same way they shoulder a shotgun, or vice versa. Still others are brand-new to shooting. With such disparity in mind, let's begin a "snap-in" session with a discussion of the basics. Where applicable, all instructions are for right-handed shooters.

Strong Side/Weak Side

Your strong side is determined by your dominant hand. If you're right-handed, it's your right side; your left hand is your weak side. You should shoot with your strong side; that is, if you're right-handed, shoot right-handed. Wield the rifle with your right hand on the pistol grip. Shouldering the gun should come naturally. If your eyes are cross-dominant that may present a challenge, but in my experience it's easier to learn to shoot with your non-dominant eye, or with both eyes open, than it is to become comfortable handling a firearm with your weak side.

Bone Support

Use your bones to support the weight of the gun. Holding a rifle takes strength no matter how light it is, and that causes muscle fatigue. Be sure the position you adopt is comfortable enough to allow you to hold the rifle in your hands, but able to support the weight of the rifle with bones in your arms.

Think "muscle on bone." In the prone position, prop your elbows on the ground and support the gun in your hands atop your forearms. In the sitting position, prop your elbows in the pockets formed by your bent knees. In the kneeling position, place your triceps over your kneecap.

Left Hand

Bend it slightly and reach forward, thumb facing forward and to the left. Place the web of your hand snug against the underside of the fore-end, palm facing upward. The proper grip ensures your elbow resides underneath the fore-end to aid in accuracy.

Right Hand

Wrap your fingers around the front of the pistol grip, your thumb across the tang. Exert firm rearward pressure on the grip to keep the butt tight against your shoulder. This also eliminates cant (tilting side-to-side) in the rifle, something that can affect accuracy.

Shoulder Pocket

A proper grip with your right hand should create a bend in your right arm, which will create a pocket in your right shoulder. That pocket is critical to getting purchase with the buttplate. Pull the buttstock tight into that pocket to steady the rifle and lessen recoil. Some shooters insist that your right elbow point outward to maintain a proper shoulder pocket. Sometimes I like to let my elbow drop to find a rest or to avoid fatigue. The situation will dictate what works best.

Stock Weld

Also called cheek weld, this is the point of contact between your cheek and the buttstock. Raise the butt to your cheek, positioning your eye at the same distance behind the sight every time. Keep your head upright at all times. Your right eye should fall into position behind the sight; never lower your head to find the sight. A proper stock weld ensures your head and rifle recoil as one, which facilitates rapid recovery and follow-up shots.

Field Note: Marine Corps Fundamentals

On the range or in the field, you can remind yourself of the principles of marksmanship by chanting an acronym the Marines have trademarked: BRASSF. Each letter stands for steps I remind myself of when an encounter with game is imminent.

B: **Breathe.** Remember to take a couple good breaths after you adopt a shooting position and before you begin your trigger squeeze. Sometimes you will have time for only one breath.

R: **Relax.** Establish your natural point of aim. Don't forget about breath control. Remember you must be able to relax properly in every shooting position; undue tension causes trembling.

A: **Aim.** Achieve sight alignment, then sight picture, then focus solely on the front sight post or reticle.

S: **Stop.** Quickly double-check the previous steps to be sure you have not forgotten anything.

S: **Squeeze.** Begin your trigger squeeze. Done correctly, every shot should be a surprise.

F: **Follow through.** Forget this step, and you can forget about hitting your mark.

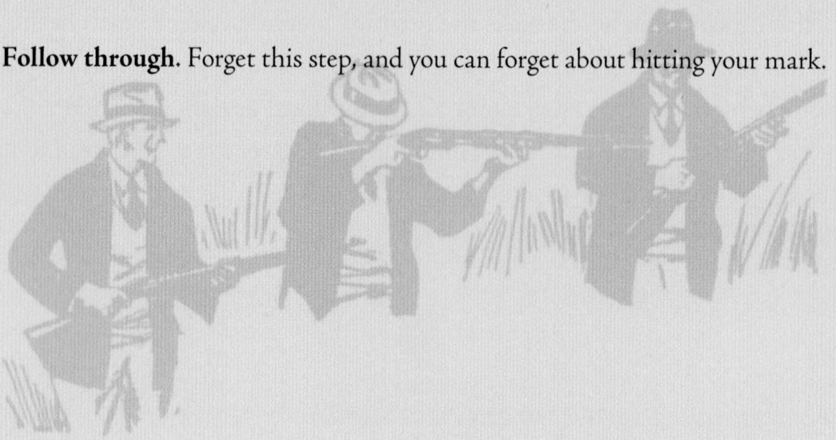

Chapter 7

Shooting Positions

Klipspringers, weighing all of perhaps twenty pounds, are diminutive members of the antelope family. Along with steenboks, duikers, dik-diks, and others, they are part of a collection of small "big" game many hunters affectionately call the "Tiny Ten." As with the other members of the Tiny Ten, klipspringers don't stand around long when they're spotted. And the terrain they like to inhabit—the high mountains—can be difficult to access.

Some years ago, professional hunter Pieter de Klerk and I stood eighty yards above a klipspringer ram high on a mountain in South Africa. Amid the boulders, there was little room for us to stand, let alone a suitable location from which to shoot. Perched above the ram, we had to act fast before the ram and its harem spotted us.

Pieter lowered his binocular, nodded at me, then motioned with his chin toward the rocks at his feet. I nodded in reply, then draped myself over the sharp rocks and managed to adopt the prone position. One shot later, the ram had disappeared from atop the rock on which he stood, and my PH was slapping my back.

"Good shooting, Scott," said Pieter. "You moved fast. This is steep here, yes? Most of my clients couldn't have made that shot."

"What do you mean?" I asked. "The range was only eighty yards; it was a steep shot, but it wasn't hard."

"I didn't have to do anything but point," he replied. "I pointed, and you laid down and found a position on the hill, on the rocks. Most guys would have taken forever to pick a position. Most guys wouldn't have been able to get comfortable. I would have had to draw them a diagram."

Pieter's point was well made. Too often, hunters expect to have all the time in the world and to be able to find the most comfortable position from which to shoot. Such luxuries come only on the range. Game won't stand around while you get comfortable.

As we approached the ram, I knew we were close enough for a shot with my 4X scope. I knew I had to take it then and there, or risk losing what was perhaps my best opportunity. I'd studied the terrain as we climbed down from the summit of the mountain where we'd first spotted the ram, and by the time Pieter motioned for me to set up and shoot, I already knew what position I'd take, and how. I set up in the prone, but by the time I squeezed the trigger my position was really a combination of prone and kneeling. Sometimes the terrain dictates the position you'll take. Years of experience gave me the knowledge to adapt a basic field-shooting position to the situation.

Your hardware does little good if you don't wield it ably; merely pointing a rifle and pulling a trigger will not bring game to bag, no matter what caliber you shoot, the price of your optic, or the construction of your bullet. Now, with your hardware chosen, it's time to focus on your body—your shooting platform. How you grip and shoulder the firearm, how and why a hunter might choose one position over another, how to drop into and climb out of it, how to contort your limbs to make best use of the terrain present—all of these factors are important to understand if you expect success in the field.

At first blush, many hunters will discount such instruction. It doesn't take a Ph.D. to understand what is meant by "prone, sitting, kneeling, and standing," and many hunters who have spent a lifetime shooting no doubt have acquired plenty of knowledge about the basic shooting positions.

But not all hunters are shooters. The average shot on game in the United States is taken at less than one hundred yards, according to surveys by game departments nationwide. What's more, these shots are often taken with a rest—that is, with the help of a tree, a rock, or the cross-bar of a deer stand. That's why, for most hunters, annual preparation for deer season at the local range may consist of no more than checking whether last year's zero still holds. It's safe to say the average hunter rarely pulls his rifle from the bench and fires meaningful shots downrange to check not only his rifle's capability but his own. Consequently, he loses sight of the basics, and after a while he can't remember the last time he adopted the kneeling position to fire at game. He grows older, his belly sags, his muscles become tight, and he can no longer snap into the sitting position even if he wants to. Then he goes on the elk hunt he's saved for years to afford. In the mountains, without a rest, he fidgets to find a suitable firing position when a big bull presents a shot. Guess what happens?

A shooter, on the other hand, has a firm grasp of the principles of marksmanship. He practices from the prone, sitting, kneeling, and standing positions because he wants to regularly test his ability. He knows his rifle, optic, and ammo will do the job as long as he does his. He knows it's the human element—not the mechanical one—that is most likely to falter. So after his rifle is sighted-in, he pulls it from the bench and challenges himself.

The following advice is derived from four primary areas of experience: my stint as an infantryman in the U.S. Marine Corps; knowledge acquired as an NRA-certified firearm instructor; training at Gunsite Academy and Sportsman's All-Weather All-Terrain Marksmanship courses; and a lifetime of experience in the field.

Lie, Sit, Kneel, Stand

The basic field-shooting positions constitute only four tools available to a hunter as part of his "toolbox" full of knowledge and technique. Nonetheless, the prone, sitting, kneeling, and standing positions are four vitally important tools. Without them, we're forever looking for a tree, rock, or fencepost, which, of course, are not always present in the field. No one is asking you to adopt all these positions on day one. If you're out of practice with the traditional stances, start slowly.

Surely most of us have fired from at least one of these positions, but how many of us have done so properly? Study the following advice closely. We'll discuss the various positions from the ground up, in order of stability. Prone, for instance, is obviously more stable than standing and shooting offhand, but that's not to say one is better than the other. The situation always dictates what position you should take to make a well-aimed first shot.

"If you cannot maintain your mechanics, you will not maintain good groups at any range," says Il Ling New of Gunsite. "At fifty yards we should be spot-on. If not, we're certainly not going to be able to do anything at longer range, say, two hundred yards. So start small, start at short range, then build to longer range."

Whenever we use muscles, they fatigue and start to move. So it's important to use as little muscle tension as possible to reduce or eliminate muscle fatigue. No matter how much your muscles scream at you, don't move during the shot. You'll affect the bullet during lock time—the time it takes for the hammer to force the firing pin to travel and strike the primer—and during dwell time—the time it takes the bullet to travel from the chamber through the barrel and out the muzzle.

Having said that, understand that our bodies have natural movement to them. We are never completely, perfectly still. You'll notice wobble. Embrace it, but control it. Wobble is the thing we want to minimize.

Don't cut corners. Adopt each position as described. Don't lethargically drop to your knees, then lie down on your belly to fire from the prone, and don't awkwardly drop to the seat of your pants to form the sitting position, either. You need to develop mental discipline and muscle memory if you expect to successfully carry these techniques to the field.

When a shot presents itself, you need to know immediately what position will work and adopt it then and there, with no fuss or change of plan. Remember, game won't stand around while you get comfortable. The more you shoot from the various positions, the more your body will know what position to take during a shot or an engagement with game. That's muscle memory at work.

Follow the procedures for getting into and out of each position step-by-step, and dry-fire from them before ever firing a live round downrange. It's called "snapping in," and it's what Marines do before they ever fire a live round downrange. It builds confidence in your physical ability, and it conditions muscles and ligaments to do things they perhaps haven't done for a long time.

The best position will provide three points of contact with the ground or a body part that rests on the ground. That's not always possible, but that's the criteria you should use, if possible, when deciding which position to adopt in the field. Two elbows resting on the ground, and one's torso and legs lying on the ground, for instance, create three points of contact in the prone position. Sitting cross-legged with two elbows rested on one's knees creates three points of contact while sitting.

After you're confident shooting from the basic positions, you can adapt any of them to suit your needs or physical limitations. Overall, remember this rule of thumb: Never stand when you can kneel, never kneel when you can sit, never sit when you can lie down. To know whether to go prone or whether to sit, kneel, or stand, you must continually assess the ground and your line of sight during a stalk. The following instructions apply to a right-handed shooter.

Prone

Prone is the most stable position you can take, since your torso and legs maintain constant contact with the ground. With each elbow planted firmly, you create three points of contact and what at times can be a benchrest-solid firing platform. Terrain, however, often rules out the position. Beware of tall brush, a rise in the ground before you, or other obstacles that will obscure your view or deflect your bullet.

How to Get There

Hold your rifle by the fore-end in your left hand, and drop to your knees. Fall forward, using your right hand as a brace. Straighten your legs, spreading them far apart. Lay your heels flat on the ground, toes pointed outward. Plant each elbow on the ground, lift the rifle with your left hand, and tuck the butt into your shoulder with your right hand. Be sure to keep your support (left) elbow directly beneath the fore-end of the rifle to provide stability. Now check your natural point of aim. If needed, adjust to it by angling your body slightly toward your strong (shooting) side. Lying prone is as close to the ground as you'll ever get while shooting. Sometimes it's too low, but you should always consider it first in terms of priority when choosing a position.

In the prone position, be sure to spread your legs wide for the best stability. Point your toes outward and lay your heels flat on the ground to minimize disturbance from wind or twitching muscles. Keep your support elbow tucked beneath the fore-end as best you can for the most stability. (Photo courtesy of Alex Sutherland/NRA Publications)

Advanced Tips

The international position provides a slightly higher line of sight and fire when terrain or vegetation present obstacles to the standard prone position. It can also be more comfortable if you find it difficult to breathe while lying on your belly because it alleviates pressure on your chest. To adopt it, bend your strong-side knee toward your strong-side elbow and adjust your elbows as needed. This raises your torso, which gives you a better line of sight. Beware: It also produces a less-stable platform, as your chest will no longer be in contact with the ground.

The Hawkins prone is the lowest and steadiest of any supported field-shooting position, but it provides the least clearance over obstacles within your line of sight and the bullet's path. To adopt it, make a fist with your support (weak-side) hand around the front sling swivel and rest your fist and the rifle's buttstock on the ground. Flatten your elbows to either side.

In any prone position, be sure to spread your legs as far as possible to make a tripod-like platform on the ground with each leg and your torso. Point your toes outward and keep your heels flat on the ground (easier in the international position) to lessen movement caused by muscle twitches or the wind. This can't be overemphasized. Physical exertion on a stalk usually precedes a shot at game; you will often be winded when you line up behind the trigger, and as you breathe heavily, the movement will transfer to your heels, making you unsteady. The last thing you need when shooting from the most stable position you can take is to induce movement.

Sitting

Next to prone, the sitting position is the most stable position you can adopt. It's usually the one most hunters take in the field when they're not using a rest because it comes naturally. Trouble is, most hunters rarely snap into it on the range, assuming they can figure it out if the situation dictates. But when they do

Cross your legs, sink low, and place your elbows in the pockets of your bent knees. This is as low as you can go without lying down. But it isn't comfortable for long. You'll compress your diaphragm and it'll be tough to breathe. (Photo courtesy of Alex Sutherland/NRA Publications)

If you are unable to adopt the cross-legged sitting position, you may choose to spread your legs. Be sure to find the right spot for your elbows—that spot will differ from the cross-legged position. This style is not as stable, but often it's more comfortable. (Photo courtesy of Alex Sutherland/NRA Publications)

so in the field, when a trophy is on the line, their muscles resist due to inactivity. If you're over the age of forty, I suggest you practice this one. Considering the vagaries of terrain and vegetation, it presents the most useful tool to a hunter without a rest, but only if one's body is prepared to adopt it.

How to Get There

Stand forty-five degrees into your strong side, your weak (left) shoulder facing downrange, and cross your left ankle over your right. Holding the rifle in your left hand, drop to the seat of your pants, using your right hand to brace your fall, and sit cross-legged. Place your left elbow in the pocket formed by your bent left knee. Hold the rifle in your left hand, and use your right hand to place the rifle butt in your shoulder pocket. Place your right triceps over your right kneecap. Now scrunch low . . . lower . . . and sink into position.

Advanced Tips

Next to prone, this is the lowest and most stable position. If you have a "pronounced" midsection, you'll never get here without practice; scrunched as you are, you'll compress your diaphragm and it'll be hard to breathe. Snap into this position on the range to stretch muscles and limber up joints. As an alternative, plant your elbows in the pockets formed by your bent knees to form a platform almost as solid. This adaptation raises you slightly higher, however, exposing you to movement caused by wind or muscle twitches.

If sitting cross-legged presents a problem, plant each foot flat on the ground and rest your triceps on your kneecaps. Be careful, as this exposes you to twitching knees.

Kneeling isn't the most stable of the field-shooting positions, but it is the one that allows you the most commanding view of the field while simultaneously providing a rest for your weak (support) elbow. You can also adjust position and even move quickly should the situation dictate. (Photo courtesy of Alex Sutherland/NRA Publications)

Kneeling

This is my favorite shooting position because it gives me three things: a stable, three-point shooting platform I can reach in an instant, a commanding view of the field, and the ability to move quickly should the situation change. With practice over the years, I've proven to myself I can be as accurate in the field from the kneeling position as I can from the sitting, mainly because it's more comfortable for me to adopt. The downside is it's hard on the knees if you must hold the position for a long time. Secondly, as much as I or anyone else wants to think otherwise, kneeling is simply not as stable as prone or sitting.

How to Get There

Hold the rifle in both hands. Face downrange with your feet shoulder-width apart. Step forward with your weak (left) leg and bend at the knee, place your

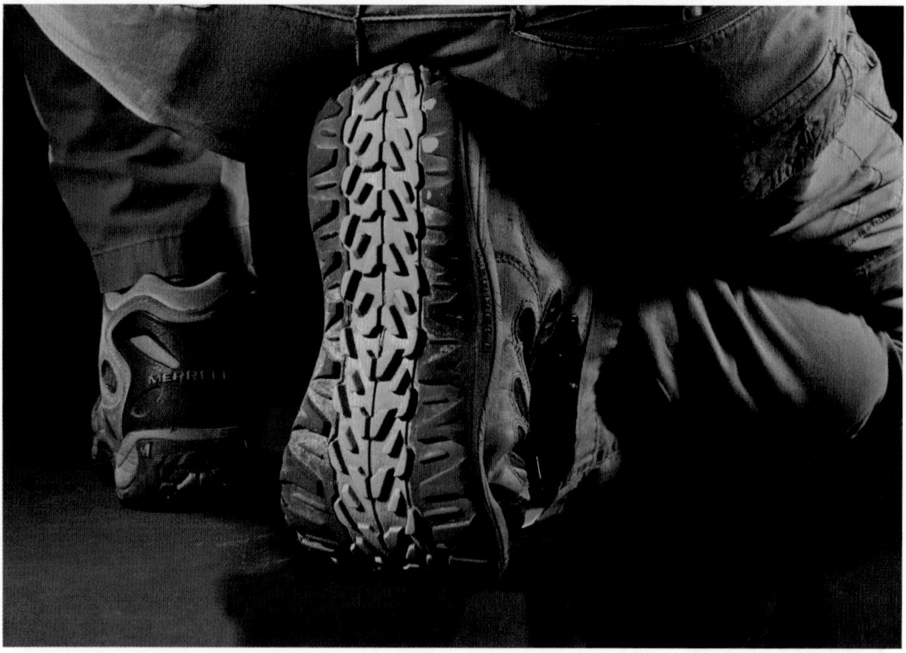

This is the most comfortable position for your heel when kneeling. But it also puts you highest off the ground. Be careful you don't sway atop your bent toes. (Photo courtesy of Alex Sutherland/NRA Publications)

If you're able to do it, you'll find the most stability in the kneeling position when you can bend your foot and sit flat on it, whether the toes are pointed inward or outward. Be aware that this really stretches the ligaments in your ankle; most folks don't like it, but it's more stable than staying up high on bent toes. (Photo courtesy of Alex Sutherland/NRA Publications)

strong (right) knee on the ground, drop onto your strong heel, and sit on it. Place your left triceps over your left kneecap. Hold the rifle in your left hand and place the rifle butt in your shoulder pocket. Lean forward just a bit, let your left triceps melt into your left knee, and let your butt sink onto your right heel.

Advanced Tips

You may also drop your right ankle to the ground and sit on either the outside or inside of it, whichever is comfortable (neither is to me). The problem with this position, also known as the international position, is your "chicken wing," your elbow as it dangles out there unsupported.

The offhand position a hunter should adopt is not like that used by competition shooters who line up in a "bladed" position toward the target. Plant your feet shoulder-width apart and bend your knees slightly. Adopt a "boxer's stance" so you're able to shoulder the gun quickly. The shot needs to be stable, yes, but mostly it needs to be quick. You will use the offhand only at one hundred yards or less. Keep both eyes open when you sight through the scope to stay aware of movement in your peripheral vision. (Photo courtesy of Alex Sutherland/NRA Publications)

Offhand

I call the standing position for hunters the "offhand" position, mainly because it leads to a shot taken rather quickly. It is the least stable, and it should be used only at close range when there is no time for anything else. Under such circumstances, it can be quite effective. Here we're interested in what works for hunters, not what works for competitive shooters. As such, don't fire from the "blade" position, with your weak-side (left) shoulder pointed downrange, as you would in competition. This will pull your shots right if heavy recoil is a problem. Instead, "square up" to the target.

How to Get There

Hold the rifle in both hands, face downrange, and spread your feet shoulder-width apart. Move your strong-side (right) foot back slightly. With your eyes fixed on the target, shoulder the rifle in one smooth motion. Firmly grasp the fore-end with your left hand, and with a firm grasp of the pistol grip with your right hand, use both hands to pull the rifle into your shoulder pocket. Keep your left elbow beneath the fore-end to prevent swaying. This stance will send recoil straight back into your shoulder, and will keep your shots from straying right.

Advanced Tips

Always bring the sights to your eyes. Never lower your cheek to attain a proper stock weld or field of view through the sights. Don't drop your head to find the sights as the rifle butt reaches your shoulder. Keep your eyes on the target. With practice, you can reliably engage targets out to seventy-five yards in a snap.

Chapter 8

Training Time

Once upon a time, the famous gunwriter Townsend Whelen said, "Only accurate rifles are interesting." I'll modify that: Only practical rifles are interesting. It's a small but significant change, don't you think? After all, it's pointless to study the fundamentals of marksmanship and various shooting positions if we go afield with rifles that, while accurate, weigh more than we are willing to bear on the hunt.

The rifle in America dates back to the first settlers. Indeed, the National Firearms Museum at National Rifle Association headquarters in Fairfax, Virginia, displays a gun that came to our shores aboard the *Mayflower*. The rifle has shaped the course of American history. It has helped us put food on the table, explore and settle a continent, and defend our homeland. In the right (or wrong) hands it is a magnificent weapon. Hunters, however, are primarily interested in its practical use as a tool.

A Practical Rifle

Webster's defines "practical" as: 1) of, exhibited in, or obtained through practice or action [practical knowledge]; 2) usable; workable; useful and sensible; 3) concerned with the application of knowledge to useful ends, rather than with theory, speculation, etc." I think that sums up our goals perfectly, both for our rifle and for us as hunters. To that end, a "practical" hunting rifle is all of the following.

Compact

This is manifested in a short barrel. Although some hunters prefer long barrels in a desire to eke out maximum velocities from magnum chamberings,

Perfect practice makes perfect: Quality training time paid dividends for the author's son, Haden, left, when the youngster shot his first game animal—a splendid South African springbok that gave the duo fits for the better part of a morning. After wounding the animal, Haden recovered, remembered the lessons his father taught him, and made a good shot from the prone position to put down the animal. He used a Kimber 84M in .243 Winchester with 100-grain Nosler Partitions.

compact rifles are best for most hunting purposes. A short barrel does not adversely affect accuracy. Further, a short barrel makes a hunting rifle easier to carry in thick cover and faster to bring to the shoulder.

Lightweight

In a standard caliber it should weigh no more than seven-and-a-half pounds; if chambered for dangerous game it should weigh about nine. Proper weight contributes directly to the balance of the rifle and its "feel" between the hands. Remember, you'll carry the rifle all day, maybe all week, and shoot it for only a few seconds.

Powerful: It should be chambered to fire a cartridge adequate to hunt all game you wish to pursue with that particular rifle. It should have as much power as is needed to dispatch game at your maximum effective range as a shooter, or to deal with the charge of a dangerous animal.

Accurate

Only practical accuracy concerns us. Combined with the qualities above, a rifle capable of delivering one minute of angle is sufficient.

This concept of a practical rifle was first espoused by Jeff Cooper, Marine combat veteran and founder of Gunsite Training Academy in Paulden, Arizona. I've modified his parameters a bit to suit my tastes; feel free to do the same. The point is, as hunters we have little use for super-accurate, heavy rifles. A hunter and his rifle must sometimes traverse severe terrain and suffer through terrible weather but still deliver optimal performance. If that doesn't define "practical," I don't know what does.

Now that we understand what makes a rifle practical, it's time to head for the range to complete the rest of the equation: developing practical marksmanship skills.

How to Zero a Rifle

Before we sight-in our rifle, it's important to understand factors that guide our desired results. There is a difference between "zeroing" a rifle and "sighting-in" a rifle, although many hunters use the terms interchangeably. Basically, when you sight-in a rifle you are establishing its zero. But you may merely sight-in a rifle at some given range without ever knowing whether you've achieved a zero with that cartridge and bullet.

Let's start with some definitions.

Line of Sight

The straight line drawn from the shooter's eye, passing through the sights of a rifle, and extending from the gun to the target.

Point of Aim

The spot where the shooter aims.

Point of Impact

The spot where the bullet strikes the target.

Bore Sighting

Refers to adjusting a riflescope reticle so the bullet fired from the rifle is "on paper." It's what manufacturers promise when they advertise a rifle with a scope that is "factory-mounted and bore-sighted." Don't trust the setup for hunting. You must sight-in the gun to be sure of bullet impact at the range you will hunt.

Zero

The distance at which your point of aim and the bullet's point of impact coincide. It's accomplished by adjusting the sighting system so the bullet impacts the aiming point exactly as intended at whatever range you determine necessary. When zeroing a rifle, shooters generally use artificial support to rule out human variables.

Sighting-In

Aligning the sighting system so the bullet impacts the target at a desired point. It may be dead-on at a particular range or a bit high or low depending on the range at which the rifle is fired.

Point-Blank Range

The distance at which the bullet will neither rise above nor fall below the line of sight by more than a specified distance, commonly three inches. The theory exploits the flat portion of a bullet's trajectory so a hunter can hit targets with almost no high or low holds. Many hunters sight-in their rifles to hit an inch or two high at one hundred yards—effectively producing a three-hundred-yard zero. With this setup they can aim dead-on at all ranges out to thee hundred yards and never miss the vital zone by more than about six inches.

Midrange Trajectory

The apex of the bullet's arc, or the highest point the bullet will ever be above the line of sight in its trajectory.

Maximum Effective Range

The greatest distance at which a rifle can inflict a killing shot with energy and accuracy.

Now that we have an understanding of the terms involved in zeroing a rifle, we can get into the nuts and bolts of the zeroing process. A rifle's sights or scope guide our eye in a straight line, but our bullet travels an asymmetric curve—its trajectory. When we sight-in a rifle, we merely take advantage of the fact that this curve is flat enough to be brought close enough to our line of sight to allow us to place a bullet at precisely the desired point of impact. When we zero a gun, we manipulate the sights or scope to coincide with the rifle's "cone of fire." The process can be frustrating without an understanding of what's at work.

Before beginning, be sure the gun is bore-sighted. Secure it in a rest so it can't move, remove the bolt, and look directly down the bore at some distant point (a spot on the wall across the room is sufficient). Adjust the scope reticle to correspond with your target so both the bore and the reticle are fixed on the same point of aim.

When sighting-in, it's paramount to use a rock-solid rest to eliminate all human variables. You can use sandbags on both ends of the gun, a tripod front rest and a leather sandbag under the buttstock, or any similar setup that will hold the rifle sufficiently. The key is to cradle and isolate the gun so you need only to press the trigger to discharge the gun. I've used a Caldwell Lead Sled for several years now, and I recommend it. If you use one, be sure to follow the manufacturer's maximum weight recommendations in the weight tray. Load it with too much and the sled will not give at all, which could lead to a cracked stock.

You may use one of three methods to sight-in your gun: a dead-on hold at 100 yards, a two-hundred-yard "hunter's zero," or maximum point-blank range. Which one you use is determined by personal choice and the chambering of your rifle. The reason some rifles shoot "flatter" than others is because the bullets they fire travel faster and cover more ground before falling to earth. Regardless of which caliber you shoot, your bullet is affected by the same law of gravity as any other bullet: It drops to the earth at a rate of thirty-two feet per second.

All bullets begin dropping as soon as they clear the muzzle. If the bore were held level to the earth when the rifle was fired, the bullet would strike the target low every time. Instead, when a rifle is fired, the bore is angled upward slightly, above the line of sight, so that the bullet rises and falls on a curve, crossing our line of sight twice.

Line of sight is the straight path from sights to target. Our vision is not subject to gravity, so our eyes and the bullet take different paths to the target. The first time the bullet crosses the line of sight occurs near the muzzle somewhere between twenty-five and fifty yards. The exact distance depends on variables like sight height, the distance to your zeroed point of impact, and the trajectory of your bullet. The next time the bullet crosses the line of sight occurs at the distance at which you zero your rifle. At any point in the bullet's trajectory other than these two points, the bullet will be above or below the line of sight.

A slower bullet takes longer to travel to a given aiming point, so it must arc higher above the line of sight than a "flat-shooting" bullet, if the two are zeroed to the same point of impact. An extreme example can be seen in the arc of bullets fired from a .45-70 and .300 Remington Ultra Magnum. The midrange trajectory of the .300 Remington Ultra Magnum zeroed at 200 yards occurs about 120 yards downrange and is only 1.17 inches. The midrange trajectory of the .45-70 zeroed at 200 yards occurs 110 yards downrange and is 13.37 inches. Total bullet drop at 200 yards for the Remington cartridge is 6.99 inches; if the bullet were fired level with the ground it would drop 6.99 inches by the time it reached the 200-yard mark. The .45-70's 200-yard drop is 51.23 inches.

The difference lies in the muzzle velocity of the two cartridges. The .300 Remington Ultra Magnum fires a streamlined bullet 3,300 feet per second that

On the range is where you want to perfect the operation of you and your rifle. It's best to work with a buddy or coach because you can't spot everything you might do wrong.

takes a mere .19467 of a second to travel 200 yards. At that distance, the bullet is still traveling 2,881 feet per second. By comparison, the .45-70 fires a squat, fat bullet that starts out much more slowly and loses velocity quickly. It starts out traveling 1,300 feet per second and it crosses the 200-yard line in .53846 of a second with 991 feet per second of velocity.

What's more, the longer the distance you select for zeroing, the higher the bullet arc. If you move the .45-70's zero back to 100 yards, its midrange trajectory occurs at 58 yards and is 2.37 inches above the line of sight. The .300 Remington Ultra Magnum peaks at .01 inch at 90 yards.

You must consider all this when choosing a zero. No one method is good for all hunting situations.

A dead-on zero at 100 yards is good in thick woods where threading the bullet through brush is the primary consideration. In this circumstance, targets are generally close. Assuming a scope-mount height of 1.5 inches, the bullet path of most cartridges will stray little more than an inch from the line of sight at 25 yards out to 150 yards. Longer shots require knowledge of the bullet's drop past 150 yards, though little is necessary with modern cartridges out to about 200 yards (a rare distance to be shooting in thick woods anyway). Be sure to mount the scope as low (as close to the bore) as possible. High mounts alter the relationship too greatly between line of sight and the bullet trajectory. You might see a clear path to the target, but the bullet path may differ significantly.

A 200-yard zero is good when hunting big game in mixed terrain where the possibility of a long shot exists. With modern cartridges, this will translate to about 1.5 inches high at 100 yards, and 6 to 9 inches low at 300 yards. If you hold the reticle high on the animal's back at 300 yards (still on hair, not air) and dead-center at lesser ranges you should hit the vitals. In the real world, most shots on game occur at 200 yards or less, which makes this method preferable for many hunters. If you zero the gun beyond 200 yards, you increase midrange trajectory, which makes it too easy to shoot over many animals.

Learn to shoot almost all targets at low power with both eyes open. There isn't much game we hunt that can't be hit with both eyes open at low power. All shots from the standing position should be taken with both eyes open. It will be within a hundred yards, after all, and you'll need both eyes to constantly assess a fast-moving situation.

Option number three involves zeroing the rifle at maximum point-blank range; the sights are adjusted so the bullet neither rises above nor falls below a certain distance from line of sight over a given range. In a six-inch zone, the bullet never rises more than three inches above line of sight during its trajectory. The bullet then crosses the line of sight a second time at your zero. When it travels beyond the zero point, it continues to drop. The distance where it is below the line of sight is the maximum point-blank range. With this method and a target zone of six inches (or whatever size zone you select) you can hold dead-on the animal's vital zone and expect to hit the vitals at any range out to maximum point-blank range. Choose the method that works best for your hunting situation, then zero the rifle as follows.

Shoot a three-shot group at, say, 100 yards. Then, after determining the center of it, adjust the scope reticle to correspond to the correction needed to bring point of impact in line with point of aim. If the rifle shoots three inches below and two inches left of point of aim, adjust the reticle so point of impact shifts three inches higher and two inches to the right.

Refer to the owner's manual that accompanies your scope to determine how many "clicks" of the turrets that might be. Quarter-minute scopes move the reticle one-fourth of an inch at 100 yards for each click of the turret. That computes to four clicks to move the reticle an inch at 100 yards. Beware: Some scopes are built with one-third and one-half minute adjustments. Also, whatever the value of the adjustments on your scope, be aware that they double as the range is halved. At fifty yards you will need to turn a turret with quarter-minute adjustments eight clicks, not four, to move point of impact an inch.

Once zeroed, your rifle should fire bullets that cross the line of sight twice. A flat-shooting magnum may be sighted-in at 25 yards to allow the bullet to rise, striking high at 100 yards, likely also high at 200 yards, and likely dead-on (along the line of sight again) at 300 yards. Sight-in that same gun to print dead-on at 100 yards, and it will be low at 200 yards and completely ineffective at 300 yards.

Remember, zeroes shift from load to load. You will need to check your zero and likely sight-in the gun for every different load you use. Remember also that you must check zero whenever you travel with your rifle. As we've discussed, riflescopes can be fickle instruments. It's rare for them to be thrown off, but if it does happen, it will occur the one time you get lazy and hunt without checking point of impact.

Practical Shooting

Once you prove your rifle is capable of delivering accurate rounds on target, move away from the benchrest and practice firing from the field-shooting positions described in the last chapter, as well as with natural and artificial rests (described later).

Perfect your mechanics by beginning each range session with facing drills, advises Doug Prichard of SAAM. Face the target, adopt a position, pop the gun to your shoulder, and aim at the target. Do this for each position. Dry-fire, or more accurately dry-practice, is key to muscle memory. There's no sense sending rounds

Practice now to always scan and assess after every shot. You can never be sure when you're "done." Sometimes game moves after the shot; you need to scan and assess the field after your shot to be sure you don't need a follow-up.

downrange right now. Relax and think about the fundamentals of marksmanship and the shooting positions you want to rehearse before loading the gun.

If you cannot maintain your mechanics, you will not maintain good groups at any range. At fifty yards you should be spot-on. If not, you're certainly not

Don't forget the fundamentals. On the range when the targets are fixed at known distance, it's easy to get lazy when bullets routinely hit the bull's-eye. In the prone position, keep your legs spread wide for stability, and your heels flat to avoid movement due to muscle twitching or the wind.

going to be able to do anything at two hundred yards. Start every range session at short range, then build to longer range.

"The more you shoot from the various positions, the more your body will know what position to take during a shot or an engagement with game. It's muscle memory at work," says Il Ling New of Gunsite.

Rehearsal

Eliminate mental mistakes with lots of practice. Pay attention to the operation of your action. You should be able to run it with little fuss. With practice, you can work the bolt and reload the chamber while maintaining any firing position.

After some facing drills, concoct field situations. These head games will pay dividends later when you're beat after a day of hiking up a mountain, when the game is skittish and rain is spitting in your face.

Practice reloads on the range so you develop muscle memory for the field. This is a low reload, which you will use when there is plenty of time. It speeds the time it takes your hand to move from your belt to the gun, but it eats up time with the lowering and raising of the gun.

"Proper rehearsal requires visualization," says Jim Land of the NRA. "For instance, if you've rehearsed right, you've already visualized a situation you might encounter in the field. You've already done it in your mind, so you know where your focus must reside: It has to be on either the front sight or the reticle.

"Competitive shooters probably dry-practice three times as much as they live-fire, if they're doing it right," he says.

"If I intended to shoot a pistol match on Saturday, on Thursday I would sit down and shoot an entire 2,700 [a 270-point match at ten points a round]. I'd remove my pistol from the case, load the magazine, shoot, make notes in my range data book, and reload magazines. I always structured the rehearsal so I would never become disoriented during a match. I did more dry-firing than almost anybody; I wasn't that good a shot, so I worked at it constantly."

You should practice until you develop the ability to reload without taking the gun from your shoulder. Muscle memory builds, and after fumbling a bit to find the cartridges and throw them in the gun you'll be able to perform not only a "position reload" but a "full tactical reload"—the ability to grab an entire magazine's worth of rounds from your belt and throw them in the gun before closing the bolt.

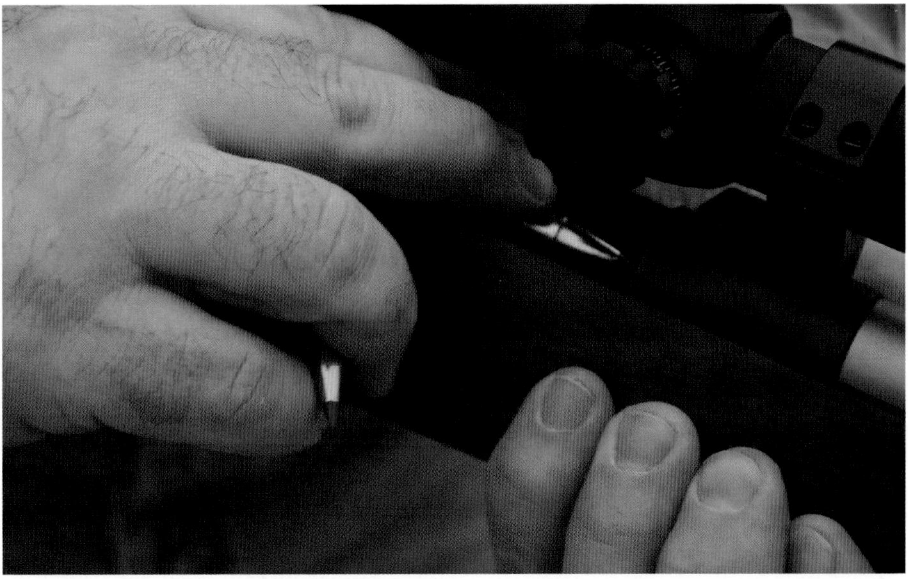

The ability to grab a complete reload of cartridges from your wallet and reload the entire magazine in one motion is an important skill to have in the field.

Watch your sights, not the target. The adage is, aim small, miss small. After you achieve sight alignment and sight picture, there is no need to look downrange. Focus intently on the reticle as the trigger breaks. Don't look at or aim at the entire target or animal.

"Pick a point on that target, or that animal," says New, "a specific point within the vital area. You can easily reduce group size by simply paying attention to the reticle."

Targets with vague aiming points help here. Eschew clearly defined grids and bull's-eyes in lieu of uniform surfaces—a paper grocery bag with a few barely discernible marks on its surface works well. Remember, an animal has no grid covering its vital zone, no neon letters that say: "Hit me here." In the field you must pick a spot, a wrinkle, or a patch of hair.

Breathing should be deliberate but natural. Remember to take advantage of the natural respiratory pause. "As I'm bringing the gun up and taking off the safety," says Doug Prichard, "I let out that breath. During that natural respiratory pause let out that breath, touch the trigger, take your last breath, let it out, and start your trigger squeeze."

Be sure to squeeze, or press, the trigger. A long, deliberate pull should be eliminated in favor of a compressed trigger squeeze. Use the middle of the first pad of your index finger to manipulate the trigger. Think about what's at work when you manipulate the trigger. Whenever you tell yourself to press the trigger, you cannot help but move your hand. If you clinch your hand and surge forward, that often leads to a low point of impact. Similarly, if a right-handed shooter uses too little of his finger (if length of pull is too long, for instance), shots will push left; if he uses too much of his finger (if he "buries" the trigger), shots will pull right.

What's more, too many hunters are anxious to see bullet impact downrange. "The biggest thing I see as an instructor is people don't ride the trigger long enough," says Prichard. "You've got to stay on it longer than you realize. Too often, I see shooters accelerate the trigger squeeze. They rush it. Don't crush the trigger—that leads to pulling the shot left or right."

Likewise, don't pull your finger from the trigger too quickly. Remember dwell time, that period of time that exists as the bullet travels the length of the barrel? Forget about it and you'll see poor accuracy downrange. Squeeze the trigger deliberately. During follow-through, hold pressure on it for an instant after the gun discharges. Then deliberately remove your finger from the trigger and move to operate the bolt.

You can get away with a little trigger smack at short range, but pulling your head away from the scope will always present a problem. Too many hunters want to see the animal drop with their naked eye, so they fail to follow through. They pull their head away from the scope. As the head rises, cheek weld is not maintained so the stock rises, the barrel lowers, and shots generally go low.

Remember that follow-through is a continuation of shooting fundamentals throughout recoil. Your eyes need to remain on the reticle. You must maintain your cheek weld. Let your finger dwell on the trigger for an instant after the gun fires.

After the shot, and after you follow through, practice keeping the rifle mounted to your shoulder and lowering the muzzle slightly to provide an unimpeded view downrange. Remove your finger from the trigger well and engage the safety, but remain ready to shoot in an instant. Scan left, right, and downrange with your eyes. If trouble materializes—wounded game you thought was dispatched, or dangerous game that charges—you need to see it as soon as possible and employ your rifle, possibly in defense of your life.

Bolt Work

Do not palm the bolt handle upward with an open hand like you might do on the bench. Sweaty hands have a way of slipping off smooth metal. Worse, it's not entirely unlikely you'll miss the bolt handle altogether. Work the bolt like you own it. Use the thumb and forefinger of your strong hand to grip, or pinch, the bolt handle. After firing, surround the bolt handle knob with a pocket formed by your thumb and forefinger. Manipulate the bolt briskly: Think of it as a two-count motion—open and back, forward and closed. The gun should never leave your shoulder; the sights should remain before your eyes. The gun should not move, and your head should not come off the stock when chambering a fresh round.

Reloads

Now's the time to perfect your cartridge-supply system. That's a fancy way of saying you should work out what you will use to carry ammo, where it will reside, and how you will move your hand between the ammo pouch and the rifle's chamber or magazine. Usually you'll have time to lower the rifle so it is close to an ammo wallet on your belt. Sometimes you'll want to keep the rifle in your shoulder while you reload. Either way, you should be able to reload quickly without looking.

Practice three kinds of reloads. All of them are begun with an open bolt. At first, watch what you're doing to ferret out problems; eventually you should be able to reload without taking your eyes off the target.

To perform a low load, maintain a firm hold on the fore-end with your weak hand while lowering the gun to waist level. Keep your eyes on the target. Use

If your shoulder tires from centerfire recoil thrown against it, think about an "understudy gun," a smaller gun similar to your hunting rig chambered in a rimfire caliber. Here is a Remington Model 700, top, paired with a Remington Model 504 rimfire; note the similar safeties, which builds muscle memory.

your strong hand to acquire one fresh round at a time. Place each one firmly in the magazine well, pushing down on each one to ensure it slips beneath the feed lips. Close the bolt on a fresh round in the chamber as you use both hands to raise the rifle to eye level. Place your finger on the trigger only after your eye finds the target through the scope.

To perform a position load, maintain a firm hold on the fore-end with your weak hand to maintain pressure on the rifle against your body. Keep the gun in your shoulder, your eyes on the target. Without looking, find your cartridge wallet with your strong hand, and acquire a fresh round. Reach up and place it in the open action, and push down on it to ensure it seats beneath the magazine feed lips. When the magazine is topped off, close the bolt and resume shooting.

A tactical load is performed similarly to the position load above, but instead of loading one cartridge at a time, you acquire a full load of rounds—enough to top off the magazine in one motion. Without taking your eyes off the target, diligently work to seat each round beneath the magazine feed lips. This takes practice. Loose cartridges don't always cooperate. Once you master this method, you will be able to top off an empty magazine and be back in action faster than you ever imagined.

Depending on rifle design, you may not be able to adequately stoke an empty chamber with a fresh cartridge, close the bolt, and fire the gun. On push-feed designs, this works just fine as there is no claw extractor that must grip a cartridge case head as the bolt locks into battery. On controlled-round-feed designs, however, it doesn't work well. You may very well be able to close the bolt and shoot the gun. You also may very well leave an empty case in the chamber when you open the bolt again because the claw extractor was unable to do its job. That could present a sticky situation when hunting dangerous game. That's why it's best to master a position or tactical load.

Managing Recoil

Learn to manage recoil. Buy and use a Past slip-on recoil pad for your shoulder. "Don't let the gun roll you," says New. "You need to be in control; don't let the gun run you or dictate what position you'll use or how much you'll shoot during a range session. It's a matter of pre-programming your body to manage recoil, to minimize the movement during recoil. If you need to shoot again, you're already on target."

If the gun kicks that much, consider a smaller caliber—an "understudy gun." A rimfire with all the characteristics of your hunting gun is ideal for range sessions. It's cheap to shoot, easy on your ears, and easy on your shoulder. Trigger time doesn't have to be miserable; it merely has to be meaningful.

Call Your Shots

You should have a good idea where your bullet hit the target before you confirm it with a look downrange. This is easy if your focus remains on the reticle when the shot breaks. Before you peer downrange through a spotting scope to check point of impact, ask yourself whether you can remember the location of the reticle when the gun discharged. Record your called shot in a range data book then compare it to the actual point of impact.

If you can't call your shots, you're likely failing to follow through. If you repeatedly call shots low, you're likely pulling your head away from the scope. Points of impact left or right might be caused by crushing the trigger or failing to maintain pressure on it during dwell time.

Other information to record in your range data book includes the location of the range; date; rifle, scope, and ammo used; wind velocity and direction; weather conditions; number of rounds fired; distance fired; the location of your final three-shot group; and other notes you deem important.

Remember that perfect practice makes perfect. There is a difference between merely sending rounds downrange and actually spending quality time on the fundamentals of marksmanship. Don't waste your time and money. You'll pay for it double when you get to the field.

Field Note: Take a Lesson from a Navy SEAL

Chip Beaman is a twenty-two-year Navy veteran, a former member of several SEAL teams, and now a trainer for the U.S. government. He's also an instructor at Sportsman's All-Weather All-Terrain Marksmanship at FTW Ranch in Barksdale, Texas. A visit with him reveals just how far the majority of us need to push ourselves to make ready for the field.

"At SAAM, our number-one goal is to be sure every shooter leaves the training facility understanding where his or her capabilities lie, given the situation. You should always train at least 20 percent farther than you'll hunt. If you determine your maximum effective range as a hunter is 300 yards, rehearse at four hundred yards. Log everything in a notebook.

"Build your house first. You gotta build that foundation regardless which position you use. The first time you do it, it might take you sixty or seventy seconds to build your house. But that time will improve each time you do it. Don't forget about your chicken wing—your strong-side elbow. If you get that right elbow pinned down you can do amazing things. If you've built your house enough times, you'll know before you shoot whether you're ready. You'll think, 'This house is not built properly. That wolf is gonna come and blow it down.'

"Find your natural point of aim. Relax your muscles by using bone support. After that it's all about FBS—focus, breathe, squeeze. And don't forget to follow through.

"This all seems so simple, but when I started shooting seriously I didn't get it. I didn't accept the fact that the human brain can focus only on one thing at a time. After the shot broke I'd ask myself, 'Where was your focus?' I figured out I was looking through the scope at the target. You've got to have crystal-clear focus on that reticle. It can melt away—and you can lose it. When that happens I move my eyes to the right, focus, then I move back to the center, to the reticle.

"Don't waste a dry-fire. The purpose of it is to execute a perfect live-fire. You have to understand what it is you're looking for. It's not just about seeing your reticle stay still when the trigger clicks. I'm always looking at my students, watching them roll their wrists, I can tell right when the trigger's gonna go. I can watch that wrist start to roll. They're not disengaging their trigger hand. You have to disengage.

"I always do a number of dry-fires before loading my rifle. Some of them are dedicated solely to my hand. Watch your hand, get it loose. I mean, this isn't a monumental thing you're doing. Get it in gear. Sometimes 'jerk drills' help. Have someone else load/not load your gun so you won't know whether you're squeezing the trigger on an empty chamber. Your reaction will tell you a lot about your state of mind.

"It breaks you of 'farming a shot,' of firing and immediately creating an excuse for a miss. The bottom line is, when you walk into the field you've got to know the dope is on, that you're on, that you're ready to rock."

Chapter 9

Long Range, the Wind, and Moving Targets

Too many hunters are too dependent on accuracy and velocity. It's hard to blame them. Enough has been written in magazines or aired on outdoor television shows about "flat-shooting" cartridges and long-range shooting to make a casual observer think all he has to do is point his wonder-magnum at game and pull the trigger to make a trophy fall. An expensive rifle, however, isn't a magic wand. Accurate shooting in the field requires at least a rudimentary understanding of ballistics, which is a science. It also requires an understanding of what the wind does to your bullet in flight, which is as much dark art as it is science.

Now that you've learned how to recognize the attributes in a rifle that determine its accuracy, how to turn your body into a shooting platform, and how to spend quality time on the range, it's time to put on your thinking cap. It's time to acknowledge that you are the weakest link in your system, because most rifles manufactured these days are capable of far better accuracy than the hunters who wield them. You are dangerous only at known ranges, which might be good for punching paper or competing in a shooting event, but it isn't enough to serve you well in the field.

Bullet drop, wind, and moving targets can wreak havoc on a hunter's success regardless of what cartridge is used. Other shooters don't have to worry about so many things simultaneously. While they do have to compensate for wind, target shooters don't have to worry about drop because in most competitions, the distance to the target is known. Before record strings are recorded in competition, the shooter fires "sighter" shots and then adjusts his sights for the known distance. A hunter, however, will get no sighter shots at a trophy bull elk. Therefore, understanding how the flight of a bullet is affected by wind, and how it arcs in its path to game, is critical to placing shots accurately at the varying ranges encountered in the field.

Exterior Ballistics

Ballistics is the science of projectiles in motion, usually divided into three categories. Interior ballistics is the study of what occurs in the chamber as a cartridge is fired, from the instant the primer ignites to the instant the bullet exits the muzzle. Exterior ballistics is the study of how a bullet flies through the air. Terminal ballistics is the study of how a bullet performs when it hits a target. We're not concerned with interior ballistics here, and we covered terminal ballistics in chapter 4 (we'll do so again to some extent when we discuss shot placement). Exterior ballistics—a bullet's behavior as it encounters air movement, barometric pressure, humidity, altitude, and other atmospheric influences—requires some measure of thought unless you're happy with shooting only at animals no farther away than your zero.

Determining what your bullet will do as it travels downrange is called "getting your dope." "Dope" refers to the data used for a particular gun and

When you first begin to shoot at long range it pays to have a spotter to help you figure out the wind. Come to think of it, it always pays to have a spotter.

load (the brand of cartridge or the kind of bullet you shoot) to accomplish a particular shot, and it also refers to the sight setting on a particular rifle used to accomplish a particular shot. Getting the dope for a shot, that is, doing the math involved to explain how your bullet is influenced by the atmosphere during its travels, can seem intimidating. You don't have to solve complex equations every time you shoot. You do, however, need to know how to account for distance and wind.

Let's define some factors at work against you and your bullet.

Air Resistance (Drag)

The resistance of the atmosphere, known as drag, has a direct effect on bullets in flight. Manufacturers account for this to achieve optimum performance, deriving a ballistic coefficient for each bullet design that maximizes flight.

Ballistic Coefficient (BC)

This is a measure of how well a bullet maintains velocity to overcome air resistance in flight. It's derived from the attributes of a bullet—its weight, cross-sectional area, and a form factor (a multiple, a control factor that compares a bullet's unique drag to that of a standard we won't explore here)—then expressed mathematically as a number usually less than one.

At long range, ballistic performance is largely dependent on how much velocity is retained by the bullet, which makes BC a critical component of bullet performance. A heavier, narrower bullet slips through air better. So BC is the most important measure of exterior ballistic bullet performance. Know your bullet's BC, and you can calculate its trajectory to determine shots downrange. You can usually find a bullet's BC in reloading manuals, or on the manufacturer's Web site.

Muzzle Velocity (MV)

This is the speed of a bullet as it exits the barrel, measured in feet per second. It will enhance or detract from exterior ballistics of any bullet of any caliber, weight, and BC. MV diminishes as a bullet travels downrange due to air resistance (drag).

Range

Range is the all-too-often unknown distance to the quarry. These days, it is foolish to hunt without a laser rangefinder anywhere shots are likely to be greater than 150 yards. If you're doing things right, the game should be unaware of your presence; you have time to get a reading. When you don't, use mental methods of range calculation.

Trajectory

This is the curved path of a bullet from muzzle to target. A flat trajectory is a relative term for minimal arcing in the bullet's flight. Generally, the faster the speed of the bullet (that is, the higher the muzzle velocity), the flatter the bullet's trajectory. It is true that a bullet begins to drop the instant it leaves the barrel, but that understanding does not account for the fact that we sight-in based on sight height. For instance, most riflescopes ride 1.5 inches above the bore line. To ensure our bullet flight coincides with our line of sight above the bore, we in effect angle the muzzle upward when we fire, producing the trajectory of the bullet.

Gravity

This is the effect of the earth's rotation on a bullet's time of flight. It is constant regardless of a bullet's weight, shape, or velocity (with the exception of a bullet fired at an extreme angle). A bullet fired from the horizontal will strike the ground at precisely the same instant as one simultaneously dropped from the muzzle. The difference is the forward velocity of the bullet fired from the muzzle. When shooting horizontally, gravity pulls a bullet directly away from the line of sight.

It also affects a bullet traveling at extreme angles relative to horizontal in another way. When the line of sight is elevated up or down, gravity still pulls the bullet straight down. So it simultaneously pulls the bullet away from the line of sight and slows down the bullet.

Wind Deflection

This defines what air currents do to a bullet. The less wind drift suffered by a bullet the better, which is another factor that suggests how important it is to choose a bullet with the highest BC possible that also shoots accurately in your rifle. Next to uncertainty about distance, our inability to evaluate the speed and direction of the wind is our biggest problem in long-range shooting. We must determine wind direction and speed to know what effect it will have on the flight of a bullet.

Altitude

This is the effect of air density on bullet trajectory. The higher the altitude, the thinner the air—a bullet flies "flatter." Conversely, the lower the altitude, the heavier the air—a bullet drops faster. Each 5,000-foot difference in elevation from your sight-in location changes point of impact by one-half to one minute of angle (one-half to one inch at 100 yards). Remember this rule: elevation up, bullet up; elevation down, bullet down.

American Hunter *managing editor Jeff Johnston uses a pack to steady his rifle in the prone position while shooting at the NRA Whittington Center in New Mexico. Shots at long range must always be supported ones. You'll seldom be effective by "winging it."* (Photo courtesy of Jeff Johnston)

Temperature

This is the effect of air temperature on bullet trajectory. The higher the air temperature, the thinner the air—a bullet flies "flatter." The lower the temperature, the heavier the air—a bullet drops faster. For every 20-degree change in temperature from your sight-in dope, point of impact changes by one-half to one minute of angle. Remember this rule: hot day, bullet rises; cold day, bullet drops.

Humidity

This is the percentage of moisture in the air that affects drag. The higher the humidity, the lighter the air—a bullet will suffer less drag. The lower the humidity, the denser the air—a bullet will drop faster. This seems counterintuitive. Most

The longest shot the author has ever made in the field occurred in New Mexico on this elk. When the author and his guide exited the pines after a long stalk, the wind shifted and the herd made a jail break. The distance was 450 yards when the shooting started. The second, third, and fourth shots were made at 500 yards. Bullets one, three, and four hit within a six-inch circle on the bull's shoulder. The author never would have made the shots without thinking about his bullet drop and compensating for the range with holdover. The rifle was a Kimber 8400 in .300 Winchester Magnum with a 180-grain Barnes MRX.

people assume that because humidity is moisture, it is heavier than air. Clouds, however, are a concentration of moisture, and they float in air. A 20 percent change in humidity from sight-in conditions equates to only about a quarter-inch of impact change at 100 yards—not a huge concern for hunters. Remember this rule: higher humidity, higher bullet.

Light

This factor affects what the shooter sees through the sights. Our tendency is to shoot high on overcast days and low in bright sunshine. Remember this rule: lights up, sights up; lights down, sights down.

Minute of Angle (MOA)

This is an angular method of measurement that describes accuracy capability in a gun, load, or even a shooter. One MOA is one-sixtieth of a degree, which subtends to 1.047 inches at 100 yards. For practical purposes, we consider that to be one inch. An MOA group, then, equals slightly more than an inch at 100 yards, two inches at 200 yards, etc.

Kinetic Energy (KE)

This is the amount of striking energy a bullet carries downrange. It is measured in foot-pounds and it's important at long range because KE is proportional to bullet mass and velocity. You should determine how much KE is required to humanely kill game, then calculate the range where the bullet falls below that threshold. Say it takes 1,000 foot-pounds of energy to kill a deer with a .30-caliber, 165-grain bullet. Now say a .308 Winchester shoots such a bullet at 2,700 feet per second. A .308 has 2,600 foot-pounds of muzzle energy, but drops below 1,000 foot-pounds of KE at 600 yards. Thus, based on this formula, past 600 yards a .308 Winchester is inadequate to kill deer.

Come-Ups

As you should have deduced by now, the concept of zero is a practical way to ease range-estimation problems. Remember the three methods of zeroing a rifle from our discussion in chapter 8:

Dead-on Zero

A 100-yard, dead-on zero is good when you can expect to engage targets at close range; you will have to employ "come-ups" to shoot beyond 100 yards accurately.

Point-Blank Range

This is the distance at which the bullet will neither rise above nor fall below the line of sight by more than a specified distance, commonly three inches.

Two-Hundred-Yard Zero (Hunter's Zero)

This is the best zero for hunting big game in mixed terrain where the possibility of a long shot exists. The gun is usually sighted-in about 1.5 inches high at 100 yards.

Based on these theories, a lot of hunters head afield with a "two inches high at 100" zero and expect to hit the vitals of any game out to 400 yards by holding over the back of game when the distance seems great. That's not always wise. It's true zeroing your rifle at point-blank range exploits the flat portion of your bullet's trajectory so you may often ignore range estimation, and it's true a hunter's zero puts you in the ballpark most of the time. When in doubt, however, do you hold on hair or air?

During any shot you should eliminate at least one variable: You can hold over for range or hold off for wind, but it's awfully difficult to do both simultaneously. It's usually best to determine distance to the target and calculate your come-up—the necessary adjustment to your scope's elevation turret—so you place the reticle precisely on a defined point of aim then hold off for wind. To calculate come-up, you need to know three things: the weight and BC of your load, and its muzzle velocity.

To do it precisely, to develop the dope for a particular bullet, you should shoot the load at various distances, in 100-yard increments, out to your maximum effective range, which is the distance you are certain to hit game with the first shot every time. Many hunters' dope cards (discussed later in this chapter) take them out to 500 yards, though such a long shot is rare. Trajectory tables on the back

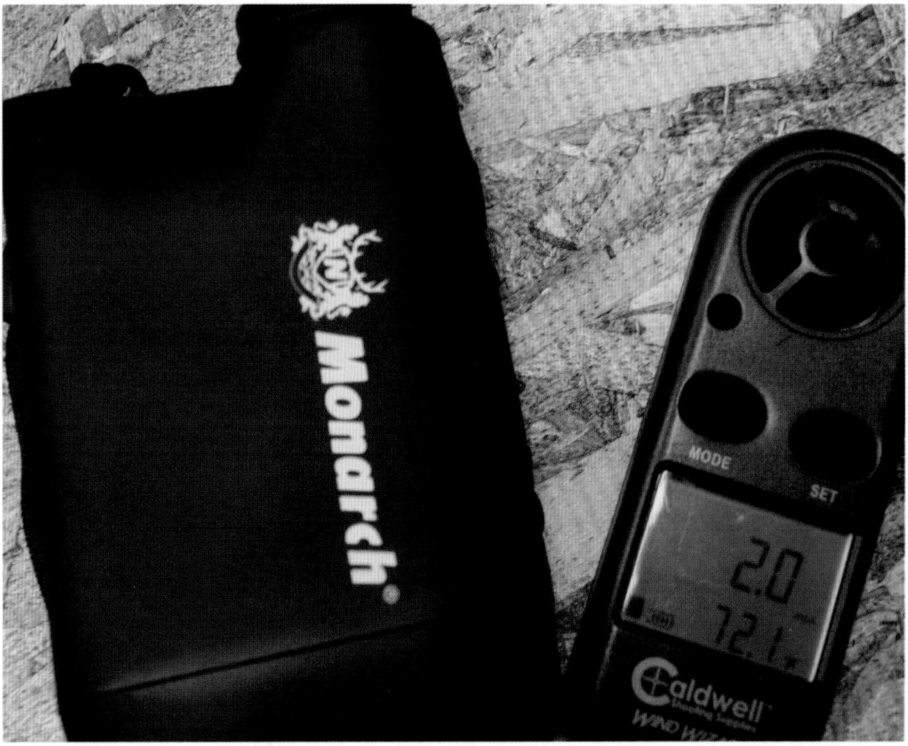

If you expect to be successful at long range you absolutely must have two tools: a laser rangefinder and a wind meter. Without both, you're whistling "Dixie."

of ammo boxes only get you started, and ballistics software is mostly theoretical. The standard deviation (the minor variation in velocity between one fired round and another) of any load can vary by 100 feet per second or more. Usually we don't need to worry about standard deviation, for the quality of factory-loaded cartridges these days is exceptional. It exists, though, and narrowing it to but a few feet per second is a primary reason some hunters insist on shooting only handloaded ammo. You should be able to rely on the muzzle velocity printed on the box of ammo in your hand, but to be absolutely sure it's wise to chronograph the load at least once in a while.

Furthermore, you should condition yourself now to erase from your mind the thought of "clicks" on your scope. Think instead in terms of minutes of angle

(MOA), which are more precise and, once absorbed, not easily forgotten. It's easy to become confused under stress if you can't turn off "clicks." If you're not careful, you might insist to yourself that the last time you touched your scope you dialed in four MOA. Or was it only four clicks? The difference is eleven inches at 100 yards, as we shall see.

For starters, we need to nail down the distance to the target. A laser rangefinder is highly useful. If you don't have one (or the batteries in yours go south) you can use manual methods of range estimation.

There are several ways to do this. You can use 100-yard increments (think "football fields"), but this is effective only to about 300 yards. Consider the size of the game (this takes experience with the actual size of the animal); bracket the distance by estimating that the object is not less than "X" yards or more than "Y" yards and then take an average; or use a combination of some or all of the above.

With range established, calculate the come-up. My Kimber 84M LongMaster Classic, a half-minute gun, is a good example to use because the cartridge it is chambered in, .308 Winchester, is used around the world. All the dope has already been developed for it. That allows me to not only check my math anytime I question my own calculations, but to hypothesize about the performance of other loads I might want to use before actually firing them. You can get the dope on any cartridge if you search manufacturers' Web sites or fiddle with ballistics programs on your computer.

The load I shoot is a Barnes Tipped Triple-Shock X bullet (TTSX) that weighs 150 grains and has a BC of .420; the .308 fires the load at 2,864 feet per second. For our purposes, let's say the gun is zeroed dead-on at 100 yards and run through a couple of scenarios at various distances.

- Range to target is 100 yards: I do nothing. My gun is zeroed at 100 yards; a dead-on hold should produce a hit on target.
- Range to target is 200 yards: I determine my bullet will drop 1.5 MOA, or 3 inches; I determine that I need to adjust the elevation turret for 1.5 minutes of elevation; each click of the turret equals a quarter-minute at 100 yards, so I dial up 6 clicks; I hold dead-on my intended point of impact.

- Range to target is 300 yards: My bullet will drop 4 MOA, or twelve inches; I adjust the elevation turret on my scope 4 MOA to compensate for a 12-inch drop, which equates to 16 clicks of elevation on the turret; I hold dead-on my intended point of impact.
- Range to target is 500 yards: My bullet will drop 9.75 MOA, or 49 inches; I dial up 39 clicks of elevation; I hold dead-on my intended point of impact.

Now, that last example is extreme. But as you can see, the math gets easier and faster to calculate the more you do it. Minutes of angle are easily multiplied by four (if you use a quarter-minute scope) to determine the come-up on elevation. You don't need to worry about the drop in inches at a given range and then think about how many clicks to the inch you need to dial up at 100 yards, then halve or quarter that number of clicks because the range is actually 200 or 400 yards. You merely determine the MOA drop and multiply by four (if you have a quarter-minute scope).

Come-ups are almost always better than holdovers because they deliver better accuracy. They produce a precise point of impact on a constant point of aim. At great distances, they are necessary. At 400 yards, it's hard to tell the difference between twenty-seven inches and twenty inches on the shoulder of a big bull moose. It's no time for guesswork.

Extreme Angles

Remember, also, the baffling effect of gravity on bullets fired in any way other than horizontal—the steeper the angle up or down, the less gravity will affect your bullet. Many folks believe that "400 yards is 400 yards" regardless of the angle at which the bullet is fired up or down, but you'll hit high when shooting uphill or downhill if you don't account for gravity in extreme angles. Remember this rule: Steeper angles mean less distance.

Remember that your rifle is sighted-in when horizontal and bullet drop is adjusted for gravity pulling the bullet perpendicularly away from line of sight. So, at slope, the bullet is pulled away from line of sight at an angle and therefore the effect of gravity is somewhat mitigated—although there is actually more math to it than that. Still, for a hunter the formula below works. Remember that in the field, the second you are not shooting horizontally, alarm bells should sound.

To calculate for steep shots, multiply the range by a constant factor. Use this chart created by the instructors at FTW Outfitters' Sportsman's All-Weather All-Terrain Marksmanship to calculate shots at extreme angles:

Angle (in degrees)	Multiplier of Measured Yards
10	.98
20	.94
30	.87
40	.77
50	.64
60	.50
70	.34
80	.17
90	.00

Note that the multiplier shrinks as the angle increases, which indicates the effects of gravity begin to kick in big-time when shooting in steep terrain.

If a 300-yard shot is fired at a 30-degree angle, we would calculate our shot:

300 (yards) x .87 = 261 (yards)

We adjust the scope for a 261-yard shot, not a 300-yard shot, because the steep terrain affects the flight of a bullet less than if the bullet were fired across level ground. If I come up for a 300-yard shot, my point of impact will be off by thirty-nine yards.

At 500 yards, the results are drastic:

500 x .87 = 435 yards

That's a miss. Make up a cheat-sheet of these angles and make it part of the dope card you carry with your rifle.

Kinetic Energy (KE)

Before we leave the subject of shooting at long distance, we should discuss downrange energy, because the amount your bullet may or may not have at a particular range may or may not kill an animal adequately. Target shooters don't care about KE because they punch only paper. To hunters, though, it's a critical measure of whether a bullet will deliver the news at the distances they may fire at game.

Remember that KE is the measure of striking energy a bullet carries downrange. It is measured in foot-pounds.

Formula for Kinetic Energy:

KE = BW x V squared / 450,800 (a constant)

Where:

KE = kinetic energy at the muzzle in foot-pounds
BW = bullet weight in grains
V = velocity in feet per second

Kinetic Energy is proportional to bullet mass and velocity. Use it by determining how much KE is required to humanely kill game, then calculate the range at which the bullet falls below the threshold. It's commonly written that 1,000 foot-pounds of KE is needed to sufficiently kill a deer, for instance. Whether that is an immutable law merits discussion, for we can all cite instances of handgun hunters killing deer using handguns that do not deliver 1,000 foot-pounds of KE at 100 yards. Still, it's an accepted measure, and useful mainly as an indicator of exactly what your bullet has left at extremely long range.

Example: Assume it takes 1,000 foot-pounds of energy to kill a deer; a .308 Winchester fires a 165-grain bullet at a MV of 2,700 feet per second. A .308 has 2,600 foot-pounds of *muzzle energy*, but drops below 1,000 foot-pounds of KE at 600 yards. Thus, based on this formula, a .308 Winchester is inadequate to kill deer past 600 yards.

My .308 TTSX, which weighs 150 grains and has a muzzle velocity of 2,684 feet per second, can be measured as:

150 x 7,203,856 / 450,800 = 2,397 foot-pounds KE at the muzzle.

At 600 yards, my .308 TTSX is traveling 1,688 feet per second. Now the formula reveals:

150 x 2,849,344 / 450,800 = 942.4 foot-pounds KE.

This is still below the established threshold to humanely kill a deer.

When considering any new rifle and caliber, you should perform the same calculation to ensure the rifle is adequate to kill the game you plan to hunt, at the distances you plan to hunt with it.

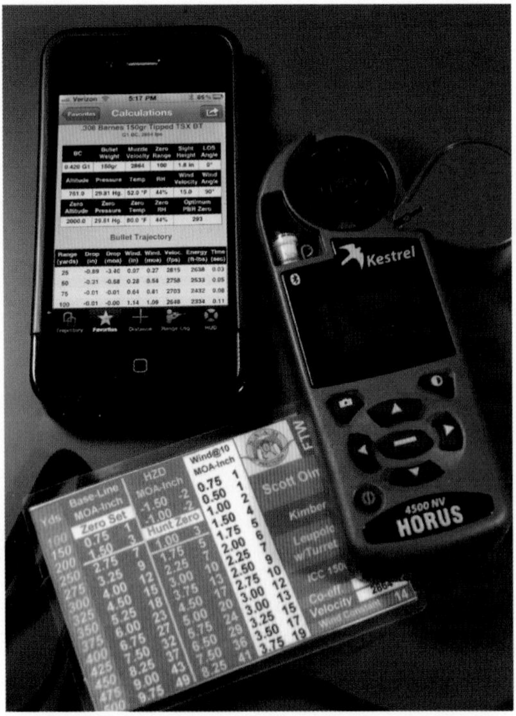

An iPhone (left), loaded with "Ballistic: Field Tactical Edition" software; a Kestrel 4500 NV weather meter (right), loaded with Horus ballistic software; and a simple "dope card." All three shortcuts are set up for the author's go-to rifle. You should have at least one of the three on hand. The dope card is the simplest to manage.

Doping the Wind

With diligent practice, a shooter can develop proficiency with come-ups. The exact distance to the target can be precisely determined, after all, with a laser rangefinder, so there's no excuse for refusing to nail down that variable. What about the wind? Crosswinds are everywhere. Vertical winds occur in hilly terrain as air currents rise and fall between slopes.

Forget range uncertainty: Our inability to evaluate the speed and direction of wind is our biggest problem when shooting long-range. To combat the problem, it's helpful to remember two facts. We know the less wind drift suffered by a bullet, the better, so we should fire a bullet with a high BC to resist wind deflection as much as possible. Still, when all else is equal we can sacrifice a few degrees of BC for the load our rifle shoots best. We know the wind deflection sensitivity of a bullet to a vertical wind is the same as it is to a crosswind, so if we can roughly determine the speed and value of wind, we can begin to account for its effects when shooting across a canyon or across a plain.

We also know the wind is ever-changing. So without the aid of electronic devices, we are seldom able to determine exactly the speed of it. There will always be some uncertainty, but we can get close.

There are two methods used to visually calculate wind speed.

Mirage

This is seen as the heat waves, or reflection of light through air layers of different densities and temperatures. With optical aids, mirage is seen even on cold days. It is best read through a spotting scope or binocular; sometimes you can see mirage through your riflescope. Find it by focusing on the target, then backing off to about midrange. A "boiling" mirage indicates the wind is at 6 or 12 o'clock. It's calm, so it has no value as far as bullet drift is concerned. Any horizontal movement of mirage is worth at least a half-minute of angle at ranges beyond 300 yards.

Sight

Use your eyes to make an educated guess. Wind speed of 1 to 3 MPH will make smoke or dust drift; 3 to 5 MPH is felt on your face; 5 to 8 MPH, trees will be in constant motion; 8 to 12 MPH raises dust from the ground; 12 to 15 MPH causes small trees to sway.

Of course not all wind blows perfectly from one direction or another, so the clock method is used to value it. Some shooters will disagree with the values below, choosing to dicker with the component value of a 1 o'clock wind, for instance. But for our purposes the system works. Remember, this is part art.

- Where the direction you will fire is 12 o'clock:
- Wind that blows from 12 or 6 o'clock has no value; no correction is needed.
- Wind from the 1, 2, 4, 5, 7, 8, 10, and 11 o'clock positions has half-value; multiply wind speed by half, so a 10-MPH wind would affect your bullet as if it were a 5-MPH wind.
- Wind from 3 and 9 o'clock has full value; multiply wind speed by 1, so a 10-MPH wind would affect your bullet as a 10-MPH wind.

The clock method will give you a ballpark estimate of what to expect downrange. Now, with wind speed and direction determined, we must determine wind deflection.

Formula for Wind Deflection:

W x D / constant = MOA correction.

Where:

W = wind velocity measured in miles per hour

D = distance measured in hundreds of yards

The constant is a control number derived for particular calibers and bullet designs. The constants for wind formulas are developed from ballistics calculators; you can find them available free online.

Constants for Popular Cartridges:

.300 Winchester Magnum: 16

7mm Remington Magnum: 16

.308 Winchester: 15
.270 Winchester: 14
.30-06: 12
.30-30 Winchester: 8

The final product will be a huge number; insert a decimal point to the first tenth (312 becomes 3.12 MOA). If the wind is blowing at 10 miles per hour from 3 o'clock, the distance is 300 yards, and the constant is 15 (the constant for a .308 Winchester bullet), we correct for the wind with 2 MOA of correction, or 6 inches of hold-off. The same wind velocity from 1 o'clock and the same distance of 300 yards would yield 1 MOA of correction, or 3 inches of hold-off.

Notice the constant changes as muzzle velocity changes and bullet characteristics change with relative cartridges. Further, the constants used here are rounded to the nearest quarter MOA to account for most quarter-minute riflescope adjustments. You should consult the spindrift specifications available from the manufacturer for the actual bullet you shoot.

Shortcuts

Although I've tried to simplify things, I'm sure your head is spinning. Trust me, this is about the simplest explanation of every variable involved in long-range shooting. If you want to be the master of your rifle at unknown distances, you need to read this chapter again, practice with your rifle and load, and learn the characteristics of your bullet's flight at various distances to target. There are some shortcuts, though.

Dope Cards

For starters, you should produce a dope card for your rifle and load. On it, you should indicate your cartridge and bullet type; its BC and muzzle velocity; your baseline zero; MOA and inch drops in trajectory in 50-yard increments; and wind-drift calculations at those same 50-yard increments for MOA and inches (with the wind constant for your cartridge near that data) out to your maximum effective range. That's a minimum.

Other helpful data to place on the card are a couple of angle corrections for common elevation grades; reminders of what different wind speeds look and feel like; and anything else you can fit on a piece of paper no bigger than your driver's license. Laminate it to protect it from the elements. Then consider it the driver's license for your hunting rifle, keep it with that gun, and never leave home without it.

BDC and Mil-Dot Reticles

Riflescopes that use stadia wires to bracket targets of known size are hardly new. And since they measure target size, they represent an easy way to determine range. Commercial ballistic-drop-compensating (BDC) reticles are more popular than ever these days, but they are merely a spin-off of the mil-dot reticle, the first rangefinding reticle system in widespread use in this country. The "mil" is short for milliradian.

A milliradian is a part of a 360-degree circle (one radian is 57.32 degrees). A circle has 6.28 radians. A minute of angle, as we've learned, is $^{1}/_{60}{}^{th}$ of a degree, so there are 3,439 MOA in one radian, 3.44 MOA in a milliradian. Divide 3.44 into 60 for a product of 17.44, about $^{1}/_{17}{}^{th}$ of a degree. The spaces between mil-dots subtend 1 mil, which equals 3.6 inches at 100 yards, or three feet at 1,000 yards.

The formula is: Height of the target in yards x 1,000 / number of mils = Distance in yards

To use a mil-dot as a rangefinder, divide a target's height in mils by the number of spaces subtending the target to get range in hundreds of yards. A deer is 10 mils at the shoulder; one that appears in the scope to be 2 dots high is about 500 yards away. Mil-dot scopes are designed to be used only at one magnification. Most tactical military-style scopes are fixed at 10X; variable scopes are usually calibrated at the top end of magnification.

The Leupold Mark 4 2.5–8X36 MR/T M1 scope on my Kimber LongMaster Classic expands on the mil-dot system with various sized and spaced hash marks on the vertical and horizontal stadia for 1-meter range-estimation. While I have used it for that, to be honest it's kind of like Spanish—if I don't use it regularly, I can't remember what I'm doing. The horizontal stadia are very handy for wind hold-off, however, because I've determined MOA measurements with them at given ranges.

Riflescopes with reticles that feature reference marks similar to mil-dots can be sighted-in for a series of specific distances. First zero the rifle at 100 yards. Then place a large target at the farthest distance you wish to shoot, ensuring there is enough paper on the target to catch flyers. Then shoot a group at, say, 400 yards. Walk out to the target and draw a large X in the center of the group. Return to the bench, align the reticle on the original 400-yard aiming point, and zoom the magnification until one of the dots lines up just below the X. Now you have a 400-yard reference point as long as you do not vary from the magnification with which you performed this sight-in. Then fire groups at 200 and 300 yards so you know where the bullets will hit in relation to the other dots, or from your original zero.

Plex reticles also can be used to indicate the maximum distance you might shoot. By setting the magnification ring on a given distance, let's say 300 yards, and

Finger-adjustable "target" turrets are all the rage these days because they allow shooters to make elevation and windage adjustments without first unscrewing turret caps.

checking the size of the animal within the posts, you will instantly know whether the animal is closer or farther than your optimum range. If you have practiced at various distances out to and past 300 yards, you will know where to hold.

For scopes with plex reticles that don't have a second set of numbers on their magnification rings, set up an eighteen- or twenty-inch-tall cardboard box at 300 yards. On the shooting bench, vary magnification within your scope until the box fits between the tip of the post and the center of the reticle—until the box is bracketed. An animal's vital zone equal to or larger than that space is within 300 yards. Write the correct holds on a cheat sheet and tape it to your rifle so you don't forget your system.

Several other gadgets deserve mention. Just remember that simply buying one and using it without understanding what's at work will rob you of the vital visualization necessary to develop proficiency, which can lead to problems down the line. My photography professors always said I had to learn to take a picture by manually manipulating the controls on the camera—the aperture and shutter speed—in order to understand what's at work. By making adjustments myself, I learned how the finished product measured up to my expectations. That way, when I used the camera on auto-mode in fast-moving situations, I knew it would produce exactly the kind of images I wanted. The same theory holds for tools that help us determine ballistic variables. It's fine to use shortcuts, but a keen understanding of the work they do for you is vital to know whether you're on the right track.

Ballistics Programs

Remember that if you change loads you will need to develop fresh dope on those loads. As I've said before, it's best to find a bullet you like and stick with it. Doing that is made easier with computer programs. If this discussion actually interests you, check out ballistics software. Buy a program, load it on your computer, and begin to explore bullet trajectories. There are a lot of such programs on the market, but they are generally available only for Windows-based operating systems. Since I've been fond of Macintosh operating systems, I've had to look elsewhere to fulfill my needs.

Nikon's new Spot-On system does a good job with either operating system; with it you can calculate trajectory and drift holds for every reticle in the Nikon lineup. You can also simply log on to several bullet manufacturers' Web sites, as they've already done the work for you. Their pages will display data only for their proprietary bullets, of course, but it's a convenient way to see how ballistics software works and determine whether you want to shoot a particular bullet.

Along the same lines, and a lot cheaper, is an iPhone app called "Ballistic: Field Tactical Edition," by Jonathan Zdziarski. With it you'll never be without a ballistics calculator again. Plug in the BC, diameter, weight, muzzle velocity, zero range, sight height, atmospheric conditions, wind speed and angle, and maximum range, and the program spits out a trajectory table complete with wind drift, energy, and time to target for your load in increments down to twenty-five yards. The program comes standard with data for numerous bullets, and you can store multiple loads as favorites. And since an iPhone is GPS-equipped, data regarding location like altitude and weather conditions are automatically loaded when you open the program. It's neat, it's inexpensive, and ever since I got it I can't stop playing with it.

Electronic Tools

Newly developed angle-compensating rangefinders are all the rage these days because they perform a calculation for you and spit out the actual distance to the target based on the angle of the shot. Models are available from Nikon, Leupold & Stevens, and Bushnell.

Wind and weather meters are useful. The Kestrel 4500 Pocket Weather Tracker has been popular with scientists and shooters for years. It measures air temperature, humidity, altitude, barometric pressure, wind speed, and wind direction, to name just a few variables. The latest model, the 4500 NV with Horus ATrag ballistics software, does more than ever. In addition to the weather data the unit measures and stores, you can plug in ballistic variables including BC, bullet weight, muzzle velocity, bore diameter, zero range, bore height, distance to target, shot angle, ground location and altitude (thanks to a built-in compass), wind speed, and wind direction, and you can load, customize, and store multiple aiming solutions for multiple guns. Information for many guns comes already loaded on the unit, but the 4500 NV can be used with any combination of gun, scope, and reticle. It isn't cheap, but it's awfully useful for avid shooters.

Moving Targets

Despite the growing legion of hunters who engage game at long range these days, the number of people who insist it should never be done is growing, I think. To their way of thinking, it's as if no one ever took a long shot at a trophy, and no one should even train for it. Same goes for thoughts on shots at running game. Lots of articles on shooting running deer were published in our forefathers' era. Once upon a time, running-deer competition shoots were standard fare at gun clubs. The Lyman sight company even used to print a running deer on its products.

As we've seen, the skills for just about any shot can be learned. If you hunt long enough, you will eventually need every trick in the book. Even if you use it only to finish wounded game, knowing how to shoot running game properly is a skill an accomplished rifleman should own. To own it, you've got to learn it, and practice it.

Unlike shooting a rifle at a fixed object, shooting at a moving target is not a thoughtful, mechanical process. It's an intuitive one. You must remain fluid and loose. Think about the techniques used in shotgun shooting and you'll get the picture. Yes, you must still squeeze the trigger and you must still be conscious of the sight picture, but to adequately shoot running game you must learn to go on autopilot.

Knowing the lead is key. Like doping the wind, this is an inexact science that is more art than anything else. You must gauge the game's apparent speed—its actual speed moderated by its angle of travel toward or away from you. It's helpful to remember the clock system used to value wind. Game running directly toward you has no apparent speed; it requires no lead. Game running at 20 MPH across your front has an apparent speed of 20 MPH, the same as its actual speed. If it is running at a 45-degree angle, its apparent speed is halved; in effect, it's running at only 10 MPH.

Range and bullet speed are important, too. If the range is 200 yards and you're shooting my .308, your 150-grain bullet leaves the muzzle at 2,684 feet per second. At 225 yards that bullet is traveling 2,435 feet per second. The game is running 600 feet distant; the bullet arrives in less than a quarter-second, .23 second to be precise. During that time, the game will run not quite 7 feet (20 MPH is roughly 29 feet per second; .23 x 29 = 6.67 feet). Swing the sights about 6 feet past the animal's shoulder and keep swinging as you squeeze the trigger.

Up close, things change. Precision becomes less important than speed. Lead still matters, though. It may be short, but you need to know it instantly.

In the field there is no time to think about either process, let alone perform heady calculations. You'll need intuition that comes from practice.

There are three ways to approach shots at moving targets.

Point-shooting is good when the range is close and the brush is thick. You plan a hit. As soon as the game appears, pick out a spot ahead of it where you think the animal will appear as the bullet arrives. Throw the rifle to your shoulder as you focus on that spot. A low-power scope is good to have for this. Keep both eyes open. Gauge target speed and direction as you shoulder the rifle. Shoot quickly, when the sight picture looks good. Build in the lead before you're tempted to aim through the scope. Your rifle should move with the animal, but don't commit to swinging the rifle.

Good point-shooting looks fluid, like an instantaneous aim with a moving rifle. You can't be caught flat-footed. Remember your boxer's stance in the offhand position, because here is one place where it will pay dividends. As sight and target merge, you must commit to the shot.

You can swing through the target. With a swing-through, you paint the game out of the picture in the same way a shotgunner pass-shoots a duck. Bring up the gun behind the game and fire when the muzzle blots it out. Swing faster than the target and keep swinging after the shot. The right lead will actually come after you squeeze the trigger as the muzzle accelerates beyond the animal and the bullet exits the barrel.

The problem here will be the brush that catches your bullet—brush you won't see until it's too late because you're focused on the sprinting animal. And

Nikon Spot-On ballistics software.

since the animal won't be in the field of view in your scope for the entire swing-through, you'll be tempted to stay on the animal when sight and target come together. Don't do it. If you do, you'll swing slowly and shoot behind the target. Again, keep both eyes open.

The last technique is sustained lead. With it, you tug the game along on a string—establish a lead, then sustain it as you squeeze the trigger. You don't have time to seek the precision you used on the swing-through. The idea is to have the proper lead no matter when you fire, moving the rifle with the target at the same apparent speed.

You'll be tempted to stay on the target too long, trying to anticipate changes in speed and direction and verify your hold and sight picture. If this happens, you won't squeeze the trigger when you should, and you'll shoot behind the game. Follow through—keep the gun moving as you squeeze the trigger and the bullet travels the length of the barrel and exits, and a bit longer.

Practice shots at moving targets on the range with a target in the center of a tire rolled downhill horizontal to your firing line. Better still is bumpy terrain that makes the tire bob and weave a little. Make sure conditions are safe. A good idea is to use a flag as a landmark the tire must pass before anyone starts shooting.

Part III

In the Field

The little things that make all the difference, the practical hunter's mindset, what a bullet does to game, and a hunter's big-game battery

Chapter 10

Field-Shooting Aids

A big-game guide once told me, "American hunters are too dependent on shooting aids. They need to learn to plop down in position and shoot rather than fumble with shooting sticks."

"No," I disagreed, "they're not dependent enough on them."

Many hunters know they probably would shoot better with a pair of shooting sticks or a sling in the field, but they often don't bother to search out the best ones for them, and they're too lazy to practice with them regularly so their use becomes second nature. All hunters owe it to themselves and the game to take the best shot possible. If that occurs by simply plopping into the sitting position, fine. Most of the time, though, you can do better.

The basic field-shooting positions should come intuitively, but none of them are comfortable without practice. Come to think of it, none of them are comfortable to a middle-aged man with a gut and bad knees. Fortunately, age and experience usually deliver wisdom, which, translated, means it never hurts to cheat a little.

Little Things Dad Didn't Teach You

Keep the barrel of the rifle from contacting anything hard that might cause abnormal vibration during dwell time, as the movement could affect the bullet's path. You never want to do anything that affects the natural vibration of the barrel. Cushion the barrel against a hard rest with your hand or a pack or something.

Set up quickly. Time is critical, but don't rush the shot. Often you'll find yourself with the wind and the range to your advantage. Remember, the first shot is the most important.

When lying prone in a supported position, release the fore-end with your weak hand; you don't need two hands on the gun. Instead, reach beneath the buttstock and grip the rear sling swivel with your fist, pulling the butt into your shoulder for stability. Be sure not to actually grasp the riflestock—grip the sling swivel only to apply minimal pressure on the rifle.

"Make sure you're as stable as possible before firing, even if it takes longer than you think it should to set up," says Doug "Dog" Prichard. He should know. He's not only a hunter but a retired SEAL sniper who served twenty-six years in the U.S. Navy, twenty-five in special ops. Today he's an instructor at Sportsman's All-Weather All-Terrain Marksmanship at FTW Ranch in Barksdale, Texas.

Use the best position possible, given field of view and terrain. Remember: Never stand when you can kneel, never kneel when you can sit, never sit when you can lie prone. Above all, never take an unsupported shot when you have time to find or build a rest. Prichard calls this "building your house."

"When hunting there is no bench or any other rest," he says. "You have to think outside the box. I take a systematic approach to the field. That starts at your feet. Then you work your way up. When you see an animal, the first thing

When sitting, you can often be more accurate by leaning into a tree or other sturdy object. If there's no tree present, lean into a buddy.

you should do is think about your feet—you've gotta get those legs squared up before you adopt any position. Whether you drop into the prone or the kneeling, you've got to get your base set up first."

There are other ways to steady yourself and take some of the wobble out of your shooting. In the prone position you need only one hand—your trigger hand—on the gun. When resting the fore-end across a pack, let go of the rifle with your left arm. Reach beneath your body and grasp the sling swivel on the buttstock and pull the rifle into your shoulder. Be careful not to touch the buttstock, as this will induce movement. You want to minimize contact with the rifle, just as you'd do on a shooting bench.

While sitting, lean against a rock or tree. If neither is present, ask your buddy to lean against you. Stuff your pack under your strong-side arm—your "chicken wing." Stuff your buddy's pack under your weak-side arm. You might look like the Pillsbury Doughboy, but you'll be rock-solid. The same trick can be used while kneeling. If it hurts to sit on your heel while in the kneeling position, place your pack under your thigh, then sink onto it to avoid the pain.

When taking an offhand shot, remember the body's most natural and therefore most balanced and strongest position is to square up with the target—the "boxer's stance" taught at Gunsite by Il Ling New and others.

"You must stabilize your shooting platform," New says. "Square up to the target; perhaps pull your strong-side leg to the rear a bit, but keep your shoulders square with the target to enable you to roll with recoil.

When shooting offhand, think: toes, knees, eyes. Square up to the target in a "boxer's stance." Remember, this will be a quick shot at close range.

"Your knees should be bent. Your knees should be over your toes, your chin over your knees," she says. "Think: toe, knee, chin—that should be the attitude of your body. This has nothing to do with strength. It's about technique."

Sometimes when game appears and you don't have enough time to drop into a kneeling or sitting position, you might have time to drop into a hasty squat, also known as the "rice paddy squat."

Square up with the game, adjusting for your natural point of aim. Bend your knees and sink so your butt rests either on or just above your heels. Keep your feet flat on the ground. The points of your elbows should rest forward of your knees, with the flat portion of your triceps rested across your kneecaps. It's a quick and stable platform, but it's not always so simple to adopt. If you've got arthritic knees or otherwise lack flexibility, the movement won't be so quick, and it may not be comfortable to sink as low as needed to make this position viable. Try pointing your toes outward to make it easier.

Natural Rests

Many people assume they'll use fenceposts or trees as rests in the field. That's a good idea, if they're available, and if you've thought about how to use them and have actually practiced with them.

Either side of a fencepost or tree can be used regardless of whether you're right- or left-handed. From either side you can build a shelf with your hand and thumb. Here's how I do it. When shooting right-handed from the right side of a tree, I point the thumb of my weak hand downward, and use the backside of my hand as a buffer between gun and tree. I stick out my thumb and use it as a shelf for the fore-end of the rifle. Be sure to keep your palm and as much of your four fingers as possible in contact with the tree to provide friction to prevent slipping under the weight of the rifle. When shooting right-handed from the left side of a tree, I reach underneath the fore-end and place my palm against the bark with my fingers pointing forward. Then I grip the bark with three fingers and my thumb while I stick out my forefinger; I rest the rifle's fore-end in the web between my thumb and forefinger. There should be some air beneath the

If you're right-handed, devising a way to support the fore-end of the rifle on the right side of a tree or post can be tricky. If you palm the tree, often your grip will hold well enough to allow you to float your thumb beneath the fore-end.

palm of your hand; contort your hand as best you can to provide the cradle for the fore-end. You'll have to press hard to maintain friction between the bark, the three fingers making contact, and your palm. Either way, be sure to pick an appropriately sized tree or post. A spindly sapling won't provide much support, as it will rock under the weight of your gun.

When shooting off the top of a fencepost, you can place your hand underneath the fore-end to buffet the gun when it recoils. I usually wrap my forefinger around the barrel to keep a good grip on the fore-end of the rifle. Sometimes, a grip similar to that used with the Hawkins prone position is best. Grip the forward sling swivel and sling in your fist tightly and rest the bottom of that fist atop the post.

Use a boulder as you would a table, sitting, kneeling, or squatting behind it and resting the gun across the top. Don't let the gun make contact with the stone. Use a pack or, lacking that, your hand beneath the fore-end to provide buffeting between the rifle and the rock. Sometimes the Hawkins grip comes in handy here, too; ball your fist around the front sling swivel and rest your fist on the rock to create a rest. If you're able, lean into the rock, melting your entire body into the stone so you can rest both elbows on something solid.

Artificial Rests

Never leave camp without a pack and shooting sticks. Either one can be used as a rest. Together, they give you multiple choices. Whatever you will use, practice with it before the hunt.

Not all packs are ideal. What's inside yours? Too many hard items in your pack won't provide a very soft rest, so load your pack accordingly. It's also not a bad idea to carry a small sandbag to camp. I have a very small, lightweight bag I pack in my duffel when traveling to some hunts. It's just enough to lay in a windowsill, the crook of a tree, or over a rock to provide a buffer between my rifle and whatever it rests upon.

When you're right-handed, supporting the fore-end of the rifle on the left side of a tree or post is simple because your hand will palm the tree naturally and without strain. It's doing the same from the other side of the tree that's a problem. Sometimes you can use a Hawkins fist to grip the sling and swivel, then place your hand on the tree. It's not perfect, but it works well for short periods of time.

At first blush, shooting sticks don't seem very stable. You can't expect them to be rock-solid. Just accept that. Even with a bit of movement, shooting from sticks is still better than shooting unsupported.

What types of shooting sticks are best for you? That depends on your circumstances. The closer to the ground you set up, the more stable you will be, but whether you can do this depends on the terrain. Kneeling or sitting with sticks is usually possible in North America. In Africa, you'll usually shoot from a standing position. Get used to doing both.

Beware of the seesaw effect that can happen with shooting sticks, especially from the standing position. If the sticks are too high, the gun will balance precariously atop the sticks; it will tend to rock back and forth, or seesaw, too easily, and you'll have to stand on the balls of your feet to see properly through the sights. Likewise, if you're set up too low, the gun will be "heavy" on the sticks and it will be difficult to shift your weight and adjust position as needed. You want the perfect stick height, which leads to a perfectly balanced stance with your legs and a perfect sight picture.

Obviously, you need to learn to manipulate your rifle and the shooting sticks without wasting time. Ideally, the crotch of the stick should reach armpit

Improvisation is the name of the game in the field. Your pack always makes a nice rest, but what's in your pack may not cooperate. Think about what makes a sandbag so nice, and be sure your pack emulates one.

Grip the forward sling swivel and the sling, then rest your fist directly on the ground. This is a good trick to use on a rock or any hard surface when another rest is not available.

level. A quick way to adjust height is to take a step forward or backward, which leans the sticks slightly forward or backward to adjust their position. If they're too low you can always crouch a bit, but if they're too high you won't shoot well from your toes.

If your guide will carry the sticks, work with him before you enter the field to make sure he sets them up properly. Rehearse your movements for placing the rifle on the sticks. Swing the gun wide when settling it in the sticks to be sure you clear them without knocking them over, and to ensure your sling does not bunch up in the V beneath the rifle's fore-end but rather settles outside it.

There are a couple of different ways to grip the rifle with your weak hand. Pull the rifle securely into your shoulder with your strong hand, and keep it in the V of the sticks by gripping the fore-end with your weak hand fore or aft of the V; forward of the V is most common. You can also place a finger or two over the crotch of the sticks to cushion the rifle and to keep a firm hold on the legs. Or, you can grip beneath the V with three fingers, wrap your thumb around the sticks, and wrap your forefinger over the top of the barrel. Either way, rifle and sticks are held as one unit to minimize the bounce of both during the shot so you can adjust before shooting or operate quickly after recovery from the first shot.

Most instructors warn against wrapping a finger or two over the top of the barrel, as this could affect its harmonics during dwell time. I suppose it does, but I've never seen evidence of it in the field. Whether kneeling or standing, I position my weak hand around the fore-end and wrap at least one finger over the barrel. Recoil has a nasty habit of "collapsing your house," especially when standing. Follow-through or reloading is problematic when that occurs. In fact, the sticks will often fall to the ground during recoil. Keeping a couple of digits over the barrel allows me to control both the gun and the sticks as one unit during recoil, allowing me to operate quickly—whether I need to shift position or move quickly for a second shot.

Lean into the sticks when standing upright to steady your shot. Throwing your weight into the sticks will help greatly, but shots at long range from the standing position will never seem steady enough. The best advice: As soon as you throw up the gun and settle on the target, take a breath, squeeze, and shoot. Your shot will never get steadier, so get it over with.

When standing with sticks you can achieve comfortable, almost benchrest-like stability if a buddy provides a shoulder to lean on. It'll take care of that "chicken wing" floating in space—that loose strong-side elbow that has nothing to rest on.

When kneeling with sticks, drop to your weak-side knee. The fore-end is already supported by the sticks—you don't need your weak-side knee for a rest. Instead, use your raised strong-side knee to support that "chicken wing," that shooting elbow floating out there in the wind.

It's true that actually grasping the barrel may alter point of impact—gripping it too hard may alter barrel harmonics. But the author prefers to wrap at least one finger over the barrel when shooting off sticks to keep both gun and sticks together as one unit during recoil. Anything less often leads to sticks lying on the ground when a second shot is needed.

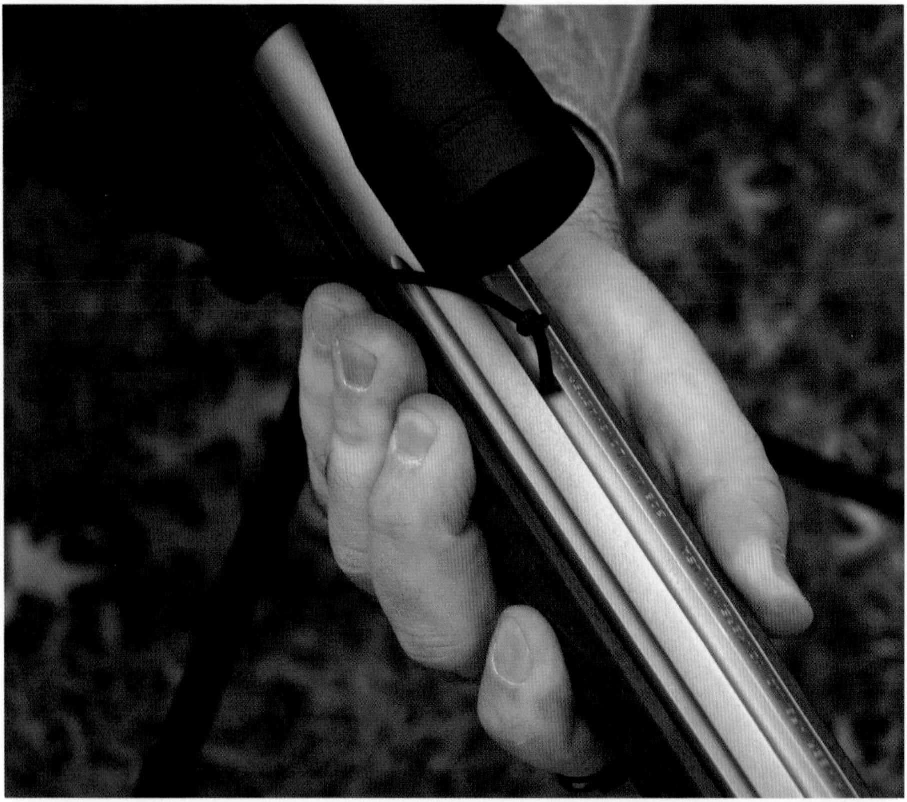

Some shooters may want to grip the fore-end forward of the V of the sticks. That may or may not work well. First, under recoil the sticks may fall when the gun rises and no weight holds them upright. Second, under recoil your hand may be pinched between the forward sling swivel and the V of the sticks.

When using sticks in the kneeling position, drop not to your strong-side but to your weak-side knee. Remember, the rifle is already supported by the sticks. You don't need to rest your weak hand on your knee. Instead, use your strong-side knee to support your "chicken wing"—your strong-side arm—to keep it from dangling out in thin air unsupported. This is amazingly stable, as it builds a shooting platform with contact in front and rear. In fact, it's my favorite shooting position. It's supported. It's high enough to provide me a higher vantage point than sitting. Also, it allows me to easily shift my weight to point the rifle left or right should the situation dictate.

Before dropping into the prone, sitting, or kneeling position, snug up the loop on a Ching Sling. You won't be able to get it above your elbow once in position.

The proper position of the Ching Sling is shown from the kneeling: Note that after running your weak-side (support) arm through the loop, you run your arm around the sling one more time before gripping the fore-end. Adjust the loop so it fits your frame when in a shooting position; it'll be loose when used at sling arms, but it should be tight in the prone, sitting, and kneeling. Don't use any sling in the offhand position.

Shooting sticks can be used to fashion a horizontal crossbar between tree limbs or other vertical support, which may provide a more stable support than the sticks by themselves.

Slings

In prone, sitting, and kneeling positions, it pays to use a sling. I'm not referring to the straps most hunters use to carry their rifles over their shoulders, but rather to a proper shooting sling. In the right hands, such an aid can pay big dividends.

In a pinch, the simple slings most of us use to carry our rifles can work to provide some measure of support as a hasty sling. Be sure to adjust the sling length before venturing afield; a loose one may not wrap tightly enough when needed. With the sling dangling beneath the rifle, insert your weak-side arm from outside in, then wrap your hand down, out, and back up to grasp the fore-end of the rifle. You've now wrapped the sling around the arm that will support the fore-end of the rifle. Push your weak-side hand as far forward as possible to achieve a snug fit.

The best "carry strap" to use as a hasty sling is the Brownells Latigo. It fits one-inch swivels and is available in a natural finish, brown, and black. There are no clips, laces, snaps, or hooks—just one piece of supple leather with two keepers and a buckle that, through a clever threading arrangement, can be set quickly to any length to carry your rifle or aid in shooting.

As long as you can brace your weak-side elbow, either on your body or some other object, a properly adjusted military-style loop sling provides excellent stability. It attaches to your rifle at two points. Detach it from the buttstock to employ it. Brace the rifle's buttstock on your hip, cradling the gun with your strong-side arm. Use both hands to rotate the loop of the sling inward and toward your weak side. Insert your weak-side arm through the loop and use your strong-side arm to pull the sling snugly above your biceps on your weak side. Slide the keeper to snug the loop tightly around your upper arm. Your weak hand then slides against the forward sling swivel as your strong hand seats the buttstock in your shoulder pocket.

The most easily employed shooting sling is the Safari Ching Sling, sold by Galco Gunleather. It creates a three-point sling out of two points of contact on your rifle, at the front and rear sling swivels. A keyhole attachment system makes fitting it to your arm length fast and tool-free. The sling is split, and a loop is strung between the two pieces. Adjust it for length, and cinch it up above your weak-side support elbow, close to your armpit, before adopting your shooting position. When the rifle is slung on your shoulder the loop also makes a nice thumb tab to keep the rifle in place. It fits one-inch swivels, it's leather (available in brown and black), and it works wonders to help you shoot more accurately.

Field Note: Never Leave Your Sticks Behind

Sometimes the best lessons are learned the hard way. By 2003 I'd already used several sets of shooting sticks with great results on various hunts. So when I went on a moose hunt in central Alaska, I made sure to pack a pair of lightweight, knee-high, collapsible tent-pole-style shooting sticks made by Stoney Point.

The terrain was steep, but doable. There were lots of trees, which suggested I'd find a natural rest should the need arise. Still, because I wasn't sure how far I might have to shoot, the knowledge of those sticks in my pack was comforting.

Several days into the hunt, my guide and I glassed a good bull high on a mountain across a river. After fording the stream and climbing for three hours, we closed the distance to a bit more than three hundred yards.

My guide said, "Let's drop our packs here, Scotty."

As I did so, I looked at my sticks and thought, *Nope, won't need 'em. We'll make it to those trees ahead.* We didn't make it another fifty yards before the bull spotted us and began to get nervous and generally let us know it wasn't hanging around much longer.

I leaned into the steep hillside and did my best impersonation of a kneeling position. The reticle of my scope danced, but my three shots landed within a six-inch circle on the bull's shoulder—enough to do the job. Still, as I pressed the trigger on each round, I thought, *You idiot! Your sticks are only fifty yards away.*

I'd carried those sticks thousands of miles, traveling from Virginia to Alaska. But when I really needed them, I abandoned them. I swore I'd never leave them behind again, and to this day I never have.

Chapter 11

Situational Awareness and Shot Placement

The game we seek needs only to drink, eat, defecate, sleep, procreate, and avoid predation. We enter its landscape—one foreign to us—and expect, on our timetable, to seek it out, close with it, and kill it. Often we outsmart it because we can find its track or determine its mating, feeding, resting, and travel habits. No matter how much wit we bring to the game, though, it still moves faster than we do. It smells and hears better than we do. Usually it sees better than we do. We can't overcome all those factors, but we can minimize them.

Movement to Contact

Like it or not, when we enter the field we engage in combat with game. That's not to suggest we make war with the animals we pursue, but consider the definition of combat: "any struggle or conflict; strife." We clearly are bent on causing trouble, at least for the game. We must enter the field with a practical mindset.

The curriculum at Gunsite advances the "combat triad" as a method to accomplish this. In the triad, mindset, gun handling, and marksmanship comprise a union of three elements essential to success. Of the three, mindset is the most important, for no amount of slick gun handling or supreme marksmanship will make up for careless behavior or a failure to recognize danger.

Always know the condition of your rifle. How many rounds are in the magazine? Is there a round in the chamber? Is the rifle on safe? How many rounds do you have on station (on your person)? Maintain muzzle awareness at all times.

Stay mentally awake. Use all of your senses. Pay attention to reflections and movement as indicators of game. Be alert to changes in shape, color, sound, and smell. In bright sunlight, remember it's difficult for our eyes to adapt to severe contrast. Be sure to check the shadows. Scan tight cover constantly with your eyes. Look for an outline by recognizing what lies just beyond your immediate zone of influence. At long range, understand that game may appear to be closer or farther away than it really is, depending on terrain and vegetation.

Create distance between yourself and a threatening situation. Meeting danger unexpectedly in the form of a charging buffalo, in tight cover, negates any advantage that lies in the power, precision, and range of your rifle.

Don't forget to focus on your reticle. In fast-moving situations and under stress it's easy to forget the fundamentals. If you train properly, muscle memory should take over in a stressful situation, so the physical

Be quiet in the field. Perform a noise check before leaving camp: Jump up and down while wearing your gear—all of it. Listen for squeaks, rattles, clanks, and rubs.

attributes of shooting should take care of themselves. At close range, however, we have a tendency to simply point the gun and pull the trigger. During the hunt remind yourself, "focus, breathe, squeeze." The last steps in the shooting process always need to be methodical.

Maintain balance. Don't get caught flat-footed while on the move, particularly during a stalk. When contact is imminent, always take steps small enough to allow you to retreat to a "fighting" stance, if need be. Never adopt a shooting position that negates physical mobility, stability, or control of your rifle. What if you need to deliver a fast follow-up shot?

Use economy of movement. The ability of game to detect movement protects it against predators, including us. Speed and sudden movements work against us. Movements we make long before we are ever close to setting up for a shot can betray us.

Choose routes that provide natural concealment. Avoid skylining yourself by walking along the "military crest," that bit of real estate below a hilltop that enables movement backed by higher ground. Stay in the shadows as much as possible, especially when the sun is brightest. Before you stalk, plan a route that allows movement from one stand of vegetation to another, when possible. Pause often to look, listen, and smell.

Pick your way through dense vegetation. When you can't avoid it, carefully navigate through it. Always try to put terrain features and vegetation between you and the game when stalking close. Once close, if you must move laterally more than a few yards, back out and move to the side, then come back at the animal rather than risk "going for it." It's called the "clover leaf" technique, and it's taught to our military. Remember, the game has only to survive. It has no idea you're present. It has all the time in the world. You need to leave your timetable at home.

When stalking, place your feet flat. Don't roll from heel to toe as in a normal step to reduce the pressure placed on a small area such as a heel. You'll spread your weight over your entire footprint, and you'll also feel twigs beneath your foot before committing the full weight of a step. As the sun rises higher, look for quieter lanes of movement. Exposed earth is always a

Choose routes that provide natural concealment. You can avoid skylining yourself if you walk along the "military crest," that bit of real estate below a hilltop that enables movement backed by higher ground. Stay in the shadows as much as possible, especially when the sun is bright. Before you stalk, plan a route that allows movement from one stand of vegetation to another. Pause often to look, listen, and smell.

good bet. Rock-strewn terrain, pine needles, and moss are ideal when present so long as you can move across the features without losing your balance.

Never step backward. It's easy to trip when you can't see to place your foot surely. Instead, pivot or whirl, depending on the situation. If you hear a noise to your right, pivot on the balls of your feet to begin to face that direction, the better to whirl and face a situation that develops there. When you want to face from 12 o'clock to 3 o'clock in a hurry, throw your weight to your right foot, raise your left foot, and pivot on the ball of your right foot, then step back down with your left foot, now facing 3 o'clock.

Be quiet. Perform a noise check before leaving camp. Jump up and down while wearing your gear—all of it. Listen for squeaks, and also for rattles and rubs. Silence squeaky sling swivels with oil or tape. Don't let a loose sling swing free to snag on vegetation. Pinch the sling against the bottom of your rifle with your strong hand, or with your support hand against the fore-end in the high- or low-ready position. Be aware that half-full water bottles sloshing in your pack sound even louder at dusk.

Sling your rifle or place it on the ground when you need to free your hands. Quiet extra rounds you carry in your pockets by using extra cartridge wallets. I have a couple from Cabela's that are ideal for hunting dangerous game. They are meant to ride in a pocket, and they hold five rounds each. I put five solids in one spare wallet and five expanding bullets in the other, then separate them in pockets on either side of my body. The cartridge wallet on my belt holds ten rounds, so with this system I carry a minimum of twenty rounds on station at all times.

When stalking, place your feet flat instead of rolling from heel to toe as in a normal step. This will reduce the pressure placed on so small an area as a heel print. You'll spread your weight over your entire footprint, and you'll also feel twigs beneath your foot before committing the full weight of a step.

Blend in. No single camouflage pattern works in all environments. If you travel to hunt, think about the landscape at your destination. Turkey hunters regularly wear one pattern on their trousers and another on their torso so they blend better against the ground and tree trunks when they set up to call a tom. Open camo patterns work well in the American West and in Africa; striped patterns work well in reedy and heavily wooded terrain; blotched patterns work well in leafy, deciduous terrain. When necessary, camouflage your equipment as well. Eliminate reflections with camo tape. Don't forget about your nose and

Stay alert when on the track of game—any game, especially dangerous game. Things can happen in an instant. Always remember you are entering the game's habitat; you operate on its timetable, not yours.

When glassing the terrain, be sure to cover at least some of the same ground in each successive area to be sure of overlap.

chin, which protrude enough to reflect lots of sunlight. Sometimes it pays to carry a facemask even if you think you won't need it.

Think about how game sees, hears, and smells. Of the five senses, an animal's ability to smell is always superior to ours. Most have a sense of smell at least as good as a dog's, which is about eighteen times better than ours.

An animal's vision, however, is not necessarily better than ours. It's just different, particularly in terms of seeing better at night and seeing into different areas of the color spectrum. Deer, for one, probably see into the blue end of the spectrum better than we do. That means no blue jeans while hunting. Deer don't see well into the red end of the color spectrum, which explains why hunter orange is safe where required by law. Remember commercial laundry detergents use ultraviolet brighteners that will, after many washings, make your camouflage garb seem to glow in the eyes of game. Wash hunting clothes in detergents marketed to hunters.

Most animals do not have acute vision, but they spot movement better than we do. While humans focus on a specific spot, animals focus on a wider area; they cannot distinguish detail the way we do. Unlike our eyes, which are constantly in motion, an animal's eyes are mostly stationary. When an animal spots us, we know it's seen something because it moves its head. Until we move, however, it's not quite sure what we are. What's more, the placement of the eyes in most animals ensures a far greater degree of peripheral vision than we enjoy. While humans have 90 degrees of peripheral vision, a white-tailed deer has 320, thanks to the placement of its eyes within its skull and rectangular-shaped pupils.

With hearing, though, humans are about equal to most animals. One study showed that deer hear about the same range of frequencies from low to high as humans do. The difference with any game animal, of course, is that it lives in the woods year-round. It knows exactly what sounds belong there,

When it's time to shoot, be sure to think about the basics. Build your house first—the foundation of any good shot. Then think "FBS"—focus, breathe, and squeeze. And don't forget to follow through. The hunter at left should be building his house. The guide at right can do all the scouting and assessing while the hunter makes ready.

whereas we enter its environment without realizing just how loud we may be when we step "quietly."

Rehearse every day during your hunt. No one said you can't get in some training time in camp. Before stepping off in the morning, step aside with your gun where it's quiet, and go over the physical and mental aspects of what lies before you. Snap into shooting positions and dry-fire. Visualize the movements needed to get into any position you might need based on expected terrain and vegetation conditions. Mentally rehearse an entire shot, from moving to adopting a shooting position to recovering from recoil, reloading, and rising from your position.

"Mental rehearsal is the best way to develop the concentration you need," says the NRA's Jim Land. "You can do that through visualization. Mentally run through 'what-if' moments; rehearse certain physical movements; visualize the moment.

"I learned mental rehearsal in Vietnam. When we left camp, we would rehearse from the time we left the wire until we returned. We functioned as if we were a football team. If we got hit, there was nobody waving their hands—'You go here; you go there'—everybody knew what to do. We continually talked with each other to make sure we knew our jobs. Same goes for hunters. In the moment of truth, the result must be the same—you know exactly what to do based on the situation because you've rehearsed. You've already embedded it in your mind; you don't have to think about what move to make. It's just there."

Search Techniques

Success in spotting game depends on your position, your skill in searching an area, how well you can maintain observation over the area, and your ability to recognize indicators presented by a target.

Depending on the situation, you may not have control over selecting your observation position. When pursuing game, hunters often end up in precarious terrain where it is difficult or impossible to shoot. Be aware of when you are in such a situation, and think about your options should you need to shoot. A

A good search is a systematic approach that takes in overlapping 50- or 100-yard strips of terrain. Start at one side and methodically search the terrain and vegetation to your front in a 180-degree arc.

good vantage point offers maximum visibility of the area while affording some concealment from game.

Move to more forgiving terrain as soon as possible. When you move to a new area, conduct a hasty search with your eyes. Don't try to absorb the entire landscape with broad sweeps of your eyes. Instead, take quick glances at specific points that attract your attention. These darting glances can be effective because our eyes are sensitive to any slight movements that occur within a wide arc of our field of view. Our peripheral vision is at work, but for it to be effective we must focus on a specific point.

Begin a detailed search if you fail to locate game with a hasty search. Use your naked eyes first, then switch to your binocular. This is a systematic approach that takes in overlapping strips of terrain from fifty to one hundred yards wide. Normally the terrain nearest you offers the greatest potential; begin there first. Start at one side, and methodically search the terrain and vegetation to your front in a 180-degree arc. Continue this pattern, progressively searching farther and farther away from your position. Be sure each new search incorporates about twenty-five yards of the previous coverage area to ensure complete coverage of the terrain. Cover all terrain between fifty yards and your maximum field of view.

Recognize shapes. In training exercises, blurry images and outlines of enemy soldiers are displayed on a screen and slowly focused while our boys in the U.S. military observe. They are taught to look at the basic outlines of aircraft and other vehicles, and to quickly notice hats, patches, and firearms to make quick decisions about what they are observing. Shape recognition also works on game. Look for oval shapes that reveal the face of an animal when it looks directly at you. The oblong ears of elk or kudu look like Christmas-tree ornaments at distance. A short, vertical line close to the ground could be a bedded buck's back. Remember that trees generally grow vertically, and they're spaced relatively far apart. Multiple short, tightly spaced vertical lines in the bush might be the legs of game.

Stand motionless, and key on movement and color. Soldiers are also taught to spot movement of arms and legs. Sudden movement can be spotted at long range even if the subject is camouflaged. Leaping deer are easy to spot, but most of us will fail to see a deer moving its head because we do not focus on details. The hair of most game blends into the landscape quite well, but it's not always a perfect match. Remember that animals secrete oils the same way we do. Even though most game will appear dull-colored, at times it's possible to spot light reflecting off the oils in its coat. A fleeting highlight deserves attention.

Never focus on one point too long. In low light if you stare at something intently enough, it will seem to move. It will grow legs, a head, and a rack, too. Your mind is playing tricks on you. Avoid the trap by never dwelling too long on one point of focus. Continue to scan, and return to the object of your curiosity only if you're convinced it will pay dividends.

Carrying the Rifle

Remember that you have a loaded firearm in your hands. The definition of "loaded" is having cartridges in the magazine—a round need not be in the chamber. Muzzle awareness is paramount at all times.

Be prepared to adopt a shooting stance quickly. Master two of the hand carries and at least one of the sling carries outlined below and you'll be able to get into position even if caught off-guard. Any method of rifle carry has its inherent risks. It's up to each of us to pick a safe, effective method befitting the situation. It's important to develop a variety of carry methods so if you grow tired of one, another is available to ease the burden on your strong hand or shoulder.

Maybe you prefer one method at a given time to make sure the muzzle is pointed in a particular direction. Maybe you must resort to a particular method because of the presence of companions. I remember while on patrol in the Marine Corps I had to use all sorts of methods to carry my rifle with the muzzle pointed in a safe direction away from my squad members, all the while keeping it ready to use at a moment's notice. That's not an easy task and not unlike the situations encountered on a stalk for game.

In the frontier carry, the rifle is carried in the crook of your weak-side elbow. Bend your weak-side arm at the elbow; use your strong arm to place the rifle in the crook of your weak elbow; cradle the gun by wrapping the forearm of your weak side over top of the gun. To dismount, use your strong hand to reach across your body, find the pistol grip, and pick up the rifle. Keep your head erect. Disengage the safety only if and when you bring the rifle to your shoulder. Keep your finger off the trigger until the sights are on target.

I almost always stalk with an empty chamber. If I'm doing things properly, the animal is unaware of my presence. When a shot becomes imminent, I have plenty of time to quietly chamber a round. This is almost always the case regardless of where I hunt. The only time I stalk with a loaded chamber is when a professional hunter tells me to, because we're on the trail of dangerous game and he's worried about an unexpected encounter. In such cases muzzle awareness is ramped up, to say the least, and my methods of carry are reduced to but one or two options.

At the outset of any hunt, it's wise to explain how you'll carry your rifle to your guide or companions so everyone is aware of what you're doing when you do it. When the game is killed or the day ends, unload your rifle completely and tell others you've done so. Always keep in mind the first two rules of NRA firearm safety: Always keep the gun pointed in a safe direction; always keep your finger off the trigger until ready to shoot. (The gun will be loaded because it's in use.)

Hand Carry

Armory Carry

This is good for short stints around camp or when moving short distances while glassing from vantage points. To mount, straighten your strong arm and

In the suitcase carry, the rifle is carried on your strong side. This method minimizes strain on your strong arm. Mount with your strong hand cupping the belly of the rifle beneath the magazine, your thumb riding alongside the magazine. For better control over longer distances, run the thumb of your strong hand between the bolt and scope, and cup your remaining fingers beneath the magazine. In either case the rifle is comfortably carried below waist level with your arm fully extended. Throwing the rifle to your shoulder is a simple matter of gripping the rifle at the fore-end with your weak hand. To dismount, reach across your body with your weak hand and find the fore-end as you slide your strong hand to the pistol grip. Do not disengage the safety unless the rifle is brought to eye level. Keep your finger off the trigger until the sights are on target.

point your hand downward so the knuckle of your thumb points downrange and the tip of it points down; acquire the pistol grip; hold the rifle upright, tight to your body in your shoulder pocket, with the muzzle just to the front of and to the side of your dominant eye. To dismount, reach across your body with your weak hand and acquire the fore-end, and raise the rifle to your shoulder. Keep your head erect. Disengage the safety only if and when you bring the rifle to your shoulder. Keep your finger off the trigger until the sights are on target.

Africa Carry

The rifle is carried on your strong-side shoulder. This is good on long treks with big bores when you tire of a sling carry or a strong-side hand carry because when game is spotted you can easily loop your strong arm over the barrel to balance the gun and grip your binocular with both hands—something done often in Africa or the American West.

Muzzle awareness is imperative. To mount, point the muzzle downward while holding the rifle with both hands; reach forward and grasp the rifle by the barrel with your weak hand, palm down; use your strong hand to lift the buttstock over your strong-side shoulder; balance the gun on your shoulder by gripping the barrel with your strong hand. To dismount, reach forward with your weak hand and grasp the fore-end; reach backward and grasp the pistol grip with your strong hand; push the rifle forward and shoulder it. Keep your head erect. Disengage the safety only if and when you bring the rifle to your shoulder. Keep your finger off the trigger until the sights are on target.

Many who don't understand the origins of this carry refuse to accept it as a viable method. Years ago, professional hunters in Africa had their trackers carry their "heavy" guns like this over their shoulders, muzzle forward, while the PH carried his "light" gun. This made for quicker target acquisition when on the trail of dangerous game. Even today the tracker is first in line during a stalk. He's focused on the ground, the tracks. The PH is right behind him, scanning the landscape before the hunting party.

With the Africa carry, the rifle is carried on your strong-side shoulder. This is good on long treks with big bores when you tire of a sling carry or a strong-side hand carry. When game is spotted you can easily loop your strong arm over the barrel to balance the gun and grip your binocular with both hands—something done often in Africa or the American West. Muzzle awareness is imperative.

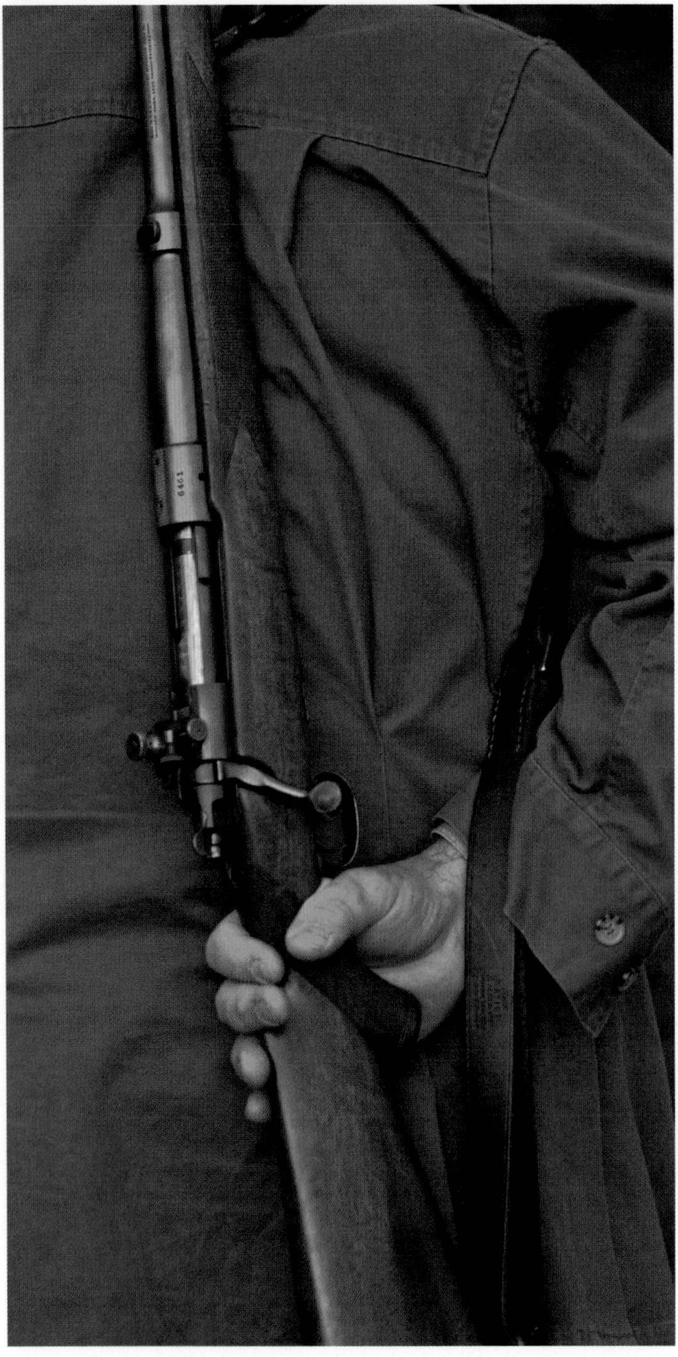

On long stints in the woods, the author often holds the rifle behind his back in the American sling carry to keep it from snagging on brush or on items on his belt.

If dangerous game is encountered, the PH is likely to see it first. He can simply and quickly grab the rifle from his tracker and shoulder it, with the muzzle already pointed in the right direction. In recent years, many hunters have adopted this style of carry. If I have companions in front of me I don't carry my rifle like this; I pick another method.

Frontier Carry

The rifle is carried in the crook of your weak-side elbow. This is popular among American hunters mainly, I suppose, because they've seen pictures of pioneers like Daniel Boone and Davy Crockett employing it. To mount, bend your weak-side arm at the elbow; use your strong arm to place the rifle in the crook of your weak elbow; cradle the gun by wrapping the forearm of your weak side over top of the gun. To dismount, use your strong hand to reach across your body, find the pistol grip, and pick up the rifle. Keep your head erect. Disengage the safety only if and when you bring the rifle to your shoulder. Keep your finger off the trigger until the sights are on target.

Suitcase Carry

The rifle is carried on your strong side. This method minimizes strain on your strong arm. Mount with your strong hand cupping the belly of the rifle beneath the magazine, your thumb riding alongside the magazine. For better control over longer distances, run the thumb of your strong hand between the bolt and scope, and cup your remaining fingers beneath the magazine. In either case, the rifle is comfortably carried below waist level with your arm fully extended. Throwing the rifle to your shoulder is a simple matter of gripping the rifle at the fore-end with your weak hand. To dismount, reach across your body with your weak hand and find the fore-end as you slide your strong hand to the pistol grip. Use both hands to raise the rifle to eye level, if desired. Do not disengage the safety unless the rifle is brought to eye level. Keep your finger off the trigger until the sights are on target.

Pistol-Grip Carry

The rifle is carried on your strong side. This method is used only for short periods when negotiating difficult terrain or thick vegetation because it is tiring. Mount with your weak hand gripping the fore-end as your strong hand reaches for the pistol grip, then wield the rifle's heft and maintain muzzle control with only your strong hand. If you wish to fire, it's a simple matter to raise the rifle to eye level. To dismount, reach across your body with your weak hand and grip the fore-end as your strong hand maintains control of the pistol grip. Disengage the safety only as the rifle reaches eye level. Keep your finger off the trigger until the sights are on target.

Sling Carry

It's true a rifle is no good unless it's in your hands, but the use of a sling does not preclude its quick employment. Despite advice I've read many times that suggests it's best to remove your sling, particularly during a stalk, the sling is a necessary component to transporting a firearm in varied terrain. Besides, a good one is a great shooting aid. Essentially, a sling is a rifle's holster.

American Sling Carry

Mount the rifle muzzle-up on the strong-side shoulder. It's the standard and most intuitive method for anyone who's ever shouldered a rifle. It's also the slowest to adopt and to dismount should the need to shoot arise. A handgun, knife, or ammo pouch on your strong side may interfere with carry or dismount. With the muzzle up, rifles with long barrels may snag on overhead brush.

Mount

Hold the rifle before you by the pistol grip and fore-end, muzzle-up, magazine well pointed downrange and a bit toward your weak side. Use your weak-side hand to grip the rifle close to the forward sling swivel so it hangs muzzle-up in front of you and a bit to your strong side. Run your strong arm through the loop between rifle and sling, as if putting on a shirt, and use your weak hand to slide the rifle, muzzle up, to your strong-side shoulder.

Dismount

Place tension on the sling and pull it forward with your strong-side hand. With your weak hand, reach across your body, through the sling, and grasp the stock by its fore-end close to the rifle's center of balance. Drop your strong hand and shoulder, and with your weak hand gripping the fore-end, rotate the rifle off your shoulder, downward, and point the muzzle downrange. Reach in from outside the sling with your strong hand and find the pistol grip. Shoulder the rifle. Disengage the safety as you bring the rifle to eye level. Keep your finger off the trigger until the sights are on target.

African Sling Carry

Mount the rifle muzzle-down on the weak-side shoulder. It presents the lowest profile in the field of any sling carry. It's quick to mount and dismount. Muzzle-awareness is key at all times. When mounted, the rifle bore may become plugged with debris when crouching or in the event of a fall. When mounting and dismounting, it's dangerously easy to cover your leg or foot with the muzzle.

With the American sling carry, the rifle is slung on your strong-side shoulder. Reach for the rifle with your weak hand and grasp it by the pistol grip or fore-end. Bring the rifle to your shoulder; don't lower your head to bring your eyes to the sights. Don't disengage the safety until the rifle is in your shoulder. Keep your finger off the trigger until the sights are on target.

Mount

Hold the rifle before you at waist level by the pistol grip and fore-end, muzzle downrange, magazine pointed downward. Point the muzzle a bit toward your weak side, and with your strong hand on the pistol grip controlling the rifle's weight, run your weak hand, palm down, to the rear sling swivel. Point the muzzle down, rotate the rifle so the magazine begins to point up, and transfer its weight to your weak hand. Let the rifle drape from the sling in your weak hand. Run your strong hand to the belly of the rifle to control the muzzle as you rotate the rifle into your weak-side shoulder with your weak hand.

Dismount

Grip the rifle by the fore-end with your weak hand. Raise the rifle, magazine pointed upward, and point the muzzle toward the target. Rotate the rifle with your weak hand, so the magazine begins to point outward toward your weak side. Find the pistol grip with your strong hand. Use both hands to raise the rifle, rotate it like a corkscrew, and shoulder it. Do not disengage the safety until the rifle is brought to eye level. Keep your finger off the trigger until the sights are on target.

European Sling Carry

Mount the rifle backward, muzzle-up, on the weak-side shoulder. It may look awkward, but it provides a quick dismount. It is especially secure when you apply slight forward pressure with your weak hand. You never have to worry about your muzzle because it's always right there in front of your face.

Mount

Hold the rifle before you by the pistol grip and fore-end, muzzle-up, magazine well pointed downrange, a bit to your weak side. Keep your weak hand on the fore-end, rotate the rifle outward, so the magazine points toward your weak side, and grip the top of the sling with your strong hand, palm down. Use your strong hand to guide the sling up and onto your weak-side shoulder. Keep your weak hand pressed against the fore-end to keep

With the African sling carry, the rifle is slung on your weak side muzzle-down. Dismount by grasping the fore-end with your weak hand; rotate the rifle as you reach for the pistol grip with your strong hand; the sling will slide off your shoulder. Bring the rifle to your shoulder; don't lower your head to bring your eyes to the sights. Don't disengage the safety until the rifle is in your shoulder. Keep your finger off the trigger until the sights are on target.

With the European sling carry, the rifle is slung on your weak side with the muzzle residing in front of your face. Reach for the rifle with your strong hand and grasp it by the pistol grip; let the sling fall off your shoulder as you rotate the rifle and reach for the fore-end with your weak hand. Bring the rifle to your shoulder; don't lower your head to bring your eyes to the sights. Don't disengage the safety until the rifle is in your shoulder. Keep your finger off the trigger until the sights are on target.

tension on the mount. With a little bit of practice you can throw the sling over your weak-side shoulder in one swoop, keep pressure on the fore-end with your weak hand, and immediately free your strong hand.

Dismount

Reach across your body with your strong hand and find the pistol grip. Use both hands to rotate the rifle so the magazine points outboard, toward your weak side, and the sling falls from your weak-side shoulder. Raise the rifle to your shoulder. Do not disengage the safety until the rifle reaches eye level. Keep your finger off the trigger until the sights are on target.

Ready Positions

When contact with game is imminent, carry the rifle in your hands in a ready position that enables you to engage targets quickly. Employed correctly, neither the low ready nor the high ready position will impede your vision. By taking a normal step with your leading leg followed by half a step with your trailing (strong) leg, you can maintain them with surefootedness while advancing or retreating.

Low Ready

The butt of the rifle is shouldered. Hold the rifle at the pistol grip and fore-end and point the barrel downward; scan the field over top of the barrel, moving your eyes and the rifle as one as you search for a target. When game is encountered, keep your head erect and stationary and raise the muzzle, bringing the sights to your eyes, and disengage the safety. Keep your finger off the trigger until the sights are on target.

High Ready

The butt of the rifle rides just above waist level to avoid contact with gear or clothing. Hold the rifle at the pistol grip and fore-end so the barrel resides in front of your dominant eye but low enough so it does not impede vision. Keep your head erect. Your eyes and the rifle move as one as you search for a

In the high ready, the butt of the rifle rides just above waist level to avoid contact with gear or clothing. Hold the rifle at the pistol grip and fore-end so the barrel resides in front of your dominant eye but low enough so it does not impede vision. Keep your head erect. Your eyes and the rifle move as one as you search for a target. When game is encountered, keep your head erect and stationary and shoulder the rifle, bringing the sights to your eyes, and disengage the safety. Keep your finger off the trigger until the sights are on target.

target. When game is encountered, keep your head erect and stationary and shoulder the rifle, bringing the sights to your eyes, and disengage the safety. Keep your finger off the trigger until the sights are on target.

Own the Shot

Maintain a constant awareness of everything within your zone of fire. Your scope should be set appropriately—usually at low magnification. If terrain and vegetation is tight, leave it on a low magnification. As terrain opens up, crank up magnification in anticipation of a longer shot. Don't forget to turn it down again when you enter thick brush. Better yet, condition yourself to shoot all game except that at very long range at your scope's lowest magnification and leave the scope set there. There isn't much we hunt that can't be hit with a scope set at 3X, as long as we've trained properly.

"We're dealing with a nine-inch kill zone—that's what we train for at SAAM," says Doug Prichard. "So when we look at our hunter's zero, we're looking at a 200-yard zero. That will allow us to hold center on a nine-inch kill zone and take it anywhere from where we are out to 250 yards. So you own a 250-yard-deep piece of property. On the magnums, it's probably going to be a 250-yard zero. That takes you out to 350 yards. So now you own a 350-yard-piece of property. Be sure you own all of it."

Constantly assess terrain and vegetation. Has the terrain before you gained any new landmarks since you studied it last? What's on your left and your right? Zap landmarks with your laser rangefinder when you have

In the low ready, the butt of the rifle is shouldered. Hold the rifle at the pistol grip and fore-end and point the barrel downward; scan the field over top of the barrel, moving your eyes and the rifle as one as you search for a target. When game is encountered, keep your head erect and raise the muzzle, bringing the sights to your eyes, and disengage the safety. Keep your finger off the trigger until the sights are on target.

time. If you set up for a long period of time, get a reading on everything you think might be beneficial to computing a shot should game appear. Carry a notebook and pen to write down the range of those landmarks. Better yet, if you've got the time, sketch the landscape, noting the landmarks and the range to each. That way you won't have to interpret the difference between "big tree, 1 o'clock, 200 yards" and "big tree, 3 o'clock, 300 yards."

Determine distance to the target, build your house, focus, breathe, and squeeze. Concentrate on these five things. When you engage an animal, the physical movements honed during training should occur automatically.

"Think STAR—shoot only at a target at acceptable range," says Prichard. "It's based on a couple of factors: the capability of the gun, the ammo, the scope, and your shooting ability. Ask yourself: 'Do I have a one-minute gun? Ammo? Scope? Am I a one-minute shooter? In this position? What about conditions?'"

Nail down all variables. If the game is within your point-blank range and you're set up with a hunting zero, you don't need to touch your scope. If the animal is outside your range, you've got to reach up and change some things—you need to adjust your scope for at least one of two variables, elevation or windage. Dial up—get elevation first—then worry about windage because you can always hold off for the wind. But you can't do both. Then analyze the wind: What's it doing?

Build your house. Choose a position and make it work. Game won't stand around while you decide your first choice won't do and fidget into another one. That doesn't mean, however, that you shouldn't take the time to build a proper foundation. Stabilize your strong-side elbow using whatever material is available, a pack, vegetation, a buddy, whatever it takes to get it right the first time. Better to take longer and build a solid foundation for that first shot than to rush and be forced to take a hasty second shot. Remember, never stand when you can kneel; never kneel when you can sit; never sit when you can go prone.

Think "FBS": focus, breathe, squeeze. Obtain sight alignment and sight picture, then stop thinking about the animal. Focus intently on the front sight or reticle. Remember, aim small, miss small: Pick a small spot on the animal—a dot, a wrinkle, whatever. Remember your natural respiratory pause. When the sights settle, disengage the safety and let out that breath. Touch the trigger. Take your last breath, let it out, and start your squeeze. The longer you wait, the more you'll wobble. Soon you'll doubt yourself, and the animal will move. So get on with it.

Don't forget to follow through. When the round fires, continue to focus on the reticle and hold your position. Reload. Deliberately lift your finger from the trigger and move your hand to the bolt. With the gun in your shoulder and your head still behind the scope, chamber another round by working the bolt in a two-stroke motion—up and back, and forward and down. Don't admire your shot, and especially don't yank your head out of the scope to see your handiwork.

Of course, no one can resist the forces of recoil completely. With practice, though, you should be able to focus on the reticle even as the gun roars, which will help you call your shot. In the field I often see the reaction of the game in my scope after I recover from recoil and while I am reloading for a second shot. Yes, I can move that fast; you can, too.

Recovery

After the shot, scan and assess the field. Before you move from your shooting position, keep the gun in your shoulder, lower it a bit, and scan the field over top of your scope. Your eyes and gun should move as one: scan left, muzzle moves left; scan right, muzzle moves right. It does little good to notice a developing situation if you are not prepared to shoot or, worse, defend yourself from danger charging in from the left or right.

Now rise. In most cases there is ample time to casually "break from character" and climb out of whatever contorted pose you've adopted for a shot. It's the times you don't that should concern you. Rehearse the right way to break position so climbing to your feet and preparing to move or shoot again becomes second nature.

Game moves, right? What if your first shot doesn't kill? What if you need to move five feet left or right, then plop back into the sitting position to fire a follow-up shot? What if you fire at dangerous game from the kneeling position at thirty yards? A grizzly can cover that distance in two bounds. Perhaps you can fire another shot at a bear while sitting, but perhaps you need to rise to clear the brush that is now between you and a charging and now very angry bear.

The following instructions might seem overly dramatic but they pay dividends.

From the Prone Position

Grip the rifle by the fore-end, release the rifle with your strong hand, and use that hand to push up off your chest. The buttstock will rest on the ground. Straighten your strong-side elbow, and when your legs enter the equation, tense their muscles and rock backward to your knees. Swing your weak leg forward and place your foot flat on the ground. Grip the rifle with both hands, and rise to a standing position, stepping forward with your strong-side leg if needed to maintain a balanced stance when upright.

Alternatively, hold the rifle by the pistol grip in your strong hand. Release the fore-end with your weak hand and use it to prop off your chest. Keep pushing with your weak hand, and when your legs kick in use them to rise to your knees and re-grip the rifle by the fore-end in your weak hand. Keep your strong hand on the pistol grip, rock back on your knees. Swing your weak leg forward and place your foot flat on the ground. Rise to a standing position.

If the terrain and your physical ability enable it, you can rock back farther when rising off your chest, and in one motion rock from your knees all the way back to a flat-footed, squatted position then stand (this is difficult). Either way, keep the rifle in your shoulder and pointed downrange, scan and assess as you rise.

From the Sitting Position

If your legs are crossed, unfold them and place your feet flat on the ground, knees up. Grip the rifle by the fore-end in your weak hand, and place your strong hand on the ground behind you. Bend your strong leg underneath the tripod formed by your weak leg and your body. Push with your strong hand and rise to your strong knee. With your weak hand still gripping the fore-end, lay your weak elbow over your weak knee, bring the rifle to your shoulder, and lean into the kneeling position. Rock forward and rise to the standing position. Keep the rifle shouldered as you rise to the offhand position.

From the kneeling position: Rock forward, putting most of your weight on your forward (weak-side) leg. Bend your strong knee inward and forward, rock forward, and rise up on the ball of your strong foot. Rise to a standing position.

Finish every recovery in your "boxer's stance," a balanced, offhand position that allows you to wheel quickly and face a target in any direction. Scan and assess the field with a live round in the chamber, your finger alongside the trigger, and your thumb on the safety. Be prepared to top off the magazine. If no other shot is imminent, leave the rifle on safe and lower the gun to the high- or low-ready position. When the situation is secure, unload and clear your gun, then visually and physically inspect the chamber to be sure the gun is empty. Always maintain muzzle awareness, even when the day is done.

What a Bullet Does to Game

We kill game quickly and humanely by destroying an organ vital to its life support. The best shots switch off the brain, sever the forward half of the spinal cord, or disrupt the oxygen supply from the lungs or blood supply from the heart. A bullet that reaches the brain will switch it off; a bullet in the neck or shoulder spinal area will sever the spinal cord. Effectively puncture the brain, spinal cord, lungs, or heart and you should deprive an animal of oxygen to the brain, and the animal should die within seconds.

Two factors within the control of a rifleman are essential to accomplishing the feat: bullet placement and bullet performance. Each factor is listed in order of importance, I believe. The best bullet ever made (if there is such a thing) will do little if placed poorly. Whether an animal stands broadside, quartering on, or quartering away, all angles present different bullet paths to consider. The best shot is a straight path through the animal that exits the other side.

When a bullet travels through tissue it creates two cavities, one temporary and one permanent. The temporary cavity is formed when the bullet forces tissue away from its path radially and/or centrifugally. It closes up almost immediately, leaving only the second cavity, the wound channel. The wound channel is caused by the expanding frontal area of the bullet as it travels through tissue, cutting and plowing its path of destruction.

The size of the temporary cavity is influenced by the velocity and construction of the bullet. The temporary cavity is also the source of most waste in meat because of bruising. Fragile bullets cause a massive entrance wound, which influences the size of the temporary cavity, but they won't penetrate very far into big game. They usually disintegrate upon impact or expand so rapidly their velocity, and thus their progress to the vitals, is arrested. We're not concerned with them. Well-constructed bullets produce an entrance wound adequate to allow them to penetrate the hide of big game, and then their solid or expanding design produces a wound channel that plows or cuts to vitals. When all goes well, they exit the animal, producing a blood trail that's hard to miss.

Shot Placement

To hit the brain, aim a bit high on the head, from eye/ear level and above. This is an ideal target because it kills instantly, wastes no meat, and requires no tracking. As long as you use a premium bullet, death is certain. The brain, however, is a small target. The head is the one thing likely to move first on nervous game. Hit a few inches off your mark, and the worst damage you might cause is a broken jaw. Take this shot only at close range to be sure of bullet placement.

A shot to the neck should be placed near the head. The neck is thinnest there and your point of aim is small but easiest to discern. Near the shoulder the target is larger, but it's risky to count on a precise point of impact. Executed perfectly, this shot wastes little meat, but it's not an easy one if the animal stands broadside with its neck extended. You must sever the spinal cord. The neck on a big-game animal can be wide and deep. Be sure of its center. If you miss, you will cause a lot of bleeding and maybe some trouble breathing, but little else for quite a while. If the animal stands a bit quartering-on, you have some margin of error vertically.

A bullet far forward in the spine, at the shoulder, ensures rapid death; it's just as effective as a neck shot. Unfortunately, the position of the spinal cord is not always easy to visualize. Don't assume it runs level with the back line—it doesn't. It runs downward toward the front of the animal, to a point near the center of the base of the neck. Also, spine shots ruin some of the best meat—the backstraps and the tenderloins, and often at least one of the shoulders.

Center-punch both lungs and they will fill up with blood quickly. If your bullet exits moments later, there should be a good blood trail. Compared to the lungs, the heart is a small target. It sits lower than most hunters imagine and it's tucked between the shoulders. A shot here kills no quicker than one to the lungs. It's difficult for your bullet to penetrate to the heart without smashing through the front leg—a difficult chore. All the plumbing in this general vicinity provides a wide margin for error.

Picture how vitals lie in an animal as it stands before you. Don't rely solely on the old adage "hit it behind the shoulder." That's fine if the animal stands broadside or slightly angled away from you. If it stands slightly angled toward you, a shot behind the shoulder may miss the lungs and penetrate the gut.

Broadside

A shot behind the shoulder and a bit high encounters no bone thicker than a rib and penetrates to the vitals. Your target is the heart or lungs. The lungs are preferable. Hit a bit low and your bullet should drop into the heart, also producing a good blood trail. Bear hunters who take broadside shots sometimes aim a bit too high. Their point of aim is the shoulder, in order to break bone on the way to the lungs and thus "anchor" the animal. This is sound strategy, but it doesn't always work. On many game animals without aiming points it's easy to mistake one wrinkle for another and hit too high, thus missing the vitals altogether.

Quartering-On

Aim for the point of the shoulder, or just inside it. Placed on the shoulder, your bullet will need to break heavy bone to penetrate to the vitals. Your target is the heart and/or lungs.

Quartering-Away

This is usually the only sound shot for bow hunters, but for riflemen it can be tricky because, again, if you mistake one wrinkle for another your bullet will find little margin for error. Hit too far to the front, and you'll break the shoulder but miss the vitals. Hit too far behind the shoulder and you'll hit only guts. In the case of a large animal like a Cape buffalo, your bullet might not make it all the way through the stomach to the vitals.

Head-On

Lungs lie to either side; the heart lies low in the middle. If you miss that, your bullet has a good chance of hitting the neck bone (spinal cord) and major arteries. Aim for the middle of the chest for a heart/lung shot. Depending on the size of the animal, you have a wide margin for error. This is an easy shot if you've practiced, and if you stand level with the game. A shot from above the animal can be tricky because the head gets in the way. Even if the head swings out of the way, there is the danger of shooting too low and penetrating nothing but a bit of brisket.

Going-Away

Often called the "Texas heart shot," this isn't as tricky as it sounds. Simply sight on the base of the tail to break the spine. In my view, however, this is not a sporting choice for the first shot on game. I subscribe to it only for wounded game—never as a first shot.

Chapter 12

The Big-Game Battery

It matters not what is written on the headstamp of a cartridge. No legendary combination of number and name will make a game animal surrender. The things that matter are impact velocity, accuracy, and a bullet's terminal performance—its reaction to impact and penetration.

"Wait a tick," you say. "Have we not learned that pinpoint accuracy and velocity are less important than bullet placement and bullet performance? Now you're putting velocity first?"

Yes I am, because any discussion of killing power isn't complete without a debate of the merits of velocity, at least as it's coupled with a certain amount of bullet frontal area. We know that calculating the ability of a bullet to fly far, shrug off the wind, and kill promptly does not produce a number on which we may always rely. True, a good way to measure flight characteristics between two bullets is to compare ballistic coefficients. A good way to measure bullet terminal performance is to measure its propensity for tissue damage. Beyond a doubt, the best way to lethally employ those measures is to fire your bullet accurately. Sometimes, though, you need power, the ability to do damage regardless of circumstance.

Velocity vs. Frontal Area

It's time to talk about speed and bulk—about velocity and frontal area—because sometimes things just don't go according to plan. Call this the "shock and awe" section. Beware: Opening this door leads to another, and another, which inevitably leads us back to some of our initial points.

One problem with relying on velocity shock, or predicting it, is the physiological state of the animal when we deliver the news. This seems to have a significant effect on how well or when the shocking blow affects the animal. Many hunters have seen many animals of the same species react differently to similar hits with identical bullets. Many more are convinced, even in the face of the irrefutable laws of physics, that indeed the "ton" of energy delivered by their bullets is responsible for great feats.

I remember a buck I shot many years ago with a .50-caliber, 350-grain Thompson/Center Maxi-Hunter lead bullet during muzzleloader season in Virginia. I hit the deer in the neck at fifty yards. It reared up as if struck by Thor and dropped dead. Being a novice, I deduced that the energy of the whopping .50-caliber bullet coupled with the effects of that big, round mushroom produced walloping knockdown power. The fact is, it didn't. It couldn't. The bullet hit the spine, which triggered a nervous reaction. I could have shot the deer in the same spot with a much smaller bullet and elicited the same reaction.

A reliance solely on bullet placement, therefore, would seem to justify the use of small calibers like the .243 Winchester for elk. Such hunting can be justified when hunters work within the limits of their arms, but for the most part, the concept of kinetic energy leads us to quickly dismiss the notion of small-caliber big-game hunting.

Remember that kinetic energy (KE) is a measure of the striking energy a bullet carries downrange. Measured in foot-pounds, it is calculated as the bullet weight (in grains) multiplied by velocity squared, then divided by a constant. It reveals that KE is proportional to bullet mass and velocity. Clearly there is a limit at any range with any combination of variables. Regardless of the predictable performance of any bullet, its propensity for damage is driven by velocity—without speed, there is no expansion, no wound channel, no humane kill.

The simple fact is sometimes the size of game on our list demands the speed and power of a big gun. The larger frontal area of a bigger bullet helps, too. The larger the animal, the greater the need for a more massive, longer wound channel despite the fact that a lot of the "need" can be accounted for in bullet placement and bullet performance. Also, it sure is fun to shoot a whopping big bullet. I don't think any of us can help ourselves. If you fire a 300-grain, .375-

caliber solid into the brain of a Cape buffalo and see the results, you'll join the club. For some, big guns produce optimism and additional joy in the hunt.

Moving up the velocity scale can be daunting, however. There are many factors to consider. One factor surrounds bullet weight: More of it produces more recoil. Some hunters prefer lighter bullets in a given caliber because of their milder recoil, recoil energy being dependent on the weight and velocity of the bullet and any unburned powder as it exits the barrel. In cartridges that differ only in bullet diameter, recoil is nearly identical in similar rifles. Shoot a .300 Winchester Magnum with a 200-grain bullet and you know about what it's like to shoot a .338 Winchester Magnum with a 200-grain bullet. So why buy a .338 if a .300 will do the same thing?

Cartridge performance listed in catalogs and on Web sites doesn't always equal what you'll get in the field. Bullet speed varies with barrel length, for one. As we've learned, it also is affected by bullet type, temperature, elevation, and other factors. The biggest big-game cartridges in any caliber-category would seem to differ so slightly in comparison to one another to make little difference which one you choose as long as you use adequate power for specific game.

On the other hand, speed and power are of little help if the rifle won't place the bullet where you want it. Some rifles don't like a particular brand of ammo or a specific load (bullet type and/or weight). For years I've fed .338 Winchester Magnums 200-grain bullets from every manufacturer in an attempt to find a more manageable load that shoots a tad faster than the 225-grain bullets that are standard for the caliber, but most .338s just don't seem to shoot light-for-caliber bullets particularly well. The only way around the problem is to find another load—in this case, a heavier one.

That's why it's not enough to simply move up the power scale to find a cartridge suitable for the biggest game you seek. You must do so carefully, ensuring you and the new rifle are compatible. The rifle in the new caliber must possess the physical and ergonomic qualities that suit you and work well with your muscle memory; it must deliver the KE necessary for the game you seek to hunt with it; and it must, I think, be chambered for a popular and widely available cartridge so ammo supply is never an issue. Its weight must not be a burden in the field; its recoil should remain manageable; and its external ballistics must be suitable.

Let's look at twenty-three cartridges with the idea of picking out a bolt-action battery that will serve us well throughout a lifetime of hunting. I must cut off this treatise somewhere, so I am including some classic cartridges that have been with us for some time as well as some newcomers that seem to have gained a foothold on crowded store shelves and in gun cabinets anywhere hunters can be found. I'm sure at least one of the newbies I mention won't survive the long run to "classic" status, but as they're "hot" now, I feel obliged to include them.

As you pore over the following, my best advice is to forget any debate between cartridges—the battle between the .270 Winchester and .30-06, for instance. Hitting "the spot" is the key, and you can't do that with power or any other single variable. Above all else, your rifle must do what you will it to do, and that brings us back to the factors I listed first and foremost—adequate accuracy, a capable shooter behind the trigger, bullet construction, and bullet placement.

.243 Winchester

The "Little Engine That Could" has introduced more people to centerfire calibers than perhaps any other. It's also dropped a lot of deer. It's one of my favorites of all time. Essentially a necked-down .308 case, the .243 Winchester was introduced in 1955 for Winchester's Model 70 and Model 88. Before long, even Remington, with its own 6mm cartridge, had to admit its popularity. It fires a 100-grain bullet at 2,850 feet per second. Today every manufacturer chambers a rifle for it. It's a good one-gun cartridge for everything up to deer-sized game. Mild recoil makes it easy to shoot well.

.30-06 Springfield

The word "Springfield" pays tribute to the rifle that introduced this cartridge to America, the 1903 Springfield, which was adopted as the U.S. military's standard-issue battle rifle in 1906. And for that reason the "Aught Six" is number one on many hunters' all-time favorites list. It's good at everything, taking smallish game with 130-grain bullets and large game like moose with 180- or 220-grain bullets.

It still rules retail sales along with the .308 Winchester and .270 Winchester. It's versatile and ammo is available anywhere in the world. A 180-grain bullet travels at 2,750 feet per second.

.270 Winchester

At the time of its introduction in 1925 in the Winchester Model 54, this offshoot of the .30-06 stirred hunters because it produced better long-range performance than any big-game cartridge in America. It sends a 130-grain bullet downrange at more than 3,000 feet per second, which is adequate for any big game in North America. Before "magnum mania" took the hunting world by storm, the .270 was the original "flat shooter." In capable hands it remains good enough for anything in North America with the exception of the big bears, although bullet weights are limited.

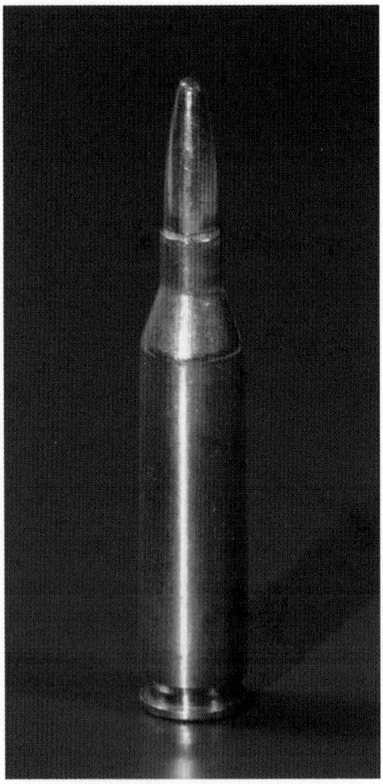

.243 Winchester.

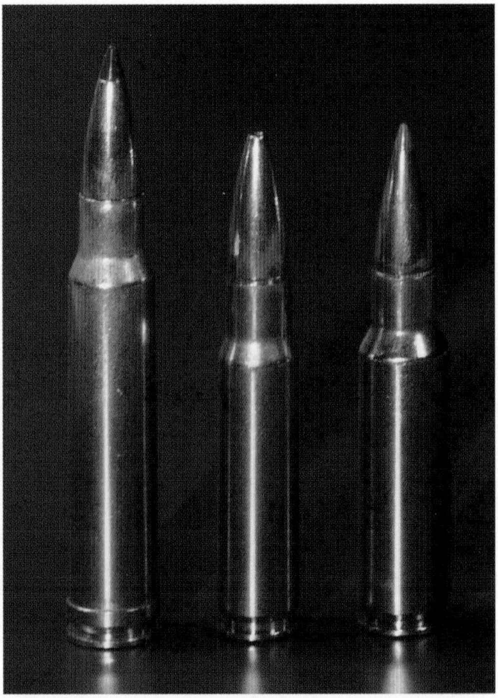

Left to right: .338 Winchester Magnum., .338 Federal, .338 Ruger Compact Magnum.

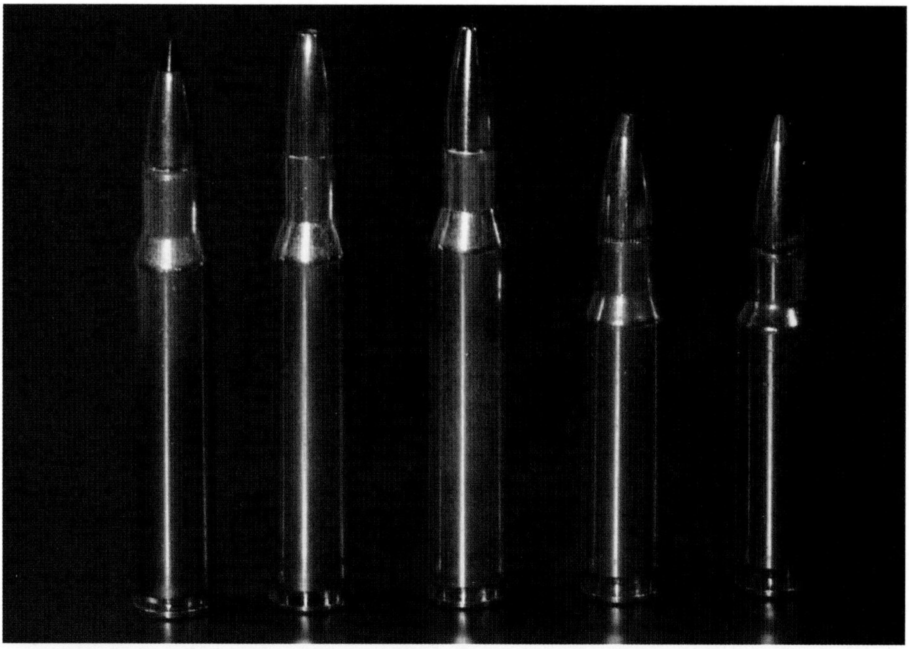

Left to right: .30-06, .270 Winchester, .280 Remington, .308 Winchester, .30 TC.

.280 Remington

Introduced in 1957 for Remington's autoloading Model 740, the .280 is the company's answer to the .270 Winchester. The Model 700 was chambered for it in 1962, and thereafter the cartridge developed a loyal but smaller following than the .270. It is a necked-down .30-06, 7mm chambering with a bullet diameter of .284 inch. It has a bit more power than the .270, and a loyal following by hunters who recognize that attribute. Bullet choices are a bit limited. A standard load is a 140-grain bullet at 2,960 feet per second.

.308 Winchester

Introduced in 1952 as the 7.62x51mm NATO, this is probably the most accurate and most efficient cartridge ever developed. Compared to the .300 Winchester Magnum or even its parent, the .30-06, the amount of powder it burns is disproportionately less than the surprising velocities delivered from its short case. Before "short, fat" magnums took off, this was the original short guy.

Competition shooters use it, and the military uses it as a sniper round, which should tell you something about its capabilities. It's available the world over. Some hunters argue it's underpowered. But when loaded with 150-grain bullets, it will do almost anything the .30-06 does, and with less recoil. A 165-grain bullet flies at 2,650 feet per second.

.30 TC

Introduced in 2007 as a joint venture of Thompson/Center and Hornady, this is the first cartridge to bear the Thompson/Center headstamp. It's a very short case for a cartridge of its capability. If the .308 Winchester is a shortened .30-06, consider the .30 TC a shortened .308. This short, fat standard caliber enhances

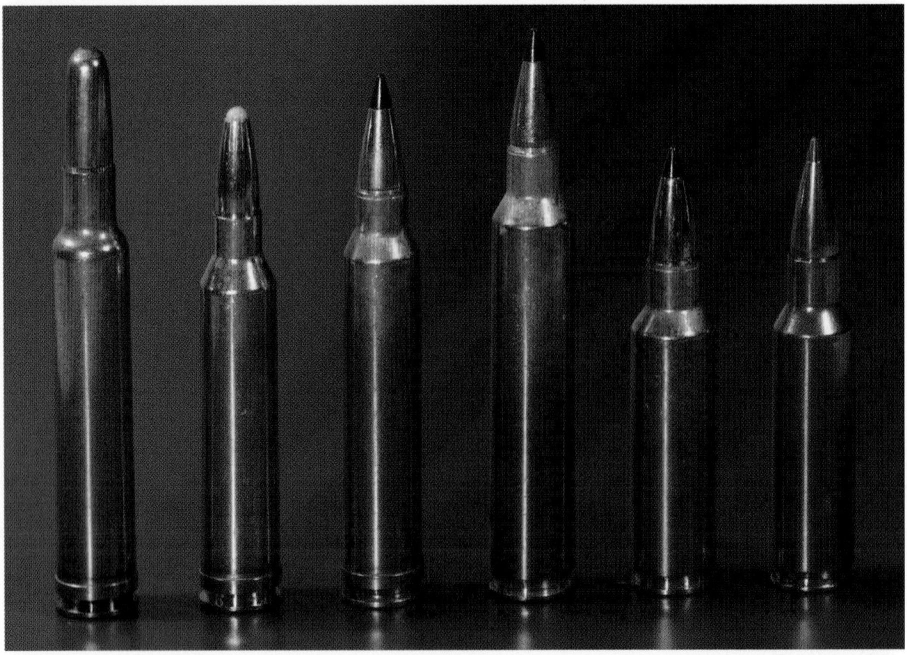

Left to right: .300 Weatherby Magnum, 7mm Remington Magnum, .300 Winchester Magnum, .300 Remington Ultra Magnum, .300 Winchester Short Magnum, .300 Ruger Compact Magnum.

performance by enhancing ignition and powder burn, which also produces less recoil. Even with 25 percent less powder than a .30-06, velocities with 150- and 165-grain bullets are similar to the older and longer cartridge: 2,920 and 2,850 feet per second, respectively. All in all, this is a pretty neat development in the world of cartridges.

7mm Remington Magnum

Introduced simultaneously with the Model 700 in 1962, the 7mm Remington Magnum quickly became a favorite of Western hunters, outselling the venerable .30-06 and everything else for about three years. In fact, it is the most popular 7mm cartridge ever introduced in the United States. Where it shines is as an accurate, powerful, long-range big-game cartridge on the plains and in the mountains. Two popular loadings are a 140-grain bullet that flies at 3,150 feet per second and a 160-grainer that travels 2,940 feet per second. Nowadays it still holds its own even in the face of so much competition from .30-caliber magnums. It is chambered by most manufacturers, and ammo remains widely available.

.300 Weatherby Magnum

The most popular and versatile cartridge in the Weatherby lineup, it was developed way back in 1944 as the last of Roy Weatherby's necked-down improvements to the .300 H&H Magnum case. It remains one of the most powerful .30-caliber magnums available today. It's also one of the snappiest; stories abound of hunters who buy one, then fear its recoil. In capable hands, however, there is nothing to fear and everything to be gained. One-gun-across-the-world hunters can do no better. Original loadings propelled a 180-grain bullet at 3,350 feet per second. Today that bullet can travel as fast as 3,240 feet per second.

.300 Winchester Magnum

If I had to pick a favorite cartridge of all time, the .300 Winchester Magnum would rate near the top of the list. Introduced in 1963 for the Model 70, it was originally criticized for its short neck because it meant heavy bullets had to be seated farther back in the case, reducing some powder space. Don't tell that to U.S. military snipers, who still rely on it as a mainstay. The 7mm Remington Magnum runs a close second to it as a fine long-range big-game cartridge, especially with today's super-premium bullets. Bullets of all types and weights are loaded for this do-it-all caliber. It can be downloaded with 130-grain lightweights at a whopping 3,500 feet per second; 180-grain bullets at 2,960 feet per second; or stoked with 200-grain heavyweights that still travel 2,700 feet per second.

.300 Remington Ultra Magnum

When Remington introduced its supersized .30-caliber magnum in 1999, the world questioned its pointless power and needless recoil, then flocked to it in droves when they saw how well it performed in the field. A 180-grain bullet travels 3,250 feet per second; a 200-grain bullet suitable for the largest game you'll hunt with this cartridge still travels at a blistering 3,070 feet per second. It is based on a .404 Jeffery case, which is larger in diameter than an H&H Magnum case and allows the Ultra Magnum to increase powder capacity without exceeding the maximum overall cartridge length capable of fitting a Model 700. It produces velocities faster than a .300 Weatherby. Today it is an extremely popular cartridge for hunters headed to Alaska; many brown bear guides cite it as their number-one client gun.

.300 Winchester Short Magnum

Introduced in 2003, the .300 WSM is essentially a .300 Remington Short Action Ultra Magnum shortened a bit more to chamber in a short-action gun. It has outlived Remington's .30-caliber short magnum. It's more than stubby—it's obese. That girth gives it great powder capacity—enough to practically duplicate performance of its big brother, the .300 Winchester Magnum, by sending a 180-grain bullet downrange at 3,010 feet per second. The trade-off is function; many hunters have problems filling magazines to capacity with the cartridges, and feeding problems have been noted. Best bet is to load one less in the magazine than maximum capacity.

.300 Ruger Compact Magnum

In 2008 Hornady teamed with Ruger to produce a couple of short, fat magnums; the first was the .300 RCM. It's a magnum cartridge that produces some pretty amazing numbers without the use of a 26- or even a 24-inch barrel—the Ruger rifles that fire this round wear 20-inch barrels. The case itself is a mere 2.1 inches long, but it measures .532 inch in diameter at its base—the same as the .375 H&H at its belt. Plus, there's minimal taper. So this fat, non-belted, distinctly un-magnum-looking magnum case holds a lot of powder to produce performance out of proportion to its size: 150-grain bullets traveling at 3,175 feet per second from a 20-inch barrel; 165-grainers at 2,964; and 180-grainers at a still-very-fast 2,840.

.338 Winchester Magnum

Based on a necked-down .458 Winchester Magnum case and released in 1958, the .338 Winchester Magnum delivers its go-to load, a 225-grain bullet, at 2,800 feet per second and produces 3,917 foot-pounds of muzzle energy. That's not bad for a magnum with about 12 percent more frontal area than the .300 Winchester Magnum but just as easy on your shoulder. This is a great cartridge for the biggest game in North America. It is only slightly less powerful than the .375 H&H Magnum, and it shines in Africa, too. It is the most popular .338-caliber cartridge in the world. One-gun hunters, take note.

.338 Federal

Based on a necked-up .308 Winchester, it was introduced by Federal Ammunition and Sako in 2006 as a big-game cartridge that offers good velocity and energy with surprisingly reasonable recoil for such a large caliber. It compares favorably with cartridges like the 7mm Remington Magnum in bullets of the same weight, and it has greater energy than the .30-06. Best of all is the fact that Federal offers four bullet weights for this new cartridge: a 180-grain at 2,830 feet per second; a 185-grain at 2,750; a 200-grain at 2,630; and a 210-grain at 2,630. If you're looking for good velocity, reasonable recoil, and lots of choices in bullet weights in a large-frontal-area cartridge like a .338, check it out.

Left to right: .375 H&H Magnum, .378 Weatherby Magnum, .375 Weatherby Magnum, .375 Ruger.

.338 Ruger Compact Magnum

This is the other 2008 incarnation from the teaming of Hornady and Ruger. The bigger short, fat Ruger Magnum takes full advantage of the greater frontal area of a .338-inch-diameter bullet. Again, it produces magnum performance from a distinctly non-magnum package, mainly a 20-inch barrel on the short-action Ruger Hawkeye rifles that fire this round. And again, it uses a short, fat powder column that holds a lot of powder. If you're looking for a .30- or .338-caliber magnum, you owe it to yourself to check out the Rugers. Hornady offers three loads: a 185-grain at 2,980 feet per second; a 200-grain at 2,950; and a 225-grain at 2,750.

.375 H&H Magnum

If African dangerous game is in your sights, get a "three-seven-five" and learn to shoot it well. You'll learn its trajectory loaded with 270-grain bullets nearly duplicates the .30-06 with 180-grain bullets. Despite the 4,000 foot-pounds of energy it sends from the muzzle, recoil is manageable. The most useful load is a 300-grainer at 2,530 feet per second. Developed by Holland & Holland in 1912, the progenitor of this cartridge family is a belted, rimless case originally released in the firm's magnum Mauser rifles for Africa. It's enjoyed a loyal following ever since, and in fact Winchester chambered its Model 70 for the cartridge in 1937. Perhaps one of its best attributes is it is not loaded hot enough to bind actions. Yet it expels power to penetrate and kill the world's toughest game. If one cartridge is meant to do it all, this is it.

.378 Weatherby Magnum

An original Roy Weatherby design released in 1953, it was created by necking-down a .460 Weatherby Magnum. It is built for super-fast flight and deep penetration on thick-skinned game and to provide a margin of error while doing it. In fact, it is the fastest and most powerful cartridge in the .375 family. It pushes a 300-grain bullet at 2,925 feet per second. At 100 yards, traveling at 2,623 feet per second, it delivers 318 foot-pounds more energy than the original does at the muzzle. When it was introduced, bullets could not withstand its impact velocities; today's super-premium bullets hold up just fine. Its recoil is more than stout—it's downright brutal. If you absolutely have to have the most powerful "three-seven-five," this is it.

.375 Weatherby Magnum

Roy Weatherby actually created this fast cartridge before he made his .378, but discontinued it after creating the .378. In 2001, Roy's son, Ed, reintroduced it. It's an improved .375 H&H Magnum with similar case taper. In a pinch, .375 H&H ammo can be fired in a .375 Weatherby. Current Weatherby ammo is loaded with a 300-grain Nosler Partition at 2,572 feet per second, giving it a significant energy edge over the hundred-year-old original.

.375 Ruger

There is no belted case on this .375, and in fact there isn't even a "magnum" in its name. Hornady and Ruger must have been teaming on this cartridge about the same

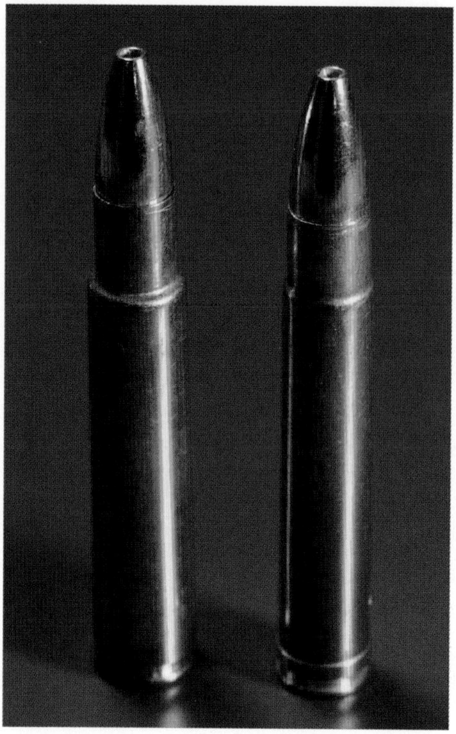

Left to right: .416 Rigby, .416 Remington Magnum.

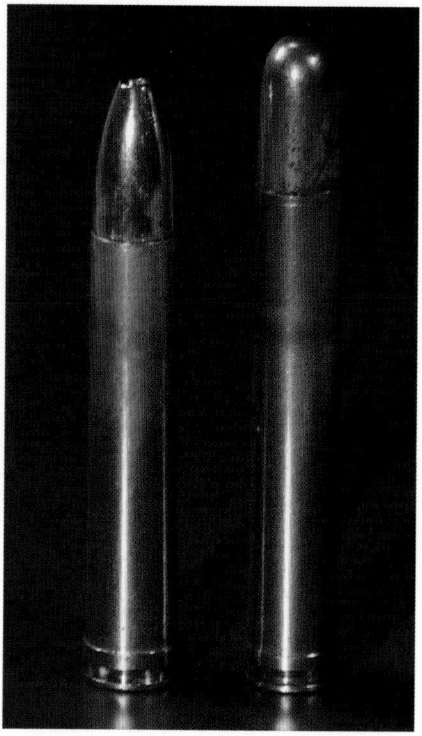

Left to right: .458 Winchester Magnum, .458 Lott.

time they were working on Ruger Compact Magnums, because the .375 Ruger came out right on their heels. The impetus for it was a desire by Ruger to offer a rifle suitable for Africa's dangerous game without the price of existing guns, including their own Mark II Magnum. Very few truly magnum-length rifles are sold in any given year; Ruger clearly thought it could hatch something if it could offer a big bore without the big price. I'd say they're on to something. The Hawkeye African that chambers this round is not magnum length, but the .375 Ruger meets and even exceeds .375 H&H Magnum performance in every way. A 300-grain Ruger bullet fired with Hornady Superformance ammo flies at 2,660 feet per second and exits the muzzle with 4,713 foot-pounds of energy. Compare those numbers to a .375 H&H with a 300-grainer and 2,530/4,265, respectively. This is a huge development in the world of dangerous-game cartridges, and I suspect it is only the beginning of things to come.

.416 Rigby

If a big bore for the Big Five is in your future, this might be the ultimate caliber. Introduced by John Rigby in 1911, it was purposely built with a large powder capacity to avoid erratic pressures in hot climates associated with the use of cordite, then the propellant in use in most British gun houses. It pushes a 400-grain bullet at 2,400 feet per second but develops the pressure of only a .30-30 Winchester. In recent years it has enjoyed resurgence in popularity thanks to commercial ammo offerings. To my mind the Rigby gets the nod over the .416 Remington Magnum because for one, it came first; two, it's got nostalgia to spare; and three, its velocity is slower and therefore more manageable for pass-through shots when shooting buffalo in herds. A 400-grain bullet at 2,400 feet per second produces almost 5,000 foot-pounds of energy. John "Pondoro" Taylor, likely the all-time authority of all things surrounding the chase for dangerous African game, would, even today, if he were alive, likely rate this cartridge as number one in the world.

.416 Remington Magnum

Based on a necked-up 8mm Remington Magnum, it was released in 1988 as a gap-filler between the .375 H&H Magnum and .458 Winchester Magnum. Of course the .416 Rigby did that job nicely, but in 1988 there were perhaps only 10,000 rifles so chambered throughout the world. The .416 Remington starts out faster than the .458 Winchester Magnum, and increases its lead in retained velocity as range increases. The standard load fires a 400-grain bullet at 2,400 feet per second; 350-grain bullets create a bit more velocity. Its trajectory is similar to the .375 H&H. Originally available only on Remington's Model 700 Safari rifle, the cartridge has proved so popular that other gunmakers have since chambered for it. Ammo is considerably cheaper than the .416 Rigby.

.458 Winchester Magnum

The "four-five-eight" hit the scene in 1956 in the Model 70 African in the face of Weatherby's success with big-bore sales, and it went on to become the dangerous-game cartridge by which others are judged today. Its 2.5-inch case length means it does not need to be chambered in only magnum-length actions, which significantly reduces cost for everyone involved. Loaded with a 500-grain bullet at 2,050 feet per second, the .458 Winchester is as good as it gets. All major ammo manufacturers load for it, and many commercial bolt-actions are chambered for it.

.458 Lott

Originally a wildcat created by Jack Lott in 1971, it is based on a blown-out, shortened .375 H&H Magnum case and is just a smidge longer than the .458 Winchester Magnum to improve performance over the Winchester cartridge with a 500-grain load. The Lott will honestly outpace the Winchester, but the price is severely increased recoil. Either cartridge can be unpleasant to shoot, but the Lott seems to win the "unbearable" prize among most hunters who try it. The beauty of this cartridge is rifles chambered for it will also safely chamber and shoot .458 Winchester, which presents a significant cost savings in ammo as Lott loads are more expensive than more popular Winchester loads. Its length also means it can be chambered in standard-length actions rather than true magnum lengths, reducing costs of manufacture and eventual price. Today the Lott is chambered by a number of commercial gunmakers that also chamber the Winchester and .375 H&H.

Chapter 13

Afterword

About the NRA

The National Rifle Association was founded in 1871 by a group of former Union officers who had noticed the poor marksmanship skills of most soldiers during the Civil War. After the war, they decided to form an association that would help educate and train the civilian populace so it would be ready to protect the homeland with skill in arms.

Many people today don't know that story. They think of the NRA only as a political organization. It's true we fight hard on behalf of all American gun owners to protect their basic right of self-defense as embodied in the Second Amendment. We fight now more than ever to protect the rights and privileges of hunters—from stopping abuse of power where it affects your right to buy, own, and use a gun, to stopping the creep of laws and regulations that infringe on hunting nationwide. Next to self-defense, hunting is the main way Americans exercise their Second Amendment right. We remain a single-issue organization so law-abiding Americans can own guns and hunt.

Americans follow gun-safety rules written by the NRA, learn from NRA-certified firearm instructors, and shoot at NRA-affiliated ranges. We have lobbied for right-to-hunt amendments in state constitutions, as well as public access and youth mentored hunting legislation. Since 1992, The NRA Foundation has awarded $180 million in grants to support youth hunter safety, Hunters for the Hungry, range construction, and conservation projects nationwide. For years our foremost mission was education and training. It still is—the NRA has a network of almost 100,000 certified instructors across the country ready to assist you with rifle, shotgun, and pistol courses. Log on to nrainstructors.org to find a course or an instructor near you.

A membership in the NRA entitles the member to receive one of three official journals: *American Rifleman, American Hunter,* or *America's 1st Freedom. American Rifleman,* in print since 1928, is aimed at gun aficionados who want to learn about the development of firearms throughout history. *American Hunter* was founded in 1973 to inform and entertain hunters who have a special interest in the way guns are used as tools of the hunt. With a circulation of more than a million readers, it is the largest-circulation hunting magazine in the world. *America's 1st Freedom* is aimed at gun owners who are not avid users, collectors, or hunters, but who care passionately about our right to keep and bear arms. Every issue keeps members up to date about developments in the fight to protect our rights.

A 2010 Gallup poll suggests there are 117 million American gun owners. But there are only about 5 million NRA members. Remember the 80/20 rule of business? It states that 80 percent of the work is done by 20 percent of the people. Clearly, when it comes to gun ownership and hunting, the 80/20 rule applies, only it's more like the 96/4 rule: 96 percent of the work to preserve Americans' Second Amendment rights is done by a mere 4 percent of gun owners—the 5 million members of the NRA.

About SAAM

As a lifelong hunter of game throughout the world, former booking agent, outfitter, and a resident of the Texas Hill Country, Tim Fallon realized he could help hunters headed on a trip of a lifetime. A couple of years ago, with the help of a couple of retired Special Operations types, he founded SAAM, Sportsman's All-Weather All-Terrain Marksmanship training, at his FTW Ranch in Barksdale, Texas. The goal is simple: Make good hunters better.

Training is conducted primarily by Fallon and Doug Prichard, a retired Navy SEAL, sniper instructor, and competitive shooter, with other experienced instructors as class sizes dictate. Both men still hunt avidly when their schedules allow, but these days SAAM training takes up most of their time.

Doug Prichard, right, instructs a student during a course at the Sportsman's All-Weather All-Terrain Marksmanship training at FTW Ranch in Barksdale, Texas.

In its short existence, SAAM's four-day Level I Precision Rifle course has graduated more than 500 students. Groups are typically small. Students fire an average of 300 rounds from 100 to 500 yards or more using range-estimation and wind-doping skills, and they practice under field conditions that require them to solve ballistic and environmental problems.

Fallon and his staff also created SAAM Level II, which builds on the skills of range-estimation and wind-doping covered in Level I; SAAM Safari for hunters headed overseas with big bores; SAAM Safari Double Rifle, which introduces students to the art and skill of handling a double-gun afield; and SAAM Pistol, which helps handgun hunters improve shooting skills with scoped and un-scoped pistols.

About Gunsite

Gunsite Academy was founded in 1976 by Jeff Cooper, retired Marine, board member of the National Rifle Association, and author of numerous books including *The Art of the Rifle,* when he founded the American Pistol Institute on 160 acres of barren Arizona land. It operated as such until 1992 when a new owner named it Gunsite Training School; it became Gunsite Academy in 1999. Today, after Cooper's passing, it encompasses 2,000 acres and is owned and run by Buz Mills, an NRA board member.

The academy trains military and law enforcement personnel as well as civilians who simply want to improve their shooting. All manner of courses are available on the academy's 2,000 acres and numerous ranges, from Defensive Pistol to Hunting Rifle, Patrol Rifle, Hunter Prep, and more. The Hunter Prep course is a two-day "safari" class of about ten students with two or three instructors. Students fire from twenty-five to several hundred yards at targets of known and unknown distance; solve ballistic and environmental problems associated with shooting; and conduct a mock walk-and-stalk for game in the field.

A Hunter's Library

Consider this list my bibliography, for I consulted every one of these books either in whole or in part to write my book. Every hunter and shooter should possess at least some of these texts. Many are out of print, but they can be found with a bit of diligence.

Barnes, Frank C., and Mike Bussard. *Cartridges of the World, Seventh Edition.* Iola, Wisconsin: DBI Books/Krause Publications, 1993.

Barsness, John. *Optics for the Hunter.* Long Beach: Safari Press, 1998.

Barsness, John, Craig Boddington, John Haviland, Richard Mann, Ron Spomer, Bryce Towsley, and Dave Campbell, eds. *Rifle Bullets for the Hunter: A Definitive Study.* Princeton, West Virginia: Ballistic Technology, 2006.

Boddington, Craig. *The Perfect Shot, North America.* Long Beach, Safari Press, 2003.

———. *Make It Accurate.* Long Beach: Safari Press, 1999.

Bussard, Michael E., Stanton L. Wormley, and John Zent. *NRA Firearms Source Book.* Fairfax, Virginia: National Rifle Association, 2006.

Carmichel, Jim. *Jim Carmichel's Book of the Rifle.* New York: Outdoor Life Books, 1985.

De Haas, Frank. *Bolt Action Rifles.* Iola, Wisconsin: DBI Books/Krause Publications, 1995.

Donnelly, John J., and Bryce M Towsley. *The Handloader's Manual of Cartridge Conversions.* Accokeek, Maryland: Stoeger Publishing, 2004.

Dunlap, Roy F. *Gunsmithing, Second Edition.* Harrisburg, Pennsylvania: Stackpole Books, 1963.

Forker, Bob. *Ammo & Ballistics 3 for Hunters, Shooters, and Collectors.* Long Beach: Safari Press, 2006.

Gresham, Grits, and Tom Gresham. *Weatherby.* Natchitoches, Louisiana: Cane River Publishing, 1992.

Howe, James Virgil. *The Modern Gunsmith, Volume I.* New York: Funk & Wagnalls, 1945.

Litz, Bryan. *Applied Ballistics for Long Range Shooting.* Cedar Springs, Michigan: Applied Ballistics, LLC, 2009.

NRA Firearms Fact Book, Third Edition. Fairfax, Virginia: National Rifle Association, 1989.

O'Connor, Jack. *The Big-Game Rifle.* Long Beach: Safari Press, 1997.

Otteson, Stuart. *The Bolt Action.* New York: Winchester Press, 1976.

———. *The Bolt Action, Volume II.* Prescott, Arizona: Wolfe Publishing, 1985.

Page, Warren. *The Accurate Rifle, Fourth Edition.* New York: Winchester Press, 1975.

Petzal, David E. *The Encyclopedia of Sporting Firearms.* New York: Facts on File, 1991.

Plaster, Maj. John L. *The Ultimate Sniper.* Boulder, Colorado: Paladin Press, 2006.

Roberts, Joseph B. Jr., and Harris J. Andrews. *The Official NRA Guide to Firearms Assembly: Rifles and Shotguns.* Accokeek, Maryland: Stoeger Publishing, 2007.

Robertson, Kevin. *The Perfect Shot: Shot Placement for African Big Game.* Long Beach: Safari Press, 1999.

Rule, Roger C. *The Rifleman's Rifle.* Northridge, California: Alliance Books, 1982.

Towsley, Bryce M. *Gunsmithing Made Easy.* Accokeek, Maryland: Stoeger Publishing, 2006.

Van Zwoll, Wayne. *The Hunter's Guide to Accurate Shooting.* Guilford, Connecticut: The Lyons Press, 2002.

———. *The Hunter's Guide to Ballistics.* Guilford, Connecticut: The Lyons Press, 2001.

Walter, John. *Rifles of the World, Third Edition.* Iola, Wisconsin: F&W Publications/Krause Publications, 2006.

Wieland, Terry. *Dangerous-Game Rifles.* Camden, Maine: Countrysport Press, 2006.